THE TWENTIES
FORDS, FLAPPERS & FANATICS

EDITED BY
GEORGE E. MOWRY

A SPECTRUM BOOK

PRENTICE-HALL, INC., ENGLEWOOD CLIFFS, NEW JERSEY

For Vera Pauline Halfhill

Current printing (last digit):
13 12 11

© 1963 by Prentice-Hall, Inc.
Englewood Cliffs, N.J.
The Twenties: Fords, Flappers, and Fanatics
Library of Congress Catalog No.: 63-19425
Printed in the United States of America
C

CONTENTS

INTRODUCTION

The 1920's have often been described by historians as retrograde years, in which little happened except the economic excesses which brought on the depression of 1929. Such an evaluation is due perhaps to the fact that most historians have concentrated chiefly on politics and, compared with either the progressive years that preceded or the New Deal reforms that followed, the Twenties do indeed look sterile. As a matter of fact, the period was one of amazing vitality, of social invention and change. And perhaps it is not too much to say that the Twenties were really the formative years of modern American society. It was during these years that the country first became urban, particularly in the cast of its mind, in its ideals, and in its folk ways. Interwoven and interacting with this change was an amazing technological development and the rise of a new type of industrial economy typified by mass production and mass consumption. Both factors speeded the breakdown of old habits and patterns of thought and prepared the way for the future. The new economy, dependent in the last analysis on the tastes and the acceptance of the crowd, had incredibly important influence upon such widely separated areas as religion, political philosophy, folk ways, dress, moral precepts, and the uses of leisure time.

Until the twentieth century, despite the more or less democratic political apparatus, the country's social goals and aspirations had been traditionally set by small groups of preachers, politicians, lawyers, editors, and teachers, and later as well by the economic elite spawned by post-Civil War industrialism. But from 1920 on, the tastes of the crowd became an increasingly important determinant, first in popular culture and later in political and economic institutions. And this new mass culture differed vastly from the traditional culture that had been inspired from above.

Societies do not give up old ideals and attitudes easily; the conflicts between the representatives of the older elements of traditional American culture and the prophets of the new day were at times as bitter as they were extensive. Such matters as religion, marriage, and moral standards, as well as the issues over race, prohibition, and immigration were at the heart of the conflict. This cultural conflict is really the central theme of this volume. The division of the sections, as well as the selec-

1

tion of the documents in each section, was made to bring out its salient aspects.

Since this volume deals only with the rise of mass culture, no effort has been made to depict the very rich activity of these years in art, literature, and more formal thought. Most social criticism, by the way, was and has remained extremely critical of the new cultural mix developing during the Twenties. But such criticism often makes little attempt to understand. And it is to be hoped that the following documents will cast light not only upon the origins of this new American society but also upon how and why it arose.

These documents were all written between the World War I and the Great Depression; many were written either by participants in the events described or by first-hand witnesses. They are thus in a way original sources. Perhaps in their totality they will destroy the myth that the Twenties was an unproductive decade and reveal it instead as one of the major formulative epochs in American history.

LET THEM EAT CAKE

The years from the end of World War I to 1929 were a time of phenomenal economic progress and change. During this period the new gospel of mass production, the amazing advances in technology, and the increasing efficiency of labor accounted for a total gain in industrial production of over sixty per cent, far outstripping the gain in population. Consequently, profits, dividends, salaries, and industrial wages all rose appreciably. With the enormous extension of consumer credit and the new emphasis upon advertising and salesmanship, the consumption level of the average American family soared. By 1928 President Hoover could talk without fear of being ridiculed about the possibility of ending all want and poverty. For the first time in world history the masses of a great nation had not only bread but cake. It is small wonder that until the crash of 1929 business and the businessman were venerated.

How this materialist Eden came about is the theme of this section. The aspirations heralded by the cult of business, the operations of the new advertising industry and the profession of salesmanship, the forces behind the rapid extension of mass consumer credit, together with their social implications, and especially the rise of the speculative (expansionist) spirit are all explored in these articles and documents.

1. BUSINESS AS THE NEW AMERICAN RELIGION

As production, profits, and personal consumption standards rose dramatically during the Twenties, faith in business as a way of life spread throughout the nation. But the business creed was not rationalized in material terms alone. A mystique developed making claims to manifold ethical and humanitarian values for business life. Lavish praise of big business as an ethical and social agent may explain the bitter criticism of it during the Thirties when it failed to produce even a living for Americans. But during the prosperous Twenties the broad claims of the following article were not atypical. Edward Earl Purinton, "Big Ideas from Big Business," *The Independent,* April 16, 1921, p. 395.

AMONG THE NATIONS OF THE EARTH TODAY AMERICA STANDS FOR ONE idea: *Business.* National opprobrium? National opportunity. For in this fact lies, potentially, the salvation of the world.

Thru business, properly conceived, managed and conducted, the human race is finally to be redeemed. How and why a man works foretells what he will do, think, have, give and be. And real salvation is in doing, thinking, having, giving and being—not in sermonizing and theorizing.

I shall base the facts of this article on the personal tours and minute examinations I have recently made of twelve of the world's largest business plants: U.S. Steel Corporation, International Harvester Company, Swift & Company, E. I. du Pont de Nemours & Company, National City Bank, National Cash Register Company, Western Electric Company, Sears, Roebuck & Company, H. J. Heinz Company, Peabody Coal Company, Statler Hotels, Wanamaker Stores.

These organizations are typical, foremost representatives of the commercial group of interests loosely termed "Big Business." A close view of these corporations would reveal to any trained, unprejudiced observer a new conception of modern business activities. Let me draw a few general conclusions regarding the best type of business house and business man.

What is the finest game? Business. The soundest science? Business. The truest art? Business. The fullest education? Business. The fairest opportunity? Business. The cleanest philanthropy? Business. The sanest religion? Business.

You may not agree. That is because you judge business by the crude, mean, stupid, false imitation of business that happens to be located near you.

The finest game is business. The rewards are for everybody, and all can win. There are no favorites—Providence always crowns the career of the man who is worthy. And in this game there is no "luck"—you have the fun of taking chances but the sobriety of guaranteeing certainties. The speed and size of your winnings are for you alone to determine; you needn't wait for the other fellow in the game—it is always your move. And your slogan is not "Down the Other Fellow!" but rather "Beat Your Own Record!" or "Do It Better Today!" or "Make Every Job a Masterpiece!" The great sportsmen of the world are the great business men.

The soundest science is business. All investigation is reduced to action, and by action proved or disproved. The idealistic motive animates the materialistic method. Hearts as well as minds are open to the truth. Capital is furnished for the researches of "pure science"; yet pure science is not regarded pure until practical. Competent scientists are suitably rewarded—as they are not in the scientific schools.

The truest art is business. The art is so fine, so exquisite, that you do not think of it as art. Language, color, form, line, music, drama, discovery, adventure—all the components of art must be used in business to make it of superior character.

The fullest education is business. A proper blend of study, work and life is essential to advancement. The whole man is educated. Human nature itself is the open book that all business men study; and the mastery of a page of this educates you more than the memorizing of a dusty tome from a library shelf. In the school of business, moreover, you teach yourself and learn most from your own mistakes. What you learn here you live out, the only real test.

The fairest opportunity is business. You can find more, better, quicker chances to get ahead in a large business house than anywhere else on earth. The biographies of champion business men show how they climbed, and how you can climb. Recognition of better work, of keener and quicker thought, of deeper and finer feeling, is gladly offered by the men higher up, with early promotion the rule for the man who justifies it. There is, and can be, no such thing as buried talent in a modern business organization.

The cleanest philanthropy is business. By "clean" philanthropy I mean that devoid of graft, inefficiency and professionalism, also of condolence, hysterics and paternalism. Nearly everything that goes by the name of Charity was born a triplet, the other two members of the trio being Frailty and Cruelty. Not so in the welfare departments of leading corporations. Savings and loan funds; pension and insurance provisions; health precautions, instructions and safeguards; medical attention and hospital care; libraries, lectures and classes; musical, athletic and social features of all kinds; recreational facilities and financial opportunities—these types of "charitable institutions" for employees add to the worker's self-respect, self-knowledge and self-improvement, by making him an active partner in the welfare program, a producer of benefits for his employer and associates quite as much as a recipient of bounty from the company. I wish every "charity" organization would send its officials to school to the heads of the welfare departments of the big corporations; the charity would mostly be transformed into capability, and the minimum of irreducible charity left would not be called by that name.

The sanest religion is business. Any relationship that forces a man to follow the Golden Rule rightfully belongs amid the ceremonials of the church. A great business enterprise includes and presupposes this relationship. I have seen more Christianity to the square inch as a regular part of the office equipment of famous corporation presidents than may ordinarily be found on Sunday in a verbalized but not vitalized church congregation. A man is not wholly religious until he is better on weekdays than he is on Sunday. The only ripened fruits of creeds are deeds. You can fool your preacher with a sickly sprout or a wormy semblance of character, but you can't fool your employer. I would make every business house a consultation bureau for the guidance of the church whose members were employees of the house.

I am aware that some of the preceding statements will be challenged by many readers. I should not myself have made them, or believed them, twenty years ago, when I was a pitiful specimen of a callow youth and cocksure professional man combined. A thorough knowledge of business has implanted a deep respect for business and real business men.

The future work of the business man is to teach the teacher, preach to the preacher, admonish the parent, advise the doctor, justify the lawyer, superintend the statesman, fructify the farmer, stabilize the banker, harness the dreamer, and reform the reformer. Do all these needy persons wish to have these many kind things done to them by the business man? Alas, no. They rather look down upon him, or askance at him, regarding him as a mental and social inferior—unless he has money or fame enough to tilt their glance upward.

A large variety of everyday lessons of popular interest may be gleaned from a tour of the world's greatest business plants and a study of the lives of their founders. We suggest a few.

1. *The biggest thing about a big success is the price.* It takes a big man to pay the price. You can measure in advance the size of your success by how much you are willing to pay for it. I do not refer to money. I refer to the time, thought, energy, economy, purpose, devotion, study, sacrifice, patience, care, that a man must give to his life work before he can make it amount to anything.

The business world is full of born crusaders. Many of the leaders would be called martyrs if they weren't rich. The founders of the vast corporations have been, so far as I know them, fired with zeal that is supposed to belong only to missionaries.

Of all the uncompromizing, untiring, unsparing idealists in the world today, none surpass the founders and heads of the business institutions that have made character the cornerstone. The costliest thing on earth is idealism.

2. *Great men are silent about themselves.* Conversely, the more a man talks about his personality, his family, his property, his position, his past, present or future achievements, the less he usually amounts to or will ever become.

We had to spend weeks of hard work to obtain personal interviews with the heads of the International Harvester Company.

They prefer the forge to the limelight. They do not want free "publicity." And they refuse to make oral statements, that might be misquoted or misunderstood; they insist that all facts and figures for publication be checked with utmost care, sometimes thru a dozen departments, to prevent the least inaccuracy.

The publicity director of E. I. du Pont de Nemours & Company was disturbed, on reading our monograph prior to publication, because he felt we had praised the company too highly! He explained that part of his job was to avoid appearance of exaggeration; and tho we stated facts, he detected a slight sound of praise. The president of the National City

Bank hasn't had a photograph of himself taken for over ten years, even to give to his friends and relatives. He accorded us a delightful interview, but requested us not to quote him directly or mention his name at all in preparing our essay on the bank.

3. *The best way to keep customers is to make friends.* Of all the assets of a business concern the chief is good will. To gain this, you can afford to spend as much as to manufacture or sell your product.

Now a fundamental rule in creating good will is to benefit the customer in a way he does not look for, does not pay for. The Western Electric Company offers to teach any woman the principles of household efficiency, mailing on request literature without charge. The science of managing a home indicates the use of electrical appliances, but the company wants to teach the science whether it sells the goods or not. This is "good business" because genuine service.

The Peabody Coal Company gladly tells the customer how to save coal. A short-sighted man would infer that the company lost sales in doing this, because the customer, using less coal, would buy less. On the other hand, the customer who follows Peabody rules of trade will buy more regularly, pay more promptly, and co-operate with the company in ways quite as important as the chance of purchasing a few more tons of coal on a single deal.

4. *Only common experiences will unite the laborer and the capitalist.* Each must get the viewpoint of the other by sharing the work, duties and responsibilities of the other. The sons of the families of Swift, McCormick, Wanamaker, Heinz, du Pont, have learned the business from the ground up; they know the trials, difficulties and needs of workers because they *are* workers; and they don't have to settle agitations and strikes because there aren't any.

Further, by councils and committees of employees, management courses for department heads and foremen, plans of referendum and appeal, offers of stock and voting power to workers, employee representation on the board of directors, and other means of sharing authority and responsibility, owners of a business now give the manual workers a chance to think and feel in unison with themselves. All enmity is between strangers. Those who really know each other cannot fight.

5. *Every business needs a woman counselor.* Better, a woman's advisory board. Nearly all manufacturing and merchandizing relates somehow to the interests of womankind.

Before E. M. Statler built the latest hotel in his big chain of hostelries, he consulted the housekeeper and matron of his masterpiece house, Hotel Pennsylvania, the world's largest inn. He wanted to know the precise arrangement, equipment and service that women guests valued most. He knew that no man could tell him.

There could be written a book of business revelations that would astonish the world. Over and over, at critical times in the development of national corporations, the hidden hand of a woman has held the huge concern at balance, or swung it in the right direction. You can no more run a business without a woman's intuition than you can run a boat without a keel.

6. *The great new field for professional men is corporation work.* Teachers, doctors, lawyers, editors, psychologists, chemists, bankers, engineers, even philosophers and ministers, now find pleasant, permanent, lucrative employment as heads of departments in famous business houses.

On my tour of the establishment of Swift & Company, I met a former editor of a big Chicago paper, a former professor and noted economist of one of our largest universities, a former engineer and author of national reputation, other professional men of high standing who were doing bigger work, for better pay, in the Swift employ than previous positions had afforded opportunity to develop. More and more, business will demand the knowledge and skill of scientists and artists of many kinds.

7. *The pleasure of money is not in having or spending it.* The pleasure is in getting it—and giving it away. Money rewards the exercize of keen brains and quick wits, but the real fun is in the exercize. I don't know of a single self-made millionaire who puts money first. There is always something bigger and better than money in his mind.

As for his heart, that is where he *gives* the most. The heart of Judge Gary is in the manifold benefits he creates for the employees of U.S. Steel. The heart of John Wanamaker is in the John Wanamaker Foundation, a beneficial organization for Wanamaker workers; and in the international Sunday School forces that he set in motion. The heart of Julius Rosenwald is in the schools he established for poor boys and girls, and the relief work he founded among the Jews. The heart of Harold F. McCormick is in the free education he gives to farmers, and the uplifting music he provides for the people of Chicago. The heart of Howard Heinz is in the Sarah Heinz Community House, maintained by him as a living memorial to his mother. The heart of every great man is in some philanthropy made possible only by his money.

8. *A family heritage of wealth alone is the worst kind.* Most parents think they are good to their children if they leave a large bank-roll, easily accessible. Others foolishly magnify the bestowal of a college education, or social position, or some other inheritance not earned, and not valued because not earned.

Founders of great business enterprizes know better. They bequeath to their sons a personal equipment of aims, principles and methods which make real men of the scions of wealth. When I asked Howard Heinz, president of the H. J. Heinz Company, to describe the ideal business man, he answered simply, "My father." When I asked him to outline his own secret of success and purpose in life, he answered, "The fulfillment of my father's plans for industrial and social betterment, by carrying out faithfully the principles he laid down for the conduct of the business."

9. *Age is nothing to a live man.* When a person gets old the calendar is not to blame—he was born dead from the heart out and the neck up.

John H. Patterson was of middle age before he really started the National Cash Register Company. He had no experience in the business either, having been a country storekeeper without personal knowledge of engineering or manufacturing. But he got a purpose—and forgot everything else. Whoever does that is young till he dies. It is never too late to make a fresh start in life.

The men who grow immortal have stopped counting birthdays. J. Pierpont Morgan, James J. Hill, Henry Ford, Elbert Hubbard, Walt Mason, Dr. Frank Crane, many others in places of high renown, didn't really get going till past forty.

This is the world-age of young old men. Look at Judge Gary, John Wanamaker, John D. Rockefeller, Chauncey M. Depew, Thomas A. Edison, Bishop Samuel Fallows, Dr. Charles W. Eliot, Dr. J. H. Kellogg, scores of other leaders who, seventy to eighty-five years old, think, feel and act like men twenty years their juniors.

10. *The most powerful preacher is, or can be, the lay preacher.*

The business manager of Gary, Indiana, the world's largest industrial city, preaches nearly every Sunday. He is called upon by the pastors and priests of churches of a dozen different faiths and nationalities, whose members are employees of the U.S. Steel Corporation, to address the congregations in some helpful, appropriate way. Because he is a fine business man, with power, skill and money back of him, the men of the city want to hear what he has to say. And because he is a gentleman, kind, thoughtful, and sympathetic, the women of the church listen gladly to his lay sermons.

I look forward to the day when professional sermonizers will be considered a relic of past incompetence, and in their place will be men who are personal vitalizers and organizers.

11. *Charity must be cleansed of poverty and sentimentality.* You are not kind to the poor when you merely give them food, clothes or money. You pauperize them when they most need energizing, organizing and reorganizing.

A leading official of Sears, Roebuck & Company hates "welfare work." He says the company won't do any. Why? Because (1) the company refuses to pose as a philanthropist, socialist, or fairy godfather; (2) a self-respecting employee hates being "welfared" by his employer; (3) charity and business don't go together; (4) the majority of welfare workers are officious, crude, paternalistic and unscientific, out of place in business; and (5) employers need welfare work, perhaps of a different kind, as much as employees, and a one-sided program of such voluntary philanthropy is unwise and unfair.

This man claims that whatever improves the health, happiness, home life or future progress of the worker improves the work, and should be considered a straight business proposition. He believes that commercialism should include idealism and fraternalism, but without mention of the fact.

12. *Industry will finally be the savior of the community.* We hear much about a decadence of morality and increase of crime. Now the person who gets into mischief and goes astray was doing nothing, or the wrong thing, or the right thing badly. Put everybody in the work he loves, teach him how to do it well, and treat him and reward him fairly; then you take away the chief components of wrongdoing, which are idleness, irresponsibility, loneliness and curiosity, aided and abetted by a consciousness of misfitness. Thomas A. Edison remarks that he never had time to break a moral law.

Even now, the brightest and best spot in the community of such corporations as U.S. Steel, National Cash Register Company, National City Bank, Heinz, McCormick or du Pont is generally the community house or center founded, built and maintained by the corporation. Happiness for a human being lies in his work or nowhere. And the way to make people good is to make them know they are good for something.

2. THE ACADEMIC ACCOLADE

The final accolade of academic respectability was granted business by the nation's universities. The University of Pennsylvania opened the first academic college of business in 1881. But it was not until the Twenties that the business school became a major adjunct of nearly all the leading educational institutions. The following article satirizes the many admitted inanities included in the study lists of the day. But it should not be forgotten that much of the change of business attitudes after the Great Depression was probably due to the civilizing powers of the university upon potential businessmen. Arlington J. Stone, "The Dawn of a New Science," *The American Mercury,* August 1928, p. 446.

. . . Today business is taught as a science at California, Chicago, Dartmouth, New York, Boston, Harvard, Northwestern, Syracuse, Cincinnati, Ohio State, Michigan, Wisconsin, Stanford, and countless others.

The main pride of these seminaries, indeed, is their scientific method. It is applied both in the lecture-room and in the laboratories of their high-powered Bureaus of Business Research. Some of the more advanced plants, such as Harvard, Dartmouth and the Ohio State, even print scientific journals, wherein they chronicle in detail, with formidable graphs and statistics, all their latest findings. And so great is the new demand for scientific business training that most of them now operate in two shifts, day and night. In fact, the volume of business they do is so large that even the most go-getting dean now finds difficulty in handling his job singlehanded. Consequently, such offices as assistant and associate deanships of business administration are not at all rare. All of these shrines of scientific business seem to be making money. Indeed, next to football teams and schools of education, they are probably the biggest money-getters in the world of the intellect. At some places, as at N.Y.U. for example, it's only the takings of the School of Commerce that enable the Chancellor to pay the university's bills.

Most of these roaring mills of the new learning manufacture their own brands of degrees. The favored one at the moment is that of Bachelor of Business Administration (B.B.A.). This is annually bestowed by such eminent Sorbonnes as Boston, Tulane, Oregon, Washington, and Texas. The next highest in demand are those of Bachelor of Commercial Science (B.C.S.), and Bachelor of Science in Commerce (B.S.C.). For the requisite research and tuition these may be obtained at N.Y.U., Denver, Georgia, Virginia, and the Southern Methodist. Some of the more conservative houses still stick to the old-fashioned B.A., or even the Ph.B., as at Chicago and the John B. Stetson University at Deland, Fla. Harvard hands out only graduate degrees, such as that of Master of Business Administration (M.B.A.) and that of Doctor of Commercial Science (D.C.S.). The latter, according to some of its holders, is more difficult to obtain than the degree of *Docteur ès Lettres* at the original Sorbonne in Paris. A few institutions, such as Stanford and Syracuse, under certain favorable conditions, now crown the business scientist with the standard Ph.D. Besides these decorations there are rafts of others, such as the B.S. in C. and F. and the M.S. in C. and F. at Minnesota, the B.S.E. at Pennsylvania, the B.S. in B.A. at Nebraska, the M.C.S. at Washington, and finally, the C.E., or Commercial Engineer, at up-to-date Cincinnati. . . .

The following is a partial check-list of [Northwestern's] offerings during 1927-1928:

Accounting Seminar (for the master's degree)
Principles of Public Utility Accounting
Capital Assets
C. P. A. Review
Federal Income Taxes
Bank Practice and Policy
Seminar in Finance (for students preparing theses)
Money Market and Security Prices
Analysis of Financial Reports
Business Barometers
Research Methodology

Fire Insurance Schedules
Land Planning
Economics of Mineral and Water Power Resources
Business Organization and Field Trips
Business Organization and Management
Seminar in Organization (methods of constructive research)
Salesmanship
Principles of Salesmanship
Sales Administration
Advanced Problems in Sales Administration
Research in Marketing and Sales Administration (open to graduate students
    only)
Foreign Sales
Oriental Trade
Latin-American Trade
Advertising
Advertising Principles
Direct by Mail Selling
Advanced Copy-Writing
Psychology of Business Relations
Business Concepts
Persuasion
Modern Opinion
Business Letter-Writing
Public Relations

Numerous other equally appetizing morsels of knowledge are to be
had at other great universities. Thus, Cornell lists Hotel Supervision,
and Syracuse bills Hotel Management, Store Management, and Practical
Table Service. Columbia offers Bond Salesmanship, the New York
Money Market, and the Business of the Theatre. Southern California
reveals the mysteries of Apartment House Management, Traffic Management, and Real Estate Advertising, with special highly scientific lectures on Billboards, Trips to Property, Golf Links, Country Clubs, and
Model Homes. Virginia's contribution is in the science of Follow-up
Methods. Under Business Administration Wisconsin teaches Business
Ethics, the Law of Sales, Livestock Management, and Cafeteria Management, the latter being spit into Large Quantity Cooking and Institu-
tional Dietaries, and Catering. Illinois has a special course in Business
Practice for Dentists. But as usual, N.Y.U. leads the pack. Besides its
famous Oil Executives' Course and its scientific research in Restaurant,
Tea Room, and Cafeteria Organization, it also has the following on
draft:

47. *Principles of Dress.* The aim of this course is not to give fashion hints or
notes on the latest mode, but to arrive at an understanding of the essentials

of taste through the study of the principles of all art in their relation to the special art of dress.

54. *Hosiery and Underwear*. This course is for the training of buyers and executives.

64. *Window Display*. This course aims to assist those who are at present decorating windows.

. . . For many years the Harvard leadership among the business schools went unchallenged. Then one day in 1925 the tom-toms began to beat far out in California and the news was flashed back to Cambridge that Stanford University had "opened the first Graduate School of Business in the West." At the outset this Pacific threat didn't bother Harvard. Why should it? Had it not withstood competition in the past? Had not Yale once tried the same sort of thing, and hadn't the Bulldog been trampled on? Obviously, Harvard had no cause to worry. Indeed, its man of action and learning, the eminent Dean Donham, even traveled all the way across the continent, just to shake the new Stanford business dean's good right hand, and to tell him and his backers that "we in Cambridge are pleased with the institution of this course at Stanford University. . . . There is a very real reason for insistence in this country on more strict graduate instruction in business."

But soon thereafter the Stanford Graduate School of Business began to grab so much publicity that even Dean Donham, no doubt, began to scratch his head. As early as 1925 it announced that under certain conditions it would be able to reward its students of the new science with full-fledged, solid gold, 14-carat Ph.D's. In the same year, too, the new seminary was able to hold the First Stanford Conference on Business Education, at which were assembled many of the high dignitaries of both Advanced Business and the Higher Learning. Drs. Herbert Hoover and Owen D. Young were specially invited, but they sent telegrams instead of attending in person. This was the occasion when Dr. Donham told Stanford straight from the shoulder that he "was a little disturbed."

But today all this excitement is over, and Harvard is once more on top, and again it's due to its Dean of Business Administration. Soon after he returned to Cambridge from the coast, he announced that if Harvard was to continue to be a leader in scientific business education it would perforce need more money. The usual campaign was launched. It was so successful that in 1926 George Fisher Baker was moved to contribute $6,000,000. The actual ceremonies of handing it over took place a year later at a great celebration, with Dr. Owen D. Young present in the flesh, and making the dedicatory address. Here is the peroration of the learned doctor's lengthy harangue:

Today the profession of business at Harvard formally makes its bow to its older brothers and holds its head high with the faith of youth. Today we light the fires in the temple which it is the trust of Harvard to maintain and from which may be renewed through generation after generation the high ideals, the sound principles, the glorious traditions which make a profession.

Mr. Baker then rose and said to President Lowell: "Mr. President, it gives me great pleasure to present to you the keys to these buildings." To which modest sentence Dean Donham replied:

Mr. Baker, on behalf of the faculty of Business Administration, and especially on my own behalf, may I thank you from the bottom of our hearts for the deeply felt responsibility you have placed, and may we renew once again the pledge we know you wish from us, that we will so far as lies within our capacities advance the intellectual basis of this new profession of business, thereby fulfilling our generous gifts and carrying on as lesser men your lifelong example?

Less than a year passed before Harvard had a chance to advance the intellectual basis of the new profession. This came in 1927, when a course in Motion Pictures was added to the curriculum, and the faculty was augmented by such men of learning as the Hon. Jesse L. Lasky, the Hon. Cecil B. De Mille, the Hon. Adolph Zukor, the Hon. Marcus Loew, the Hon. Samuel Katz, the Hon. William Fox, and Elder Will H. Hays. That some of the less keen-sighted Harvard *studiosi* might not become suspicious, their good dean hastened to assure them:

It must be remembered that to the student this story is quite as full of business case material as it is of human interest. . . . The sudent must dig deeper and discover underlying principles of general application in the business world.

With the dean's reassurance, much work has been done in the new course. The keynote of it all was sounded by Elder Hays when in the Harvard *aula* he told his eager student-listeners that the movies "contain a potency of life in them to be as active as the soul whose progeny they are." Also that the new Hollywood additions to the Harvard business faculty "realize that they are the responsible custodians not only of one of the greatest industries in the world, but of a most potent instrument for moral influence, inspiration, and education." And finally that "in no other commercial activity is there such conclusive demonstration that honesty is the best policy."

3. ADVERTISING: THE MODERN BLACK ART

What the alchemist in the Middle Ages failed to do, making a silk purse out of a sow's ear, the advertiser attempted during the Twenties with more success. For despite the "truth in advertising" movement, much of the old chicanery in a more sophisticated form persisted during the decade. Still, mass production and mass consumption depended to a great degree upon the beguiling wiles of the "ad" man. In a very real sense advertising was at once the ignition system of the economy, the dynamo of mass dissatisfaction, and the creator of illusions in a most materialist world. In an extract from the article "The Tragedy of Waste," *The New Republic,* August 19, 1925, Stuart Chase examines the economics and the place of the industry in the life of the decade.

A ROUGH ESTIMATE OF THE OUTPUT IN NEWSPAPERS, MAGAZINES, BOOKS, pamphlets and circularization matter, reveals the fact that nearly two quadrillion words come off the printing presses of the United States in a year's time. Eleven billion linear miles of words—enough to go clean around the solar system. It would take a shell 500 years to go from the first headline to the last. To consume them all, every man, woman and child in the country over seven years of age would have to read some 60,000 words a day—a sizable bookful. And well over half of them are advertiser's copy.

Advertising might be termed the big brother of most of the forms of illth I have already described. It is the life blood of quackery, and the patent medicine industry. It enters largely into the output of super-luxuries, fashions, commercialized recreation. It is an invaluable adjunct in mobilizing a nation for war. Though the manpower engaged directly and indirectly in advertising is not so large as in certain other forms of wasteful consumption, nevertheless its power, prestige, and ramifications are such as to merit a separate discussion. Furthermore, its position is slightly different from the forms of illth heretofore enumerated. It is not an end product. No one consumes advertising directly. It is an inter-mediary service which points the way to consumption and which enters into the cost of consumption—whether the product be soap or lingerie, motor cars or pink pills.

Mr. Edward Bok, writing in the Atlantic Monthly, has estimated the total annual outlay for advertising as follows:

Newspapers, $600,000,000; direct advertising (mail matters, hand bills, etc.) $300,000,000; magazines, $150,000,000; trade papers, $70,000,000; farm papers, $27,000,000; sign boards, $30,000,000; novelties, $30,000,000; demonstrations, $24,000,000; window displays, $20,000,000; posters, $12,000,000; street car cards, $11,000,000; motion pictures, $5,000,000; programs, $5,000,-000; total, $1,284,000,000.

Over $1,250,000,000 involving, at an average wage of $2,000, the labor power, direct and indirect, of upwards of 600,000 workers. Mr. Bok's estimate is not excessive, for it checks with all other estimates we have seen, which run in the neighborhood of a billion a year, or better.

Whether this total includes under the caption of "direct advertising" all of the doctrinal matter on and about package goods and bottles, we do not know, but we suspect that it does not. Such outlays are more likely to be charged direct to the cost of manufacture.

So-called "national advertising," which discloses the merits of a single product to the whole country from California to Maine, amounts to over $600,000,000 a year—or about one half the total for all advertising. A poster campaign covering the country with 17,196 lithographs, duly placed at proper scenic spots along the public highways, will cost about $140,000 per month to operate.

More than half of the output of the country's printing presses is advertising matter. In newspapers, the ratio of advertising space to total space runs from 40 to 75 percent. Thus of the 2,600,000 tons of newsprint pulp consumed annually well over 1,500,000 tons goes into advertising. It has been estimated that 80 percent of all mail matter consisted of advertising material. The proportion of this which finds the wastebasket unread must be very considerable. One concern appropriated $12,000,000 for advertising in 1923. In the same year the Investment Bankers' Association spent $40,000,000. Meanwhile, a single page in the Saturday Evening Post costs $11,000 per insertion. The Wrigley gum electric sign at Times Square, New York, consumed $108,000 of current a year. On the top of the Cleveland Credit Company appears this legend: "This sign burns more current than the entire town of Illyria." Illyria has a population of 30,000.

. . . the elimination of certain forms of cheating and chicanery is good from the public standpoint, but the public will have to carry the load of the 600,000 non-producers just the same. They may turn from the stimulation of "Black Draught" and "baby killer" soothing syrups; but only to increase the stimulation of svelte lines, motor cars, and skins you love to touch. An advertisement was recently noted to the effect that "hard water had ruined more hands than hard work"—an advertisement put out by a water-softening concern. It had duly passed the official "Truth" censorship. A man of science wrote to the censorship and inquired what chemist had verified this statement. As a chemist himself he knew that it was not true. Nothing is harder than sea water, and nothing is better for the skin. The Truth movement replied that they had no technical backing for the statement, and invited the man of science to furnish the necessary vouchers!

In America one dollar is spent to educate consumers in what they may or may not want to buy, for every 70 cents that is spent for all other kinds of education—primary, secondary, high school, university. And yet when all is said and done, advertising does give a certain illusion, a certain sense of escape in a machine age. It create a dream world: smiling faces, shining teeth, school girl complexions, cornless feet, perfect fitting union suits, distinguished collars, wrinkleless pants, odorless breaths, regularized bowels, happy homes in New Jersey (15 minutes from Hoboken), charging motors, punctureless tires, perfect busts, shimmering shanks, self-washing dishes—backs behind which the moon was meant to rise.

4. SALESMANSHIP

The salesman, of course, did not originate in the Twenties. But the new academic emphasis produced a host of textbooks which ostensibly drew upon psychology and other sciences. They purported to instruct the neophyte in new ways of the ancient art. The noted criminal lawyer, Clarence Darrow, examined some of these volumes in a critical spirit, and clearly brings out the appeal of the salesman to the irrational elements in his clientele. Whatever his effects upon the rational individual, the salesman, like the "ad" man, was an inseparable part of the institution of big business. The following extracts are from Clarence Darrow, "Salesmanship," *The American Mercury,* August 1925.

A FEW DAYS AGO I PICKED UP A POPULAR MAGAZINE AND READ THE ADVERtisements. I was surprised to see the number of schools and universities offering courses in salesmanship. These advertisements all featured in large type such expressions as: DON'T ENVY SUCCESSFUL SALESMEN—BE ONE! and BECOME A SALESMAN—BIG JOBS OPEN! The headings were followed by seductive reading matter about men "who make from $5,000 to $30,000 a year, who travel first class, stop at the best hotels, and are in daily contact with Prosperous Business Men." Often there were pictures. Two boys were represented, starting out with equal chances and equal ability. In the next picture they had both grown old, but one was associating with Prosperous Business Men and the other was still a laborer. One had studied Scientific Salesmanship. The other had stuck to hard work.

It was not with the idea of getting a job, but mainly through simple curiosity that I sought to find out what all this was about. All my life I had been interested in books, but somehow I had overlooked books on salesmanship. Literally hundreds of them, it appears, are now on the market, and used by our colleges, universities and Y.M.C.A. night schools in the laudable business of giving hope and cheer to the overworked and underpaid. The topics they deal with range from those which might properly be placed under the heads of calisthenics, physical culture, hypnotism, phrenology, psychology, dress, and deportment, to specific directions for the treatment of hard customers and tricks for getting the unwary to buy.

Here I shall let these books speak for themselves, with only such comment as will be necessary for clarity. There is a matter of terminology which we must get straight before the show begins. Among the first things which attract attention in this literature is the fact that a prospective purchaser is not regarded simply as a human being, or even referred to in terms of his occupation or social position. For the salesman all men are Prospects. It seems to me only fair, then, that we look upon every one who attempts to sell anything as a Prospector.

Obviously, if a Prospector is to be successful, he must prepare himself for his arduous life of gold-digging. All the books thus start out with chapters on the general subject: "How to Get Ready and Why." The first thing the aspiring salesman must do, it appears, is to develop the physical basis for the combative spirit necessary in forcing a Prospect to buy:

> Many young men are not highly developed in the faculty of combativeness and in order to become good salesmen they require this faculty brought into positive function, that they may not give up or become undecided and discouraged. Combativeness functions through the shoulder and arm muscles as shown by the soldier, prize fighter, athlete, etc., and, well developed, it imparts a feeling of enthusiasm, physical vigor and power of decision that no other faculty can give; the best way, then, of bringing it into proper function is to take up some form of exercise that will call into use the shoulder and arm muscles, each morning immediately upon arising, devoting ten or fifteen minutes to this. The same amount of time may be devoted with profit in the evening if one feels the extra need.

But this is not enough. No ambitious salesman will be content with the development merely of his physical powers. He will also cultivate his spiritual gifts for the contest. Thus he is instructed to say to himself: "I *will* succeed. I will *awaken* tomorrow feeling good. I will go through the day doing work better than I have done it before. I will meet every one with a feeling of good will!"

It is a good idea, we are informed, to keep on repeating this formula until one falls asleep; then the subconscious can carry on while one is sleeping. By morning, one will thus have made as much progress as if one had stayed awake repeating the formula all night! . . .

II

All this mental discipline, of course, is possible only if the salesman has some training in and understanding of psychology. Accordingly, each one of the books I have examined devotes a few pages to explaining the fundamentals of that recondite science. . . . One of them sagely advises the student to "spend a few evenings studying psychology." Out of that study, brief as it is, he is supposed to attain to complete control of the Prospect:

> To master conviction it is essential that you have knowledge of the human mind and how it works. You must know what takes place when a customer deliberates. What change takes place in his mental consciousness, what is his mental attitude, and what is his state of mind while being convinced.

One would think that with all this subtle knowledge the scientific salesman would be ready for the fray. But no. He must next carefully prepare a Selling Talk. All the books lay great stress on this. It is never even suggested that people buy goods because they want them. They must be told that they want them. The only exception I have been able to find in the literature is in a few sentences distinguishing between the business of a salesman and that of a mail-order house. We are told that "some goods are sold without salesmen. Mail-order houses use a catalogue in selling their merchandise. *The individual who orders from a catalogue usually* WANTS *the goods and utilizes the catalogue to ascertain the price.*" But the scientific salesman is above selling merchandise to those who actually want it. What he must do is put in a simple way by one of the most popular books on the subject:

> You get an order from a prospect because of what he *thinks.* Signing an order or handing over money must be a *voluntary* operation. The prospect must be *willing;* he must think certain thoughts. *You* must lead him *to think those thoughts.*

Another author calls this process "uncovering a need for the goods." We are informed, however, that merely uncovering the need is not sufficient, for it might result in the customer buying some other person's goods and fail to convince him that he should buy *now.* The Selling Talk, therefore, must induce the prospect to make a favorable decision at once. In fact,

> The one and only purpose of a Selling Talk is to get the order. . . . All that a salesman says to a Prospect can be printed in a circular or typed in a letter and mailed to the Prospect, but the salesman can bring to bear in the personal interview every power of language and every bit of force that is in words, and focus them on the mind of the customer while he demonstrates his goods. The whole purpose of the Selling Talk, then, can be summed up in: 1. It must uncover in the Prospect's mind a need for the goods. 2. It must convince him that *your* goods are the goods he needs.

3. It must bring him to the point of *deciding* that he needs your goods more than he needs the money they cost. 4. That he must have the goods as quick as he can get them—so he orders. Any Selling Talk that does not accomplish this purpose has missed the mark.

In many of the textbooks, the salesman is carefully instructed as to the use of particular words and as to their proper pronunciation and warned against errors in grammar. However, he must understand, too, that it will not do to be over-particular about grammar. He must be democratic and despise the snob. One of the best books gives this suggestion:

I know a man who found it helpful with his general methods to deliberately cultivate a few incorrect habits of speech, such as dropping the *g's* in words ending in *ing*—saying *goin'* for *going* and *advertisin'* for *advertising;* and saying "there *ain't* any" for "there is none" (*sic*). By *unaffected* use of these expressions and careful use of otherwise *good* grammar and pronunciation, they secure an added impression of *earnestness* in what they are saying.

. . . Having mastered all these principles, the student is ready for his first Prospect. But before he can make Selling Talks, he must manage to run his quarry down. If the Prospect is a business man in a downtown office, a careful plan of attack must be formulated. If the Prospect is a housewife or a farmer, a different and perhaps more subtle method must be used.

In discussing the stalking of a business man, many of the books give full instructions for getting past what they refer to as the Outer Guards. These guards are generally office boys and stenographers. Some none too astute salesmen hand the office boy a card reading:

Mr. B. Clyde Edgeworth,
Boston, Mass.

with the inscription in the corner, "Representing the United Bond Co." But this is bad practice, for

The office boy takes this to the inner office and returns a few moments later with the answer that the president is too busy today to see you. You have committed an error in your approach. There is nothing for you to do but leave and try at some future time when you have worked out a more unique method of getting the interview.

Here it is perfectly plain that the Prospect was warned that he was expected to part with money. He should not have been told in this abrupt way. The next time you call, if you are a good salesman, your card will read simply:

Mr. B. Clyde Edgeworth,
Boston, Mass.

The Prospect will be glad to see Mr. B. Clyde Edgeworth from Boston, Mass. If he is a lawyer, for example, he will probably surmise, or at least hope, that Mr. Edgeworth has come from Boston, Mass., to give him money. So Mr. Edgeworth is at once ushered in, and once he gets in he can take his choice of any number of approaches. One book suggests that he may even forget his card and explain to the office boy that he has none. This may induce the Prospect to think he has a client waiting outside. It is even suggested that "many will insist on using a name so difficult that the office boy will forget it. Something like this is used by a clever salesman with a national reputation who enters the outer office and gives the name of Mr. Eishenhimmel." No office boy can remember this name, so the manager hears only that some gentleman from Boston wants to see him. This arouses his curiosity and the interview is granted.

Sometimes the Prospector finds an office unprotected. The proper method of procedure in this case is to stroll carelessly in, "indicating by this attitude that he is familiar with the surroundings." When the Prospect appears, the salesman informs him that he has been waiting for some time. This immediately puts the Prospect on the defensive. Still another way is for the salesman to walk up to the girl in charge and ask for the Prospect and then walk right in to his private office. This will lead to the belief that the girl has sent him in. "While the Prospect is wondering what is wrong with his office system, the salesman is getting warmed up on his talk."

The methods which are suggested for getting into the home and talking to the housewife are even more interesting. We are assured that the following plan is used with great success by the talented representative of a large canned soup company. He carries a thermos bottle filled with hot soup. He rings the bell and the door opens:

"Good morning, Madam."

He pours a small portion of the hot soup into a paper cup which he has handed her.

"I just want you to try this soup."

While she is tasting the soup, he gives a brief explanation and then endeavors to book her order for three or four cans. He explains that the order will be given to her grocer and delivered the same day. She need not pay until the end of the month.

The farmer, it appears, must not be approached too abruptly. If you are to get his money you must break the news to him gently. You should first talk about horses, soil and market conditions. This conversation will show that you are interested in things close to him and likewise give you a chance to study his temperament and "to learn his likes and dislikes and *discover his weaknesses.*"

III

When the Prospector gets well in touch with his Prospect then all his learning in psychology is called into play. To persuade or hypnotize the Prospect, it is of first importance to get his attention. This does not mean that he merely listen politely, but that he give Real Attention to the salesman. Giving him a mental shock is sometimes valuable.

This you can do by dropping your pencil or striking the table. The effect of this is very good providing that the instant you have his attention you drive home some selling point.

. . . Some methods are a little more drastic. One book tells of excellent success following making the Prospect angry.

It was up to me to get their attention. What did I do? I tramped on their corns. I reached over and plunked down on their corns. I really did this; I am not stuffing you. When they got red and mad all over, I knew that I had their attention. Then I would say: "I was clumsy, wasn't I? But profits, profits for you today and profits you haven't dreamed of. . . ."

After the salesman gets the attention of the Prospect, he is ready to unlimber all of his psychological artillery. Of course, he understands that no sale can be made unless he first induces a Desire to Buy. This is a fundamental axiom in all the textbooks:

There must be enough desire in any particular instance to over-balance all obstacles and make the man desire to do the thing more than for some reason—either concealed or expressed—he desires not to do it. The whole question is, can the salesman produce this much desire? If he can, he can sell. There is the whole problem of salesmanship in a sentence.

Nothing could be clearer than this. Contrary to the political economists, sales are not made because the purchaser needs the article and wants to get it, but because the Prospector creates a Desire to Buy in him—a desire which the Prospect never had before, or which at least lay dormant in his unconscious. We are instructed that for creating this desire suggestion is much more important than argument. The Prospect should be in a passive and receptive mood to get the best results

For example, it is easier to make a sale if you are sitting in a semi-dark room than if you are in one brightly lighted. Impressionability and sensitiveness are apt to be overcome by bright lights.

When one really understands this principle, the rest is very simple. So simple that one can't help wondering how a Prospect ever keeps his money. To quote again:

Another stratagem successfully used by a great many salesmen, especially in so-called "high pressure" selling, is to get the Prospect into an agreeable frame of mind just as soon as possible, and then lead him on from one agreement to another until he has the habit. Then, when you ask him to agree to give you an order, he is just that much more apt to do so. This is called the "yes" method of closing.

A life insurance salesman, for example, starts in by getting the Prospect to agree that it is a nice day, or that his offices are very bright and cheerful. Then he leads him on, tactfully and adroitly, from that small beginning to agree that life insurance is a good thing. The next step is to get him to agree that every man should invest a percentage of his income in insurance, and so on up the ladder until finally the salesman gets him to agree to be examined.

In working such sorceries, considerations of age and sex are important.

The young are more readily influenced than the mature, because their fund of knowledge on a given subject is smaller. Women are more liable to succumb to suggestion than men because they are impatient of deliberate process and like to reach conclusions quickly. In business transactions the common citizen is more easily swayed than the professional buyer. Fatigue increases susceptibility, as shown by laboratory experiments. Intoxicants also increase it.

. . . Now we have our Prospect in a passive state of mind and ready for suggestions. To the untutored, the simplest and most direct way to awaken the Desire to Buy in him might seem to be by telling him something about the excellence of your wares and his crying need for them. But there are subtler ways, and the books are nothing if not subtle. Let us go back to their theoretical training in psychology.

Salesmanship is the science and the art of influencing the mind through the five senses. The number of senses that can be played upon depends on the line or the article to be sold.

A wine merchant or salesman can play upon all five senses. The sense of sight is played upon by the merchant's or salesman's manner, expression, gestures and the color of the wine. The sense of smell by the bouquet and the flavor of the wine. The sense of feeling by the generous warmth imparted by the wine to the feelings. The sense of hearing by the salesman's voice and argument.

Operating upon the sense of hearing is by far the most important, for through hearing the salesman can persuade the mind that the other senses are mistaken in their perceptions, or that the consensus of opinion favors the direct opposite of what his mind conceives.

The voice can be trained to become so strong and forceful that its very force carries conviction to the mind of the hearer. It can be trained to become so even and matter of fact that its very tone suggests truth, and the mind of the hearer unconsciously adopts the suggestion that the proposition is entirely as represented. The voice can be trained to become so subtly soft and low that it deadens the resistance of the brain like a soothing narcotic.

It is only fair to add that the book in which all this appears was published before the Eighteenth Amendment and not by the Y.M.C.A. But singers, speakers and actors have long observed these effects of the human voice. Many a man has been charmed by an oration and after going away from a meeting has been unable to remember a single idea that the speaker suggested. Nature creates such magical voices, but art should not be neglected. People, it appears, are taken quite unawares when the great gifts of the rhetorician are suddenly launched against them by one selling mouse-traps or cockroach powders.

Meanwhile, the scientific salesman must not overlook the power of the magnetic eye. This power was first used by snakes in charming birds, and it has been long used in taming lions and other wild animals. Here is its modern application:

Can you look a prospect straight in the eye? Can you keep him looking at you while driving home a point? If you can't, learn how. If you want to be master of the situation, if you want to cast an influence over his mind that will be hard to resist, do it with the eye. If you can hold your gaze on a man without wavering, you can practically persuade him in every instance, unless your proposition is too unreasonable.

While looking a prospect straight in the eye, *it gives him no chance to reason or reflect.* An idea is planted on the subjective mind. It is not analyzed. It is not compared with some past experience. *It is taken as a truth.*

• • • • •

IV

The real purpose of all the foregoing is "to make *your* will the Prospect's will." He must not be allowed to make his own decision, nor even think about it. He may not need your goods or want them, but *you* want him to buy them. You must be the complete master in the whole transaction. Now and then, it would seem, a Prospect shows fight. He has a foolish idea that he ought to have something to say himself about how he spends his money. A good salesman is alert to catch the first sign of this untoward resistance. The Prospector is carefully enjoined, to quote the words of one of the books, that

> If you keep a tight rein on a skittish horse, you can handle him, but the minute you let him grab the bit and feel he is boss, then you have a dangerous chance of a runaway.

This admonition is followed by a touching story of a clever salesman whose Prospect began to take the lead in the conversation. Disregarding all the rules, this Prospect forced the salesman to follow in *his* lead. Promptly the salesman shut him off.

> At the first sign of unruliness in the Prospect, he began to pick at his thumb nail. As the Prospect got further out of control he would examine the supposedly afflicted thumb anxiously. Then in the middle of the Prospect's remarks he would say, "Pardon me, but have you a sharp knife?" The Prospect produces a knife and generally apologizes for its not being very sharp. The salesman says that it will do and begins to cut at an imaginary hang-nail and complains of what a nuisance hang-nails are. The Prospect generally sympathizes and as he draws up to look at the operation, the salesman says, "There, I guess that's fixed," shuts the knife and with a sigh of relief looks up at the Prospect again. "Let's see, what were we talking about? Oh yes, about so and so. . . ."

One's mind wanders to the question of the fairness of this subtle method. What chance has an ordinary man when a Prospector so deeply learned in psychology has at him? However, this point is covered in a perfectly logical manner by the textbooks.

> When a Prospect has granted you an interview; when he has given you his attention at its best or comes into your store, or when a woman has opened her house door to you, that interview is *yours* and you have a right to manage it and direct it according to your own particular plan.

Fair enough! The impudence of a Prospect having anything to say about spending his own money! Especially in his own home!

The whole procedure may be summed up in one sentence, taken from a leading textbook: *Do not permit the Prospect to reason and reflect.* A scientific salesman must always bear in mind that it is his first duty to get control.

> The salesman must not be entirely confined to one method of approach, or a single talking point, or to any particular and exact program. He must be

versatile. If he can't get his customer one way, he must get him another. A thoroughly trained psychologist, by observing the facial expression of his Prospect, his feeble remarks, his wariness, and his show of fight, ought to be prepared at any moment to change his tactics. The expert fisherman tries out the fish—if one kind of *bait* doesn't get the strike, he changes. And if one kind of hook doesn't *land* them he changes hooks. If he is alert, aggressive, masterful, persistent and a thorough psychologist he perseveres. He carefully lays his snares, places his bait and, then the unsuspecting Prospect falls into the trap.

No matter how good an approach you have made, regardless of how clever or how perfect your Selling Talk may be, it is all of no avail unless you close the sale. Therefore, you should have a Reserve Talk in readiness if the need should arise. In large letters the salesman is told that "many Prospects must be led; others driven. The closing argument must be directed at the Prospect's *weakness*. Tie your Prospect up so that he must act. The majority of salesmen make it too easy for their Prospect to slip away. Tie him up so that he cannot *possibly* back down."

5. A DOLLAR DOWN: CONSUMER CREDIT

The personal tensions built up in this mass production, consumption-on-credit process, as well as the inevitable economic debacle it foreshadowed, were scarcely considered by its chief promoters during these years. The effects on the local merchants of the mandate to sell goods on almost any terms is illustrated in the following "confessions" of an automobile dealer. "Confessions of a Ford Dealer" as told to Jesse Rainsford Sprague, *Harper's Monthly Magazine,* June 1927, p. 26. Copyright 1927 by Harper & Row, Publishers, Incorporated. Reprinted from *Harper's Monthly Magazine* by special permission.

THE FORMER FORD DEALER SAID:
Things have changed a lot around here since 1912, when I bought out the man who had the Ford agency and paid him inventory price for his stock, plus a bonus of five hundred dollars for good will. A dealer didn't have to hustle so hard then to make both ends meet. You kept a few cars on your floor and when you needed more you bought them. You were your own boss. There weren't any iron-clad rules laid down for you saying how you had to run your business.
Sometimes I wonder if Mr. Ford knows how things have changed. I have just finished reading his book, and in one place he says: "Business grows big by public demand. But it never gets bigger than the demand. It cannot control or force the demand."
Understand me, I think Mr. Ford is a wonderful man. They say he is

worth a billion dollars; and no one can make that much money unless he has plenty of brains. Still and all, when Mr. Ford says businss cannot control or force the demand I can't quite think he means it. Or maybe it's his little joke. You *can* force demand if you ride people hard enough. And, believe me, you have only to get on the inside of a Ford agency to learn how.

Take my own case, for instance. Like I say, when I first took the agency I was my own boss like any other business man, selling as many cars as I could and buying more when I needed them. I didn't have to make many sales on installments, because people who wanted cars usually saved up in advance and had the cash in hand when they got ready to buy. Occasionally some man that I knew would want a little time, in which case I just charged it the same as if it was a bill of dry goods or groceries, and when the account fell due he paid me. There was no such thing then as putting a mortgage on the car and taking it away from him if he didn't pay up. If I didn't believe a man was honest I simply didn't give him credit.

I did a pretty good business this way and by 1916 was selling an average of about ten cars a month. Then one day a representative of the Company came to see me. I'll call him by the name of Benson, though that was not his real name. In fact wherever I mention a man's name in giving my experiences I shall call him something different because some of them probably would not like to be identified. Well, anyway, this man that I call Benson came into my place at the time I speak of and said ten cars a month was not enough for a dealer like me to sell. It seems the Company had made a survey of my territory and decided that the sales possibilities were much greater. Benson said my quota had been fixed at twenty cars a month, and from then on that number would be shipped me. . . .

Well, I finally decided to take a chance on twenty cars a month rather than lose the agency. I had read a lot of nice things about Mr. Ford in the newspapers and I felt sure he wouldn't ask me to do anything he wouldn't be willing to do himself. Benson said he was glad I looked at things in a businesslike way and promised me plenty of assistance in moving my twenty cars a month. He called it "breaking down sales resistance."

I guess I should explain that out West here an ordinary Ford dealer doesn't do business direct from the factory in Detroit, but works under a general agency. The agency that I worked under was located in the city about a hundred and fifty miles from here, and I suppose the manager there took his orders from the factory. During the fourteen years I was in business there were eight different managers, and some of them rode us local agents pretty hard. I always thought I wouldn't have so many troubles if I could have done business direct with Mr. Ford, but

I can realize how busy a big man like him must be, and I guess it is necessary for him to leave things pretty much in the hands of his managers that way. A few times when I thought they were riding me too hard I wrote in to the factory and complained about certain things, but I never got any answer. My letters were sent on to the branch manager, and of course that got me in bad with him. I found that if I wanted to hold my agency I had better do what I was told. Out of the eight managers six were transferred to other branches and two threw up their jobs to go into other lines of business. I met one of these fellows after he had quit and asked him why there were so many changes. He said he guessed it was because the Company believed a man had a tendency to get too friendly with the local agents if he stayed too long in one territory, and to see things too much from the agents' viewpoint. Personally, he said he quit the Company's service altogether because he couldn't stand the pace. . . .

I sure got it in the neck when the slump of 1920 came on. If anyone wants to know what hard times are he ought to try to do business in a Western farming community during a panic. Almost overnight half of our sheep men went bankrupt when wool dropped from sixty cents a pound to twenty cents, and hardly any buyers at that price. The potato growers couldn't get enough for their stuff to pay freight to the Chicago market, and most of them let their crop rot in the ground. Of our four banks in town two went into the hands of receivers and the other two had to call in every possible loan in order to save their own necks. A lot of our Main Street retailers fell into the hands of their creditors that year, too.

I was in about as bad a fix as anyone else. By then I had agreed to take thirty Fords a month, which was a pretty heavy job to get away with in good times, to say nothing of the sort of a situation we were going through. These cars came in each month, regular as clock work, and I had stretched my credit at the bank about as far as it would go in paying for them as they arrived. The bank kept hounding me all the time to cut down my loan, which I couldn't do with my expenses running on all the time and hardly any business going on. From September to January that year I sold exactly four cars.

Pretty bad? I'll say it was. But the worst was yet to come. Altogether I had more than one hundred and forty new cars on hand, besides a lot of trade-ins, and no immediate prospect of selling any. Then all of a sudden came notice that a shipment of fifteen Fords was on the way to me, and that I would be expected to pay for them on arrival. I thought there must be some mistake, and got the branch manager in the city on the long distance. He was a pretty hard-boiled egg named Blassingham.

"What's the meaning of these fifteen cars that are being shipped me?" I asked. "I've already taken my quota for the month."

"It don't mean anything," Blassingham answered, "except that you're going to buy fifteen extra cars this month."

I tried to explain to him that I was in no position to get hold of the cash for such a purchase, and even if I was I wanted to know the whys and wherefores.

"You know as much about it as I do," he snapped. "Those are the orders, and my advice to you is to pay for those cars when they arrive."

Of course I sensed the reason later on, when it came out in the newspapers about Mr. Ford's little tilt with the money sharks down in New York, how they tried to get a hold on his business and how he fooled them by getting the cash without their help and then told them to go chase themselves. . . .

I am willing to confess that we rode the public a little ourselves while we were getting rid of our big surplus of cars. There are always some people that you can sell anything to if you hammer them hard enough. We had a salesman named Nichols who was a humdinger at running down prospects, and one day he told me he had a fellow on the string with a couple of hundred dollars who would buy a car if we would give him a little extra time on the balance. This prospect was a young fellow that had come out West on account of his health and was trying to make a living for his family as an expert accountant. Just at that time the referee in bankruptcy was doing most of the accounting business around town, and I knew the young fellow wasn't getting on at all. He had about as much use for a car as a jack rabbit. I told Nichols this, but you know how plausible these go-getter salesmen are; he told me it wasn't our business whether the young fellow had any use for a Ford or not; the main thing was he had two hundred dollars in cash.

Well, we went ahead and made the sale, but we never got any more payments. The young fellow took to his bed just after that, and the church people had to look out for him and his family until he died. In the final showdown it turned out that the two-hundred dollar equity in the car was everything they had on earth, and by the time we replevined it and sold it as a trade-in there wasn't anything at all. I gave twenty dollars toward his funeral expenses. I know this sounds pretty tough; but when it's a case of your own scalp or some other fellow's you can't afford to be too particular. . . .

About the most nagging thing to me were the visits of the expert salesmen who came around every so often to show us how to sell cars. It seemed to me that so long as I was taking my quota every month I ought to be the best judge of how and who to sell. There was one expert I specially remember by the name of Burke. Among other things I had to do was to keep a card file of people in the territory who had not bought cars, and usually on these cards we wrote items like "says maybe will be in market this fall," or "not ready to buy yet." Burke was always raising

Cain because we didn't make people give more explicit reasons for not buying. I remember once he laid me out because a card said only "Can't sell him." The man was a poor devil of a renter seven or eight miles out of town who never had enough cash ahead to buy a wheelbarrow, but Burke insisted that one of my salesmen go out there with him to try and land a sale. When they got there a couple of the children were down with whooping cough and a hailstorm had laid out his bean crop, but Burke came back and told me he would expect me to put over a Ford on the fellow before he came on his next trip. . . .

You do a lot of things when someone is riding you all the time that you wouldn't do under ordinary circumstances. Beans and clover seed are the farmers' principal money crops around here, and one fall in September and October we had one heavy rain after the other that practically ruined everything. Business was terrible because the farmers hadn't recovered yet from the bank failures and the slump of 1920; and one day I wrote in to the Company, telling what bad shape the farmers were in and asking if my quota couldn't be reduced for a few months until things picked up. All I got for my trouble was a letter stating that "such farmers are not the people to sell to."

Of course it was easy enough for them to write such a letter, but I always thought Mr. Ford ought to realize that in a country community when the farmers are broke the doctors and dentists and storekeepers are in about the same fix. Not being able to get my quota reduced, I had to take business wherever I could find it, and it was about this time that I had my experience with the army captain. It seems this captain had been kicked by a horse in the course of his duties and came to our town for treatment in the hospital. He showed up at my place one day and said he wanted to buy a Ford coupe. He had a dented-in place on the side of his head from the accident, which I suppose was the reason for his acting so queer. There were some big used cars in the place that belonged to customers, and while the salesman was showing him Fords he would hop into these cars and start the engines and then say he wanted to buy one of them instead of a Ford. It didn't make any difference when the salesman told him the cars belonged to other people. Finally the salesman came to me and asked what to do. I had a talk with the captain and at first was inclined not to sell him, especially when he said he only had fifty dollars to lay down as a first payment. We are supposed to get a third down on a new car, but of course when the branch manager is riding you all the time you sometimes make deals that are not strictly according to Hoyle, and with my quota of thirty cars coming in every month and no farmer trade in sight I was inclined to take chances. The upshot was that I took the captain's fifty dollars and off he drove.

He had promised to bring in another hundred dollars when he got his salary check, but the first of the month rolled around and no captain. We wrote him letters but he didn't answer, and the collector never could catch him in at the place where he was staying. When it strung along for another month I set a private detective on his trail and found the captain went three times a week to the hospital for treatment, from ten to twelve in the morning. We have duplicate keys for all the cars we sell, so one morning I sent one of my mechanics out to the hospital and when the captain parked his car at the curb and went inside the building this mechanic just unlocked the car and drove it back to the garage. Of course I didn't have any right to do this but possession is nine points of the law, and when the captain threatened to make trouble I reported him to the army authorities as a deadbeat. I guess he was a little daffy anyhow, from the dent in his head, because it turned out he had been buying a lot of other things on installments. People said he was a real nice fellow before his accident, but in the investigation that followed he lost his commission and was fired out of the army. The last I heard of him he was bootlegging.

If Mr. Ford knew personally some of the things that go on I am sure he would call a halt to his branch managers riding the local agents the way they do. Like I say, when you are crowded all the time to make your quota under all sorts of business conditions, you do things you don't like to. There are some pretty tough characters in this town just as there are everywhere else; but a quota is a quota and you can't stop to pick your customers. One thing I have noticed is that the hardest boiled eggs are most likely to come up with their time payments. Only last year I sold a car to a big colored fellow and of course as he had no visible means of support I took a mortgage on it so I could replevine it in case he didn't pay, but every month he came in right on the dot with the cash. Naturally I'm not bragging about it, and I'm not saying anything was wrong; but during that time a street car conductor was held up at the end of the line a couple of times and there were some other bits of devilment of a like character.

● ● ● ● ●

If manufacturers were happy about the massive sales on credit, others were less so. Bankers and credit institutions warned that the overuse of the new instrument might bring disaster. In 1926, as the following article points out, the national association of credit men warned the country about the "explosiveness of credit" if improperly used. "Living and Dying on Installments" by Hawthorne Daniel, *The Worlds Work,* January 1926, p. 329.

. . . The installment business has been built up largely by manufacturers desirous of increasing their output. So far it has worked, but there is an interesting possibility that seems to have been overlooked by many whose sales have been increased by this method.

Let us imagine a person who purchases everything on the installment plan. Let us suppose that, in doing so, he pays on the average 10 per cent more for the goods that he buys. It is obvious, then, that 10 per cent of his expenditures goes to pay the operating costs and profits of finance companies or whatever takes their place. Thus the customer can buy only nine tenths as much as he could if he paid cash, and consequently the manufacturers who serve him, reduce by 10 per cent the goods they can produce for him. Carried to extremes, then, the installment plan may end by forcing a reduction in output, which is the exact opposite of what it is supposed to do. Before the widespread use of the system this was not possible, but today, with more and more merchants utilizing it, there is a real possibility that it will end by killing the goose that lays the golden egg.

Recently the National Association of Credit Men, an organization representing 30,000 merchants and manufacturers, adopted, at its national convention at Atlantic City, a carefully prepared statement concerning installment credits. It is a clear exposition of the conservative credit man's viewpoint and reads as follows:

Many business executives in their zeal for distribution have failed to understand the explosiveness of credit when it is improperly used. The events of recent years clearly show that the stimulation of business by the unwise use of credits is merely a temporary measure and has a reaction in the serious disturbance of business and prices.

Selling goods at the expense of safe credit tends to cheapen it, to make serious losses, and to disturb business morals. Selling goods on the installment plan when these goods are used for further production or to fill economic needs is perfectly proper, provided the contract has reasonable conditions. Selling goods on the installment plan for individual consumption or for mere pleasure is highly dangerous unless the distribution is reasonable and the credit used in such transactions causes no disturbance of the credit supply.

Making it easy for people to buy beyond their needs or to buy before they have saved enough to gratify their wishes tends to encourage a condition that hurts the human morale and supports a form of transaction for which credit is not primarily intended.

There has been built up in our country a large peak of installment credits, and it is wise for our business people to exercise caution, for undoubtedly in a credit pinch this condition would prove a very disturbing factor.

Some distributors have taken exception to this attitude of caution upon the part of the National Associaion of Credit Men, but it must be recognized that the preservation of credit is our chief obligation. We must be fearless in pointing out the dangers in the present situation, even though we should, in doing so, go against the ambitions of some for an extended distribution on long and installment credit terms.

6. SOMETHING FOR NOTHING: SPECULATION

During the Thirties it became fashionable to blame most of the speculative urge which contributed to the Great Depression on Wall Street and on other New York financial institutions. That the speculative fever was endemic to all classes in the country is well evidenced by the great Florida land boom of 1925-26. The boom was essentially caused by hundreds of thousands of small operators, doctors, lawyers, shop-owners, and retired people. They flooded the state feverishly buying property at sky-high prices in the hopes of selling it a few months later at enormous profit. The following extracts are from an article by a would-be female speculator, who, like millions of others saw pie in the Florida sky. Gertrude Mathews Shelby, "Florida Frenzy," *Harper's Monthly Magazine,* January 1926, p. 177. Reprinted by permission of Harper & Row, Publishers, Incorporated.

THE SMELL OF MONEY IN FLORIDA, WHICH ATTRACTS MEN AS THE SMELL of blood attracts a wild animal, became ripe and strong last spring. The whole United States began to catch whiffs of it. Pungent tales of immense quick wealth carried far.

"Let's drive down this summer when it's quiet," said canny people to one another in whispers, "and pick up some land cheap."

Concealing their destination from neighbors who might think them crazy, they climbed into the flivver, or big car, or truck, and stole rapidly down to Florida.

Once there, they found themselves in the midst of the mightiest and swiftest popular migration of history—a migration like the possessive pilgrimage of army ants or the seasonal flight of myriads of blackbirds. From everywhere came the land-seekers, the profit-seekers. Automobiles moved along the eighteen-foot-wide Dixie Highway, the main artery of East Coast traffic, in a dense, struggling stream. Immense busses bearing subdivision names rumbled down loaded with "prospects" from Mobile, Atlanta, Columbia, or from northern steamers discharging at Jacksonville. A broken-down truck one day stopped a friend of mine in a line. The license plates were from eighteen different states, from Massachusetts to Oregon. Most of the cars brimmed over with mother, father, grandmother, several children, and the dog, enticed by three years of insidious publicity about the miracles of Florida land values.

The first stories of the realty magicians had been disseminated through small city and country newspapers, particularly in the Middle West.

Systematic propaganda stressed the undeniable fact that Florida was an unappreciated playground. Yet that was far less effective advertising than the beautiful, costly free balls given by one subdivision in certain cities. Those who attended shortly afterwards received a new invitation, to go without charge and view lots priced from one thousand dollars up.

Lured by the free trip, many went. Those who bought at the current prices and promptly resold made money. Other subdivisions met the competition, offsetting the overhead by arbitrary periodic raises in all lot prices. Whole states got the Florida habit. The big migration began.

Millions—variously estimated from three to ten—visited Florida last year, investing three hundred million dollars, and bank deposits swelled till they neared the half-billion mark in July.

The newcomers found themselves in a land where farming was practically at a standstill. Fresh vegetables were almost unobtainable; everybody uses canned goods. All food brought top New York prices. Railroads and steamships were inadequate to carry enough food, supplies, and passengers. For more than thirty days at midsummer an embargo was effective against building materials because a food famine (not the first) threatened. In September the prohibition extended to household goods, bottled drinks, and—chewing gum! . . .

Joining the great migration this summer, I went inclined to scoff. Were the others also confident that they possessed average good sense and were not likely to be fooled much?

Probably. I was lost. I gambled. I won. I remained to turn land salesman. Not only with no superiority, but with defiant shame rather than triumph, I confess—not brag—that on a piker's purchase I made in a month about $13,000. Not much, perhaps, but a lot to a little buyer on a little bet.

In June an old and trusted friend turned loose upon our family a colony of Florida boom bacilli. It was a year since I had heard from this particular friend. He was down and out, owing to domestic tragedy topped by financial reverses. Suddenly he bobbed up again rehabilitated, with $100,000 to his credit made in Florida since November, 1924. His associate made more than $600,000 in six months.

Had they been successful in 1923 in forming a $250,000 syndicate to buy the entire Florida part of the coast-wide canal, which included alternate sections of land in what is now a high-priced neighborhood, they would have been multi-millionaires. Failing to do this, they afterwards secured mere remnants of these lands at $22 an acre, selling promptly at an average of over $200. Now they wish they had had writer's cramp and had been unable to sign contracts of sale, for the same land is held at ten times the price at which they sold. . . .

We sailed from Philadelphia. On the boat I was amazed to find myself already a "prospect." Brokers on shipboard enviously assumed that our friend, like the usual land-octopus, had encircled wealthy prey in New York. A protectively inclined Philadelphian warned me in private, "Don't be drawn in. I wish I'd never seen Florida. It's a magnificent state. Money is to be made still. But speculation is hog-wild. People do things they'd never be guilty of at home. I've done them myself. I'm sewed up now in a company whose president, I've discovered, is a crook who failed at everything but bootlegging. If you enjoy a good night's sleep now, stay out." His protectorship was rather unflattering. Feeling superior, I thanked him. But when I landed at Miami I saw the significance of his warning. The whizzing pace of the people in tropical heat (for it *is* hot in Florida in summer—dripping hot) showed their frantic excitement. There was a sparkle in every eye, honest or dishonest. At the hotel, humming night as well as day with unwonted activity, a man in the next room took advantage of the after-midnight rates joyfully to long-distance New York.

"Momma! Momma! Is that you, Momma? This is Moe! I bought ten t'ousand acres today. Yes, ten t'ousand. Vat? Vat you say? Vy—Momma! How should I tell you where that land iss? I don't know myself!"

When, in those first days as a prospect, I was rushed by motor car and boat all over the Gold Coast, that millionaire-jeweled strip seventy-two miles long and two to seven miles wide from Miami and Palm Beach, between the Everglades and the Ocean, I was confronted everywhere by evidences of boom hysteria. On a street corner a woman selected a choice lot from a beautiful plat shown her by a complete stranger and paid him fifteen hundred dollars in crumpled carefully hoarded bills. He gave her a receipt, but vanished. There was no land.

On two minutes' acquaintance disciplined men and women boiled over to totally unknown chance companions on purely personal matters. A corner policeman of whom I asked a casual question burst out, "My God, I wish I was out of this! My mother died yesterday in Chicago." The current excitement had undermined his usual self-control.

On one of the innumerable Florida busses, bumbling overbearingly down the blisteringly hot Dixie Highway toward Miami, my neighbor was a young woman of most refined appearance, an exceedingly pretty brunette in white crêpe de chine gown and hat. Only her handkerchief-edge hinted at mourning. As usual, the bus joggled loose all reserves.

"Florida? Wonderful! Came with a special party two weeks ago. Bought the third day. Invested everything. They guarantee I'll double by February. Madly absorbing place! My husband died three weeks ago. I nursed him over a year with cancer. Yet *I've actually forgotten I ever had a husband. And I loved him, too, at that!*" Values and customs are temporarily topsy-turvy in Florida.

What happens to Florida "sourdoughs" on arrival? Few come fortified with even the names of reliable firms. Notorious as well as honest promoters lie in wait for the gambling horde. Like wolves, they stir up the sheep, stampede them, allow them no time for recovery. They must decide instantaneously.

Again and again I declared that I had no intention to buy, but nobody let me forget for an instant I was a prospect. As upon others, the power of suggestion doubtless worked on me. It is subtly flattering to be the implied possessor of wealth. The kingdoms of the world appeared to be displayed for my choice. To help me choose, I, like everyone else, was accosted repeatedly on Miami streets, offered free dinners and bus trips, besides a deal of entertainment, conscious and unconscious, by high-pressure salesmen.

The boom bacillus thrives on prodigality. The price of good food brings many a prospect to the point of spending thousands. Two unusual concerns rewarded only real purchasers *post hoc*. One gave them an airplane ride, the other a free soft drink.

On account of an inherited notion of conduct towards those with whom one breaks bread, I refused all such bait. On my independent investigations salesmen found me unusually inquisitive. One, trying to sell me a $3500 lot, reproved me. "Those things don't matter. All Florida is good. What you are really buying is the bottom of the climate. Or the Gulf Stream. All you've got to do is to *get the rich consciousness*. There's the dotted line—you'll make a fortune."

Authentic quick-wealth tales, including innumerable lot transactions, multiplied astoundingly. They were not cases of twenty-five-dollar land proved worth one hundred dollars, but of prices which had pyramided high into the thousands. When I saw the sort of people who were making actual money my hesitation appeared ridiculous. I resolved to invest. I tried to assume an attitude of faith. I said aloud, indiscreetly, "Resisting enthusiasm and using intelligence—"

I was interrupted scornfully. "That's just it. The people who have made real fortunes check their brains before leaving home. Buy anywhere. You can't lose."

Those last three sentences, boom-slogans, were mainly true in 1924. But I for one refused to credit them in 1925. Clinging to such wits and caution as remained to me, that first week I studied the land itself from Miami to Fort Lauderdale, to Palm Beach, to Jupiter and Fort Pierce. Like everyone else I yearned to own a bit of the ocean rim. But shore acreage was held mainly in parcels priced at a million or worse. Beach lots for the little piker in good subdivisions cost now from $7000 to $75,000, according to location. Even on good terms that sort of thing was not for me. Biting off too much leads to acute financial indigestion.

Perhaps I could find a doll-ranch—the traditional five acres with orange trees.

I searched. Some orchards still stand. Many have been mowed down by subdivisioners with an eye to front-foot prices. The fields, the wilderness, are side-walked and handsomely lampposted. The main ocean boulevard of the little city in which we were staying at the moment has not yet a sidewalk, yet checkerboards of cement, often approached through a showy archway, mark the strangely empty site of many a sold-out backwoods subdivision. The raw land is being laid out as if for an exposition. Surveyors' theodolytes are seen everywhere. Roadmaking is a great industry. The available supply of wood is used up for lot-stakes.

Yet, houses, usually of hollow tile, pop out like the measles—they weren't there yesterday. Florida's table, I concluded, was being spread as rapidly as possible for an immense population, invited to occupy not only what it is believed will be a continuous pleasure city seventy-two miles long between Palm Beach and Miami, but the entire state, with twenty-two million acres capable of development.

Searching continually for some deal to fit my modest purse, I found that the only ranch tracts priced within my reach were six or seven miles back in the Everglades. No Everglades for me, I decided, until reclamation is completed.

I then was offered by a reputable firm a great bargain in a city lot for $1000, an unusually low price. Well-located $3000 fifty-foot lots are rather scarce. This bonanza turned out to be a hole, a rockpit—and I reflected on the credulous millions who buy lots from plats without ever visiting the land!

But to set against this experience I had one of exactly the opposite sort which left me with a sharp sense of personal loss. An unimportant-looking lot several blocks from the center of Fort Lauderdale (whose population is fifteen thousand) on Las Olas Boulevard had been offered me about a week before at $60,000. I didn't consider it. It now resold for $75,000.

"It doesn't matter what the price is, if your location is where the buying is lively," I was told. "You get in and get out on the binder, or earnest money. If you had paid down $2500 you would have had thirty days after the abstract was satisfactorily completed and the title was approved before the first payment was due. You turn around quickly and sell your purchase-contract for a lump sum, or advance the price per acre as much as the market dictates. Arrange terms so that your resale will bring in sufficient cash to meet the first payment, to pay the usual commission, and if possible to double your outlay, or better. In addition you will have paper profits which figure perhaps several hundred per cent—even a thousand—on the amount you put into the pot. The next man assumes your obligation. You ride on his money. He passes the buck to somebody else if he can."

"But what happens if I can't resell?"

"You're out of luck unless you are prepared to dig up the required amount for the first payment. You don't get your binder back. But it's not so hazardous as it sounds, with the market in this condition."

Imagine how I felt two weeks later still when the same lot resold for $95,000. By risking $2500 with faith I could have made $35,000 clear, enough to live on some years. Terror of an insecure old age suddenly assumed exaggerated proportions. Right then and there I succumbed to the boom bacillus. I would gamble outright. The illusion of investment vanished. . . .

● ● ● ● ●

The stock market was the main arena for the speculative urge, a market uncontrolled except for the self-regulation of the governing boards of the exchanges. Consequently the cupidity of the brokers was equaled only by the stupidity and the avarice of the customers. Below is the account of a businessman who in 1928 spent two months in the office of a "reliable and honest broker." His astonished concern at the "normal practices" on the street, of course, had no effect upon the big bull market that roared on to its cataclysmic crash just a year later. Robert Ryan, "Brokers and Suckers," *The Nation*, August 15, 1928, p. 154.

DURING THE SPRING MONTHS OF THIS YEAR THE CUSTOMERS' ROOMS OF Wall Street's brokerage houses were overflowing with a new type of speculator. In these broad rooms you could see feverish young men and heated elders, eyes intent upon the ticker tape. The ranks of the inexperienced—the "suckers"—were swelled by numbers of men who had been attracted by newspaper stories of the big, easy profits to be made in a tremendous bull market, of millions captured overnight by the Fisher Brothers, Arthur Cutten, and Durant. At first these newcomers risked a few hundred dollars with some broker they knew, discovered that it was easy to make money this way, and finally made their headquarters in the broker's large customer's room, bringing with them their entire checking and savings accounts.

These amateurs were not schooled in markets that had seen stringent, panicky drops in prices. They came in on a rising tide. They speculated on tips, on hunches, on "follow-the-leader" principles. When a stock rose sharply they all jumped for it—and frequently were left holding the bag of higher prices. They would sell or buy on the slightest notice, usually obeying implicitly the advice of their broker.

Out of this combustible desire to trade in and out of the market, abuses have arisen. Some brokers, none too scrupulous, have taken advantage of the helplessness of the small customer. The broker can make more commissions by rapid trading than by holding stocks for real appreciation in value, and he knows that this particular type of customer is here today and gone tomorrow. He must make commissions while the money shines.

Sometime ago I spent about two months in a busy broker's office. I had been offered a position as customer's man (to get new accounts and keep them posted on the market's doings). As I wanted to see whether I would like this work, I asked for a two months' period in which to learn the business. The broker with whom I became associated is considered reliable and honest, and the offer was supposedly an attractive one. I sat in the private office of the president and was thus able to follow quite minutely the methods by which he conducted his business. Years of experience with ordinary business had given me no hint of the practices I saw occur as everyday procedure—in the main practices highly prejudicial to the average customer's interest. So astonished was I that I questioned several other Wall Street brokers, only to find that the practices I saw were common enough on the Street, indulged in more or less generally by large and small firms. . . .

I shall list here a few of the incidents I witnessed while in the office. On Thursday the partner of Mr. X, whose name I shall conceal, had bought some shares of Arabian bank stock at $440 a share. This stock was not listed on the Stock Exchange but was dealt in by over-the-counter houses (houses which deal in unlisted securities). These firms make their own prices, determined solely by the demand for the stock. There is usually a marked difference in quotations by these houses, and the practice is to call several of them before buying in order to get the best price. On Friday morning a customer of Mr. X telephoned an order to sell 50 shares of Arabian bank stock. Mr. X obtained his permission to sell "at the best price." He called to his partner, "Want any more of that Arabian bank stock?"

"At what price?" answered Mr. Y. "I paid $440 a share yesterday."

"You can have this for less," said Mr. X. "I've got a market order. The market is 415 bid, 445 offered. Want it at 415?"

"Sure," said Mr. Y. And the customer was informed that it was too bad he got such a low price—but after all, "we sold it at the market."

The dishonesty of this transaction lies in the fact that if several firms had been called and the stock offered for sale, a better price could have been obtained, for this was an active stock in good demand with a wide difference between the bid-and-ask prices.

Incident No. 2: This firm was "bullish" on a certain stock—they believed its price would go higher. Suddenly a panic developed in the stock and it began to decline at a rapid rate. The large and small customers who owned the stock all began selling at once. When the selling confirmations came in, Mr. X announced that no selling prices could be given out until all the orders were checked. In the next half hour Mr. X and his partners selected those sales which had brought the best prices, allotted these best prices to their larger customers, and allowed the small fry to get what was left. This is obviously unfair discrimination. A record is kept by the order clerk of the sequence in which the selling orders are placed. Consequently, the prices of the sales should have been allotted in that order. "Of course," Mr. X remarked, "we make most money from our large customers, and we must keep them satisfied."

Incident No. 3: The broker charges a standard—and substantial—commission on the orders he executes, yet it is common practice among all firms to borrow money at, let us say, 5 per cent and charge 6 per cent to their customers who buy on margin. The Stock Exchange has ruled that brokers may charge their customers the exact amount of interest, or more than the exact amount, that they themselves have to pay when they borrow the money in the open market or from banks; but in no case may brokers charge the customers *less* than the brokers pay in borrowing the money. This rule has been promulgated in order that brokers may not offer the extra inducement of a reduced interest rate to large speculators in order to acquire them as customers. This rule does away with a great deal of cut-throat competition; but in practice the large customer is actually charged the same amount of interest as the broker pays or very little more, while the small customer pays an average of $\frac{3}{4}$ of one per cent additional on all money which he uses when buying on margin. This $\frac{3}{4}$ of one per cent, various brokers have told me, is intended to cover the entire overhead cost of their business. This means that the commissions which are paid for buying or selling the stock are net income to the brokerage house. It is easy to understand why brokerage houses insist that they are justified in charging this so-called "service fee" for negotiating a loan for a client.

Incident No. 4: Mr. X stepped into the customers' room and announced with a great show of sagacity that "Pomegranate A" was a purchase at current prices, and that he advised immediate purchase. His advice was quickly followed; there was general buying by the customers who thought they saw an opportunity to make some quick money. A few minutes later Mr. X notified one of his large customers that he had sold 1,500 shares of "Pomegranate A" at excellent prices, and received the client's congratulations for a good "execution." Those customers in the big room who bought on Mr. X's advice paid 6 per cent or more on their money, and watched the stock drop in value. The story behind this transaction was enlightening. Mr. X's large customer had heard from a director of "Pomegranate A" that the quarterly dividend would **not be** paid and that this fact would be announced in a few days. Knowing that the stock would drop in price after such an announcement, Mr. X's customer gave immediate orders to sell at the current prices. Mr. X knew that "Pomegranate A" was a volatile stock and that if he dumped 1,500 shares on the market it would break the price of the stock. So, by getting his small customers to buy these shares, he placed a cushion under the stock to absorb the 1,500 shares he was selling. He sold at no sacrifice and induced his smaller customers to buy stock which he knew would decline in value.

Incident No. 5: A "pool" is made to maintain current prices in a certain stock or push those prices higher. Mr. X was in a pool to raise the price on "New York Rug." This pool had made a substantial profit by the time its price had been shoved up to $212 a share. Thereupon the members of the pool decided to liquidate their holdings and take their profits. Mr. X knew that this stock was not worth $212 a share and that when the pool had distributed its holdings the stock would drop in value. Mr. X had put a large number of his customers into this stock at high prices. When any of them called to inquire about it he answered cheerfully, "It's good for $250 a share. Yes, I'm holding mine." So his customers held on.

When Mr. X and his friends had finished taking their profits by selling the stock and the news had come out on the floor that the pool had disbanded there was a great deal of "short selling." (If you believe a stock is selling at a price above its real value, you sell it and buy it back at a lower price—if you are lucky.) These "short sales" forced the stock down, and it was only then that Mr. X telephoned his customers that he understood the stock was a sale at once, and watched his customers receive much lower prices.

Incident No. 6: Mr. X advised all his customers to buy "Rotton Apples Common." Since Mr. X's firm helped to finance the stock issue their interest in selling this stock could hardly be wholly disinterested.

It would be simple to multiply these incidents and cite other practices, but what I suggested in the first part of this article has, I believe, been amply shown: in every case under my observation the broker felt that he must give the advantage, even though it were a dishonest advantage, to his large customer, for the large customer is his bread and butter and his profits. The small investor or speculator remains completely unaware of these practices. In a rising market such methods may be employed without losing the customer's business, for a speculator will overlook small irregularities as long as he continues to make money; while in a declining market the broker gets away with an equal amount of dishonesty, the customer blames the results on market drops. If a customer loses all his money, or so dislikes the actions of Mr. X's firm that he withdraws his business, Mr. X is completely unconcerned. As he remarked to me: "Suckers are born every minute; the glamor of easy money gets them all. One goes, two come in. Win or lose, we get our commissions." It is an easy-going philosophy which has been so completely proved true by many Wall Street brokers that they have no reason to revise it.

How such practices can be stopped I do not know; nor do I imagine that it is within the power of the Stock Exchange authorities to prevent them. I do believe that one step ahead would be to forbid all brokerage houses or their employees to transact business for themselves, to compel them to act solely as customers' agents. Surely this would make them a trifle more disinterested in the advice they give their clients.

In the meantime Mr. X's firm is making money hand over fist. In another month they will move to quarters three times their present space.

TECHNOLOGICAL CULTURE

One of the most important social results of the new industrialism was that it supplied leisure time to the masses. By the end of the Twenties the work week of sixty hours was cut to forty-eight. As technology supplied time, it also furnished instruments and institutions by which the newly leisured masses were beguiled off the job. The automobile, the moving picture, and the radio were all taken up en masse during the Twenties. Of the three it is difficult to say which had the greatest impact upon the rapidly rising urban culture. The automobile gave the population an unaccustomed mobility unknown since the pastoral hordes had wandered across the grasslands of Asia and Europe. And the ways and institutions of mobile peoples have always sharply differed from those of the more sedentary populations.

The movies gave another dimension to mobility, offering the spectators an easy escape into worlds not their own. Some of these new worlds were constructed of pure fantasy, but others reflected the life of the rich, the smart, and the profligate. Thus an intimate knowledge of how the other half supposedly lived became the common property of the masses. Radio did in a way for the ear of the crowd what the movies did for the eye. It brought the world to the middle-class home and to the tar-paper shack with an immediacy never before known. Simultaneously the compelling tones of the advertiser were declaiming to the crowd that these once unattainable worlds were a part of the their inheritance. A chicken in every pot, a car in every garage, film star beauty for every adolescent girl, and perhaps an adultery for every marriage—these were the promises and the expectations of the Twenties.

The new income levels and leisure also made it possible for the crowd to participate in fads and fashions, a preserve hitherto of the wealthy, since both depended in part upon an expensive factor of rapid obsolescence. Just as quickly as the working girl zestfully bought a cheap copy of a carriage trade dress she took up Mah Jong and almost as quickly discarded both as the wheels of fad and fashion turned. And occasionally the crowd invented its own fads. Marathon dancing and flag-pole sitting were phenomenal in popularity one year and forgotten the next. The following articles and documents comment as much upon the social results of this bright new world of mass leisure as they do upon its construction.

7. THE AGE OF PLAY

Contemporary authors were aware that the new technology, affording the masses both leisure time and money, was basically responsible for a major social revolution in the country. Almost overnight the amusement and recreational industries became big business, the proportions of which are pointed up in the following article. Robert L. Duffus, "The Age of Play," *The Independent,* December 20, 1924, p. 539.

. . . IT IS DIFFICULT TO ASSIGN AN EXACT DATE FOR THE BEGINNING OF THE Age of Play. If we seek the influences which brought it about we may go back half a century or more with profit; if we are looking for its external symptoms, a quarter of a century is nearly enough. Obviously the first prerequisite for play is leisure, although animal spirits and some economic leeway are desirable. Play on anything like the American scale would have been impossible except for the short working day, the Saturday holiday or half holiday, and the annual vacation. These are gifts of a century which also presented us with the World War and the Newer Pessimism.

With a decrease in the amount of human energy actually required for earning a living has gone a prodigious increase in wealth, thus upsetting what was once held to be an ethical as well as a mathematical law. In 1850, the national income per capita was $95, in 1918, $586—a rate of progress which far outruns any inflation of the currency. In 1900, according to Mr. Julius Barnes, the average American family spent sixty per cent of its income for the basic necessities of life, but in 1920 had to devote only fifty per cent to the same purpose. Thus there was not only leisure to devote to play, but money to spend on it. There was also, no doubt, an increasing restlessness, growing out of the uninteresting nature of the mechanical tasks to which larger and larger armies of workers were being assigned. So the stage was amply set for the Age of Play.

The first unmistakable sign of the coming era was the development of interest in games, a phenomenon faintly manifested in the United States for a decade or two prior to the Civil War, and slowly gathering strength thereafter. Baseball first appeared in something like its modern form about 1845, but did not produce its first professionals and thus start on its career as a great national spectacle until 1871. Lawn tennis, first played in America in 1875, and golf, introduced early in the last decade of the century, remained games for the few until very recently. Now there are said to be 2,000,000 golfers and from a quarter to one half as many tennis players. These are conspicuous instances of a general tendency. The playing of outdoor games was formerly either a juvenile or an aristocratic diversion; it has now become practically universal. There are golf links upon which horny-handed men in overalls play creditable games. And the number of onlookers at professional sports is legion. In a single year there are said to have been 17,000,000 admissions to college football games and 27,000,000 to big league baseball games.

A second phase of the development of play in America is the community recreation movement, which arose from the discovery by social workers that training and organization for leisure were becoming as necessary as training and organization for work. In 1895, the city of Boston took the radical step of providing three sand piles for the entertainment of young children; model playgrounds came about ten years later, and the first "recreation centers" were not established until the middle of the first decade of the budding century. As late as 1903, only eighteen cities had public playgrounds of any description. Then the growth of such facilities began with a rush. Last year there were 6,601 playgrounds in 680 cities, with an average daily attendance of about a million and a half.

In eighty-nine cities there were municipal golf courses on which any man or woman who could afford clubs, balls, and a small green fee could play. Besides golf courses and tennis courts, upon which many a commoner became proficient in what had been "gentlemen's" games, there were municipal swimming pools, ball grounds, theatres, and, in forty-five instances, summer camps under municipal auspices. Municipal expenditures for public recreation have nearly trebled since 1913, though they are as yet only about one third of the national chewing-gum bill.

But no spontaneous play and no disinterestedly organized recreation program can for a moment be compared in magnitude with what are commonly known as the commercialized amusements—"the greatest industry in America," as James Edward Rogers of the Playground and Recreation Association has called them. The motion picture, the phonograph, and the cheap automobile came into existence, like the cheap newspaper, because a public had been created which (consciously or not) wanted them and could pay for them. Each had been the object of experimentation during the last quarter of the Nineteenth Century, but each attained social significance only after the opening of the Twentieth, when multitudes, for the first time in history, had money and leisure they did not know how to use.

The most significant aspect of the Age of Play, however, is not in its inventions, good and bad, but in an alteration of an ancient attitude—a veritable change in one of the most fundamental of folk ways. For uncounted generations man has survived and made progress, in the temperate zones, only by unceasing industry; in tropical and subtropical areas, where climatic conditions did not encourage industry, he survived without progress. At first the industrial revolution did not seem to break down this antique scheme of nature; but in this country, at least, and within this generation, it has become evident that unremitting toil is not necessarily a law of human destiny, and that a thimbleful of brains is worth at any time an ocean of sweat. The mechanical multiplication of labor power by ten, twenty, forty, or a hundred, the replacement of a man by two cents' worth of coal, has struck a fatal blow at the ancestral faith in mere hard work.

Less than a hundred years ago the merchants and shipowners of Boston were able to answer the demand of their employees for a ten-hour day with the argument that "the habits likely to be generated by this indulgence in idleness . . . will be very detrimental to the journeymen individually and very costly to us as a community." Fifty years ago a United States Commissioner of Patents, Mortimer D. Leggett, declared amid the applause of well-meaning persons that "idleness . . . stimulates vice in all its forms and throttles every attempt at intellectual, moral, and religious culture." The first break in this armor of conservatism occurred when it was discovered that play added to the worker's efficiency and was therefore of economic value. Through this chink heresy has crept in, and it is now apparent that play is coming to be looked upon, whether athletic in character or not, whether "commercialized" or not, as an end justifiable in itself. Blindly, blunderingly, yet with more intense conviction than appears on the surface, the masses of the people are uttering a new moral law. The chains of necessity have been loosened; they are nearer a frank and full enjoyment of life than any people that ever lived.

I do not maintain that all their amusements are wholesome, nor that the excessive standardization and mechanization of work and play alike is without its dangers. I do maintain that such evils as exist are minor in comparison with the great gain for civilization that took place when millions learned to play where only thousands played before. These evils are not to be cured by curbing the spirit of play. Reformers and educators must accept this spirit as more sacred than anything they have to give; they can help by guiding, not by restraining.

The right to play is the final clause in the charter of democracy. The people are king—*et le roi s'amuse.*

8. THE COMPULSION TO WHEELS

The compulsion to buy an automobile in the early Twenties seemed to afflict all classes, the rich and the poor alike, irrespective of need and of personal budget. This national mania can probably be explained in part by the nation's overwhelming acceptance of the automobile as the ultimate status symbol, in part by the feeling of mastery and power it gave the new owner. What the "auto mania" did to personal budgets and for the pride of the owner is discussed below by a small-town banker who himself fell before the new contagion. William Ashdown, "Confessions of an Automobilist," *Atlantic Monthly,* June 1925, p. 786. By permission of the *Atlantic Monthly.*

I AM A SMALL-TOWN BANKER, AND I AM EXPECTED TO ACT THE PART, LIVING well, dressing well, and patronizing all our local affairs, as a banker should.

As a dispenser of credit, I have many opportunities to study human nature and to observe how men get ahead and how they fall behind. I believe my bank has handled more automobile propositions than any bank of its size in the country. We have made a specialty of loans on automobiles and have watched the agencies as they have grown from nothing to substantial business concerns. In this connection we have acquired a large amount of experience, suffered no losses, and learned not a little of the weaknesses of human nature as reflected in the automobile.

I am not a "tightwad." I am careful and I am thrifty—at least I was until I became a motorist. I am not a good spender. I have always worked for my money and I part with it only for value received. I have always saved part of my earnings, from habit rather than from necessity. I have never earned "big money," but I have always had enough. I have never celebrated a stroke of good fortune more riotously than by buying a new suit of clothes and a necktie. But several years ago, when I was getting into my stride, I was told by my friends that I had arrived; and I wanted to believe them. Perhaps the moment had come to paraphrase General Pershing and tell the world "Ashdown's here!" How could I tell it more effectively than by the purchase of a car?

At that time the automobile had not yet become a popular fad. The streetcar was still the common method of local conveyance and the railroad still the common medium of long-distance transportation. There were no finance companies especially equipped to handle time-payments on cars. The banks were highly skeptical of the automobile as a credit-risk, and the man who borrowed in order to buy a car was looked upon as dangerous. Even the humble Ford had to be sold, instead of selling itself as it now does. The dealers were inexperienced and without adequate resources. A car was considered distinctly a luxury, not, as at present, a rudimentary necessity.

After a severe battle with my thrifty conscience, I persuaded myself that I could afford a car. Absolutely ignorant of cars and car values, I finally decided upon a modest secondhand machine, of a make that was neither standard nor popular. The price represented about one tenth of my yearly income, and I had never before spent half so much on a luxury. Theretofore my greatest single extravagance had been a bicycle, which, while bearing at the time about the same relation in cost to my earnings, carried with it no upkeep or heavy depreciation, no social obligations or incidental expenditures; its first cost was its last.

It is a rigid rule with me not to buy what I cannot pay for, and whenever I drive a new car out of the salesroom it has no lien upon it; but it was not without trepidation that I drew my check in payment for that first automobile. . . .

At first I carefully set down all expenses connected with my car. I was curious to see if my budget was working out, but the figures mounted up so fast that I dared not look the facts in the face and so closed my books. Ignorance is bliss and bliss is expensive.

Having a quick method of locomotion, it was easy to run out into the country of a Sunday for dinner, or of an evening for a drive and a "bite." Then, too, my friends expected me to do the honors, as chauffeur and host, and this added to the mounting costs. But I had started something that I could not stop gracefully or consistently. My thrift habits were steadily giving way to spendthrift habits.

After eight years of experience I find that the psychological processes of car-owners are much alike. First you want a car; then you conclude to buy it. Once bought, you must keep it running, for cars are useless standing in a garage. Therefore you spend and keep on spending, be the consequences what they may. You have only one alternative—to sell out; and this pride forbids.

The result upon the individual is to break down his sense of values. Whether he will or no, he must spend money at every turn. Having succumbed to the lure of the car, he is quite helpless thereafter. If a new device will make his automobile run smoother or look better, he attaches that device. If a new polish will make it shine brighter, he buys that polish. If a new idea will give more mileage, or remove carbon, he adopts that new idea. These little costs quickly mount up and in many instances represent the margin of safety between income and outgo. The overplus in the pay envelope, instead of going into the bank as a reserve-fund, goes into automobile expense. Many families live on the brink of danger all the time. They are car-poor. Saving is impossible. The joy of security in the future is sacrificed for the pleasure of the moment. And with the pleasure of the moment is mingled the constant anxiety entailed by living beyond one's means.

Time was when the leading men of the community vied with one another as owners of houses. The mansions of an earlier day, with their mansard roofs and spacious outbuildings, are mute evidence of the race for prestige years ago. A man expressed himself and his tastes through his home and its surroundings. If he owned a span of horses and a few carriages and hired a coachman, his entire investment was not half that often covered by one car today. The upkeep was small and could be figured with reasonable certainty. The coachman got board and lodging and perhaps two dollars a day; now a chauffeur gets five dollars a day and meals wherever he happens to be.

The paramount ambition of the average man a few years ago was to own a home and have a bank account. The ambition of the same man today is to own a car. While the desire for home-ownership is still strong, I believe people are giving less thought to the home and more to the car as an indicator of social position. The house stands still; only a chosen few can see the inside. But the car goes about; everybody sees it, and many observers know what it cost.

Given the choice of a fine home without a car and a modest one with a car, the latter will win. Real-estate men testify that the first question asked by the prospective buyer is about the garage. The house without a garage is a slow seller. While the country makes an appeal of its own, it has an added lure if it can be enjoyed through the medium of the car, and many a man has moved from city to country in order to get away from the high cost of maintaining an automobile in the city. The whole scheme of domestic life centers about the motor-car.

Dangerous rivalries among friends and in families are created by the motor. If one member of a family makes a bit of money he must advertise it to the rest of the family and to the world by the purchase of a car. Or, if his social scale seems a bit below that of the rest of the family, he seeks to lift himself higher through the medium of a car. The result is a costly rivalry that brings the whole group into debt.

Not only is the car a symbol of the social and business status of the owner, but its loss is a calamity. I have never known a man to give up an automobile once owned, except to buy a better one. The experience of the finance companies is that only an insignificant percentage of the cars financed by them are ever repossessed. In other words, the car stays sold, no matter what hardships may attend its keeping. It takes courage of no mean order to confess to the world that you have had a motor and have lost it. Therefore the car is the last sacrifice to be offered on the altar of reverses. I know a man who did not have the price of his next month's commutation ticket and yet he kept his automobile.

The ambition to own an automobile does not confine itself to the upper classes and those with substantial incomes, but reaches down into the "white-collar workers"—the clerks and salaried men on limited incomes. In my own bank fifty per cent of the force own cars and drive to work in them. I do not believe the middle classes are getting ahead as they once were. What formerly went into the bank now goes into the motor-car. The thought in the minds of many workers is not how much they can save, but how long it will be before they can have a motor.

I had occasion not long ago to check up a number of automobiles on the time-payment plan with a New York company. We found that the owners were carpenters, masons, bricklayers, and so on, living in inaccessible suburban places, who used their cars—all new ones—to go to and from their work. Perhaps their investment is justified by the high wages they now earn, but time was when the humble bicycle or the trolley-car was good enough for them. Walking today is a lost art. Even my laundress comes to work in a taxi and goes home by the same route. No doubt I pay the bill. To go to the village shopping on foot is now a social error, even though the distance be but a few blocks.

True, many automobiles are now sold to those who can afford them, but the competition is so keen and the driving force behind the dealers is so insistent that many who would not ordinarily buy are persuaded that they should do so. I use our own town as typical of many others. During a period of about four weeks I saw the following sales made: (a) a $1500 touring car to a small tailor, who had no place to keep it, had nothing to pay down on it,—except an old Ford in exchange,—and who could not in the course of two years pay a note of seventy-five dollars at his bank; (b) a similar car to the policeman on the post, who went in debt for half his monthly salary for a year in order to pay for it; (c) a sedan selling for about $2000 to a restaurant keeper who had just gone into business for himself. He had saved $1000, purchased a place for $5000, borrowed $2500 from the bank, and gave notes for the balance in order to take possession. After the first season, with a hard winter before him, this man deliberately—or through the efforts of a good salesman— plunged into debt for $1200. The result is that all he earns must be applied to his debts, and he now has no margin of safety at all. Before, he was sure of his ground and free from anxiety. Now, he must not only work, but he must also worry.

Some will blame the dealers for sharp selling practices; others will blame the finance companies for accepting any risk that is offered; still others will blame the buyer for being an easy mark. But, whatever the reason, the result is the same—debt, debt, debt, for a costly article that depreciates very rapidly and has an insatiable appetite for money. To be sure, the money goes out in small lots, but the toll is large if it be reckoned for a year, and this the average man has not the courage to face; or, facing it, he has not the courage to quit. He must keep his car.

The avalanche of automobile-owners is not a good omen. It signifies that the people are living either up to their means or beyond them; that the old margin of safety no longer obtains; that the expense account must constantly increase. The race to outdo the other fellow is a mad race indeed. The ease with which a car can be purchased on the time-payment plan is all too easy a road to ruin. The habit of thrift can never be acquired through so wasteful a medium as an automobile. Instead, the habit of spending must be acquired, for with the constant demand for fuel, oil, and repairs, together with the heavy depreciation, the automobile stands unique as the most extravagant piece of machinery ever devised for the pleasure of man.

But—

I still drive one myself. I must keep up with the procession, even though it has taken four cars to do so.

9. GO SOUTH, OLD MAN

America had always been a transient country. And in a way the Twenties simply substituted the Ford for the prairie schooner. For many the trek to Florida held some of the same lures that the trails to the West once had—a chance to start over, a possibility of sudden fortune. This 1925 migration was the first, but not the last, to take place on rubber wheels and gasoline power and it betokened the future; it also was prompted by a new American reason for trekking. The frontiersman had gone West knowing that he was to be faced with privation and, at the journey's end, hard work. Many of the Florida migrants, however, came seeking the sun and the soft life out of a desire to escape the harsher features of their old homes. For the first time in the national life masses of Americans sought not opportunity but indulgence. This phenomenon is discussed in the following article. C. P. Russell, "The Pneumatic Hegira," *The Outlook*, December 9, 1925, p. 559.

IT WAS IN A GROVE OF OAK AND PECAN TREES ON THE EDGE OF A NORTH Carolina cotton farm that I came upon a roadside camp of automobile tourists on their way to the new promised land—Florida. Night was falling, and there were a sound of clattering dishes and a smell of cooking in the air. Tents of white or brown were slowly rising like angular camel's humps. Children's voices mingled with the barking of small dogs.

There were fourteen cars in the camp, ranging all the way from dusty Fords to big and glittering limousines with balloon tires and tremendous horse-power. Included were two large caravans built on truck frames. One housed a family of eight persons, and the other contained a single elderly couple, whose wheeled abode was fitted up like a Pullman car. One automobile drew a trailer laden with a substantial stock of canned goods. Its owners were taking no chances on running short of food in the unknown South.

The States represented were Maine, Vermont, Massachusetts, New York, New Jersey, Pennsylvania, Ohio, Montana, and Washington. The population of the camp was perhaps sixty, including dogs, cats, and ukeleles. Children were numerous, and there was a fair sprinkling of old people—the parents of young couples who had sold out everything "up

North" and were on their way to the far South to make their fortunes, to find work, or just to "locate."

The tourists included men of almost every occupation. Carpenters and bricklayers—attracted by tales of high wages—were numerous, but there were also engineers, lawyers, doctors, schoolteachers, salesmen, and proprietors of small-town stores.

As they drew in and stopped their heated engines, some of them threw themselves flat upon the ground and lay there as if exhausted, some walked around stiffly for the purpose of limbering up cramped limbs. Others immediately began to erect their tents, set up cots, and lay out their cooking utensils, for your motor tourist, after a long day's drive, has but two thoughts—first to eat, and then to rest under shelter.

After being rested and refreshed, nearly everybody was willing and even anxious to talk. A gathering around a central camp-fire was turned into an experience meeting. There were few without a tale of calamity to tell, for Florida-bound cars are heavily loaded, and the continuous driving imposes a strain on men and machinery which manifests itself in more or less troubling accidents.

There were stories of inhuman hills, of unsuspected holes, of terrifying detours, of blow-outs and broken parts. Nights of horror in storm-beset camps were described. A lady camper told how she had been kept awake for an hour one night by a stealthy gnawing and pulling at the corner of the tent. She was afraid to move or to call her husband. She recalled stories of the wild beasts of the semi-tropical South, of cougars and catamounts, of alligators and bears. Finally, she summoned strength to arouse her husband. He woke peevishly and criticised the race of women, but on listening to the menacing sound drew his revolver and got out his flashlight. He cautiously raised the flap of the tent and pointed both revolver and light in the direction of the intruder. The glare revealed a bewildered kitten.

In the course of the discussion it was brought out that one or two of those present had been over the Florida trail before. They were instantly made the targets of multitudinous questions.

Was it true that a cordon had been drawn around Miami and that no more strangers were being admitted? Was it true that you had to wait in a long line to buy food there? What about the mudholes in south Georgia and the sandbanks in north Florida? Was it true that the natives fixed up these traps on purpose, so as to be able to draw the stuck cars out with mules at $10 a draw?

There were assertions and denials, rumors and fantasies, arguments and disputes. And above and around it all was perceptible an air of suppressed excitement. It was evident that for most of those present this was the Great Adventure. Some of them had never been far from their native towns before. They were quiet, sedate, settled people who prefer life that runs in an accustomed groove, and to whom change with re-adjustment to new conditions is upsetting. A few of them confessed that they had sold out everything, including the ancestral home, had bought a car and a camping outfit with the proceeds, and were staking all on Florida.

Some declared that they were in search of a climate in which cold and industrial smoke would not afflict bronchial tubes made tender by Pittsburgh or Chicago winters; some avowed with astonishing frankness their failures as laundry superintendents or grocery-store proprietors and their intention to start all over again; others announced that they were "goin' to be a-goin'" or "just to look around." None would admit that he hoped to get rich quick by speculation in land.

It is improbable that the country at large grasps the extent of the present National hegira to Florida. For nearly a year the road on which this particular camp was situated has been traversed by perhaps an average of one hundred cars a day. In the middle of the summer the average climbed up to perhaps two hundred. In September and October the movement attained a crescendo, which was checked only by the advent of chilly and disagreeable weather.

And yet this route is only one of the three favored by motor tourists bound south from the North Atlantic States. The other two carry scarcely less traffic.

The movement promises to bring momentous changes in its train. Southern States, long negligent of their roads, have been stimulated into transforming rough or sandy rural thoroughfares into straight and stately hard-surfaced boulevards, with a consequent fillip to internal intercourse. Old-fashioned Southern villages have been awakened out of their sleep, with an ensuing desire to paint up and brush up. And for the first time in history the common, ordinary "fo'kes" of the North and South are meeting one another on a really large scale, mostly by means of the National chariot—the Ford car.

But what is most striking of all is the setting in motion of a current which may result in a National shift of population scarcely less important in American history than the rush to California and the far West in the days of '49. Though unwarlike and less violent, this movement may have effects as far-reaching as other celebrated hegiras; such, for instance, as the descent of the Goths on Rome, the Mongols on China, the Dutch on South Africa, or the Mormon trek from Illinois to Utah.

Observers of social movements will probably see in it the manifestation of the stampeding instinct which at times seems to seize human beings as well as cattle. Cynics may see in it the aberrant pursuit of a chimera or the sordid desire to get something for nothing. But, whatever its cause and source, there is no doubt about its presence and its probable increase. There are prophets who assert that the South-bound rush of the past summer and autumn will be repeated next year on an increased scale, and there are some who foresee a long motor highway stretching from Bangor to Miami and lined with auto accessory shops, filling stations, Greek lunchcounters, and hot dog stands. This trail will be strewn, not by whitening bones, but by discarded inner tubes and heaps of salmon cans.

Certainly it is the first time in history that a hegira has been carried out on pneumatic tires, upholstered seats, and patented gasoline stoves. Never before have trail-breaking pioneers been able to cover such distances in such *de luxe* style. By carefully selecting their routes they are able never to be long out of sight of ham and eggs or a quart of medium oil. The fortunate go through from New York to Tampa without the labor of even lifting an automobile hood or a hardship beyond a punctured tire.

A new Mark Twain will doubtless arise to record some of the picturesque history of the route to Florida. But he can never use the title "Roughing It."

10. SPECTACLES FOR THE MASSES: THE MOVIE REVOLUTION

The two articles following give some impression of the enormous strides the motion picture industry made. The rapid change from pictures made at the start of the decade costing $50,000 and exhibited in nickelodeons, to ones budgeted for millions and produced in picture palaces in 1930, marks the economic growth of the industry. Aside from noting the effect of the movies upon the legitimate stage and questioning their effects upon the morals of the young, the Twenties had little to say about their impact upon American mass culture. The second article below does, however, hint at some of the psychological results of this democratization of the stage. The first extract is from a staff report to *The Forum*, January 1920, p. 16.

WE HAVE ALL OF US WONDERED HOW MUCH REAL MONEY THEY PUT INTO productions at California. At the studio they had just completed a big production, and I was able to copy off the expenditures from the actual final tabulated cost sheet. Here they are:

COST OF PRODUCTION

Director and Assistant	$3,926.30
Cameraman and Assistant	3,615.85
Raw Stock	395.48
Developing and Printing	3,048.53
Sets	5,579.12
Stills	369.35
Props	4,263.79
Rental of Props	3,111.40
Rental of Lamps	1.00
Rental of Autos	5,384.85
Regular Actors	15,266.96
Extra Actors	24,255.35
Locations	21,914.18
Electricians	516.60
Propertymen	1,352.50
Wardrobe and Drapery	3,174.55
Studio Rent	3,000.00
Office Expense and Telegrams	775.19
Standby	121.00
Titles and Inserts	1,774.24
Administration	1,983.68
Publicity	1,522.99
General Expense	305.47
X—— Y——, Director	13,500.00
Total	$119,158.38

But, of course, any such staggering outlay of money is the extraordinary. That picture is what Movieland calls a "special"—a production which the backers fondly hope will play week runs at theatres and gross them anywhere from half a million to a million dollars. And it was possible to learn at the studios how much real money goes into the average movie as you see it; it is a range from $25,000 to $50,000.

We went into one of the great sheds, called studios, that had a floor space 100 x 220 feet upon which "sets" could be built. Here stood three walls of a ship's salon, the fourth (non-existent) being the opening through which the camera photographed the scene to be played therein. And just across the studio floor stood the massive oaken walls and staircase of a manor house, and, beyond that, one glimpsed the interior of a "church." At the far end of the studio, carpenters were building Napoleon's tomb in the Invalides—the circular visitors' gallery towering above it.

"First," they told us, "the director, after reading the story, decides what scenes will be required. Then he sends a memorandum to his Art Director. (In this studio, by the way, that person turned out to be a famous architect, graduate of the Beaux Arts, who is known for the Italian studio he built in the home of Mrs. Harry Payne Whitney.) The art director then makes rough sketches of his conception of the scenes. Once these are approved by the director they are done again as finished drawings. From these, blue prints are made and sent to the shop."

The "shop" turned out to be a young furniture factory or place where portable houses are built—a large building, buzzing with machinery. Sawdust flew from electrically driven saws only to be sucked in by great ventilators, depending from the ceiling like inverted bowls.

"The walls of the sets," our guide explained, "and all woodwork are built here—also, incidentally, any period of furniture that may be called for by the specifications of the pictures,"—he dipped a prodigious wink—"yes, we all have our bungalows furnished very nicely."

It was in another studio shed that we saw how the sets were prepared for the players. There they stood, four sets of wooden walls in various stages of completion. Here painters were staining the woodwork the color of mahogany; there, men were hanging wall paper; over there where a set was all papered and painted, interior decorators were draping it with curtains and hangings; while in a last set furniture was being arranged, pictures hung, and knickknacks placed with cunning eye to make it look "lived in." And the business manager of one of the companies later showed me his cost sheet for a recent production. One was staggered to see that "props" alone, the dressing of the bare sets, had cost $6,333.57; and that the construction of the sets came to $21,-271.93—a total of $27,605.50, so that your eye would be pleased by attractive backgrounds. And you, who have been told of the fabulous salaries of movie actors and actresses, consider that in this big special picture this total of $27,605.50 had been paid for scenery, so to speak, whereas the total expenditure for performers, including "supes," was but $19,470.71; and that one man, the director, got $15,375—or more than all his actors and actresses, excluding supes, put together. And while the business manager is good enough to let us glimpse at the secret figures of movie production, we pick up the fact that of the $100,000 spent upon this production, 6½ per cent of it was for camera negative, developing and printing, that the hire of automobiles claimed 4½ per cent, that the cameraman and his assistant got about 3 per cent, that lighting lamps and electricians in the studio cost about 2 per cent and studio rental almost 3 per cent. So it is obvious that the big movie, you may see, drew most heavily upon the producer's bankroll for sets, actors and director.

● ● ● ● ●

Lloyd Lewis, "The Deluxe Picture Palace," *The New Republic*, March 27, 1929, p. 175.

THE LEGITIMATE THEATER, USUALLY KNOWN AS "BROADWAY," IS IN A PANIC today, with many of its temples dark and many of its priests and vestals rushing about the streets of the walled city, crying out that the movie vandals are at the gates of the citadel at last.

To hear them wail, one would suppose that the old battle between the drama and the films is about to result in the extinction of art, culture and the revered British accent. The movies, armed now with new electrical catapults and strange talking devices, have all but taken the modern Rome. Years ago, out in the provinces, the films conquered the legitimate theaters of "the road." Not only that: the barbarians clubbed and chased those pious missionaries, the Chautauquans. Next they captured Broadway's strolling half-brothers, the vaudevillians, enslaving them to work four and five times a day in the pagan temples which the vandals have erected everywhere. And now, as the Visigoths prepare to take the capital, it sickens the priests and vestals to discover that the cold-blooded bankers of the citadel itself are financing the invasion.

Superficially, it is the advent of talking pictures, backed by enormous capital, that has caused the panic. In reality it is the success in New York of that provincial institution, the big moving-picture theater, that is responsible.

Only in the past year has Broadway awakened to the fact that the colossal film house, known to the trade as the "de luxe" theater, has been as successful in New York as it was for a decade previous in the "sticks." Ten years ago, when the Capitol Theater, itself immense in size, opened on Broadway, the legitimate drama viewed it as a sort of amiable behemoth, likely to attract little more than the chronic movie-going public. Which was about what happened. But the Capitol was not a typical "de luxe" film house, as that institution has since become standardized over the country. Two years before the Capitol opened, the progenitor of the now accepted type was built in Chicago, a 2,200-seat theater, the Central Park, which some determined and imaginative boys from the nearby Ghetto—the Balaban brothers and Sam Katz—had started, as an experiment upon which they were willing to risk their combined savings. As though inspired by the spirit of audacity which seems contagious in Chicago, they planned their new theater on an unprecedented scale, lined its interior with crimson velvet and marble, adorned the walls with paintings, and filled the lobbies with uniformed and bowing ushers. In a swirl of color and splendor, they experimented with prologues, singers, dancers in diaphanous robes, and "presentations"—in fact, almost everything that the most gorgeous of the 6,000-seat "de luxe" houses offer, on a still vaster scale, today.

As it turned out, magnificence paid well, and, by 1921, the Balabans and Katz had added three other, similar theaters to their list. Presently the clink of money dropping into their box-offices had become such a siren song that moving-picture exhibitors over the country were deserting the old-time "nickelodeons," to make round eyes at the finer and bigger things themselves. By 1926, almost every large city had its "de luxe" house, seating from 2,500 to 4,500 people. Small picture houses died around them like flies. In cities of less than 200,000 inhabitants, the legitimate theaters wilted; vaudeville houses closed or added pictures; Chautauqua circuits shrank.

But each year the "de luxe" houses were more thronged. That pioneer, the Central Park, played to 750,000 patrons in its first year. In 1928, the circuit of Chicago theaters, to which it still belongs, had expanded to include twelve, the other eleven all larger than their progenitor, and had checked over 30,000,000 admissions in the year.

Most of these 30,000,000, of course, were women and children; perhaps not more than 25 per cent of all the patrons were men, and many of these were there chiefly in the role of escort. What had the Chicago pioneers put into their temple that was so seductive to American women?

In the dim auditorium which seems to float in a world of dream and where the people brushing her elbows on either side are safely remote, an American woman may spend her afternoon alone. Romantic music, usually played with a high degree of mechanical excellence, gives her a pleasant sensation of tingling. Her husband is busy elsewhere; and on this music, as on a mildly erotic bridge, she can let her fancies slip through the darkened atmosphere to the screen, where they drift in rhapsodic amours with handsome stars. In the isolation of this twilit palace, she abandons herself to these adventures with a freedom that is impossible in the legitimate theater, where the lights are brighter and the neighboring seat-holders always on the edge of her vision: the blue dusk of the "de luxe" house has dissolved the Puritan strictures she had absorbed as a child.

All of this splendor has been planned for her delight, and with a luxuriance that she had imagined was enjoyed only in Cleopatra's court, oriental harems, or Parisian and Viennese society. She strolls voluptuously through lobbies and foyers that open into one another like chambers in a maze; her feet sink in soft rugs, she is surrounded by heavy Renaissance tables, oil paintings, and statues of nudes. She enjoys the sense of leading a sophisticated, continental life, with none of the practical risks. For she sees church members and respectable householders savoring the same delights about her.

When she goes home that evening, she will perhaps clean spinach and peel onions, but for a few hours, attendants bow to her, doormen tip their hats, and a maid curtsies to her in the ladies' washroom. She bathes in elegance and dignity; she satisfies her yearning for a "cultured" atmosphere. Even the hush that hangs over the lobbies means refinement to her: voices that have been raucous on the street drop, as they drop on entering a church. . . .

The royal favor of democracy it is: for in the "de luxe" house every man is a king and every woman a queen. Most of these cinema palaces sell all their seats at the same price,—and get it; the rich man stands in line with the poor; and usually tipping is forbidden. In this suave atmosphere, the differences of cunning, charm, and wealth, that determine our lives outside, are forgotten. All men enter these portals equal, and thus the movies are perhaps a symbol of democracy. Let us take heart from this, and not be downcast because our democratic nation prudently reserves its democracy for the temple of daydreams.

11. THE FREE AIR: RADIO

The radio, like the movies, became a major stimulus and conveyor of the new mass culture. By the middle of the decade few people were out of earshot of the loud speaker. And since the industry combined the functions of purveying free entertainment and selling advertising aimed directly at the national market, it became an indispensable prop for the mass consumption economy. Its only antecedent in social function was perhaps the patent medicine show of the nineteenth century, and many of the "snake oil" characteristics of the old institution persisted in the new. But to a great degree the mass public became the arbiter of the kind of entertainment which went out over the air. The programs put on were determined in most instances by the size of the listening audience, and thus this new major cultural dynamo was dominated largely by considerations of quantity and not quality. The first of the two following articles traces the rise of the industry and its early connections with the institution of advertising; the second illustrates the power of the public, even in the early days of radio, well before the Hooper ratings, in determining what sort of sense and nonsense went into the microphone. George W. Gray, "Signing Off on the First Ten Years," *World's Work*, December 1930, p. 46.

FROM A FEEBLE WIRELESS TELEGRAPH SERVICE IN 1920 RADIO HAS GROWN in ten swift years to the billion-dollar industry it is today—surely something new under the sun!

At the beginning of 1920 radio was merely a device for sending messages without wires—a means of communicating between ship and shore, and thereby dramatized as the savior of many a shipwreck—an incorporated public service offering transatlantic wireless communication at so many cents per word. Strange magic, of course, but still just another electric way to send a message.

Today wireless telegraph service is more extensive and more widely used than ever before, but who thinks of it when he thinks of radio? Most of us think of WJZ, or of some other cryptic combination of letters. We recall the garrulous antics of Amos 'n' Andy, the pious anecdotes of Seth Parker, the inanities of the Nit-Wits, Dr. Cadman's booming voice. Radio means King George's speech coming over from London in the early morning, it means overhearing Adolph Ochs in Schenectady chat with Rear Admiral Byrd in New Zealand; it means Graham McNamee, Roxy, Floyd Gibbons, Lowell Thomas, the barrage of vocal advertising. It means, in one word, broadcasting.

It's a modern postwar baby, this broadcasting industry. When the boys of the A. E. F. came trooping home from overseas the movie had set up its flickering screen in every crossroads village and the airplane was already carrying the mail on regular schedule, but there was no broadcasting. The radio world consisted of the wireless telegraph stations, a few experimental laboratories, and some thousands of eager amateurs scattered over the globe.

One of these amateurs, whose station had grown from a small homemade receiving set into a full-fledged experimental laboratory, was Frank Conrad. He lived in a Pittsburgh suburb, and his station occupied the upper room over his backyard garage.

Doctor Conrad of the Westinghouse Electric & Manufacturing Company is an eminent engineer and inventor, but I list him here among the amateurs because he entered the wireless field as an amateur. Indeed, he told me he set up his first radio apparatus in 1913 in order to get Naval Observatory time signals and thus keep tabs on the accuracy of a new watch; but he was soon led into the fascinating realm of radio experimenting. By 1915 he had applied to the government for a license, struggled through the requirements until he could receive ten words a minute in Morse code, and obtained a license for experimental station 8XK.

When the United States entered the war in 1917 all amateur licenses were suspended. But because of the work his company was doing for the government, the Navy authorities decided that Conrad's station might continue, relicensed as 3WE. It became an important center of radio research. Day and night the work went forward here and at the station established at the Westinghouse plant five miles away. Conrad's studies were focused mainly on problems of the Army Signal Corps. And especially did he work toward the perfecting of radio telephony.

After the war this backyard laboratory became one of the most powerful amateur stations in the country. Conrad had rigged up a phone transmitter—not many amateurs had that—and it became an exciting game to launch his voice into space and see how far it would carry. Even more exciting was the thrill that came to the distant listener when he picked that voice out of the air. Here was a message that he did not have to decode; anyone could understand it. In many an amateur's home there was the excited calling of members of the family: "Listen. You'll hear a man talking."

The man talked twice a week, Wednesday and Saturday nights. He played phonograph records before the microphone. His high school sons enlisted a quartet of singers from among their classmates, and these became a regular feature. Between musical selections were announcements of news, baseball scores, and other gleanings from the evening paper. In dozens of homes people began to write letters to their faraway entertainer, thanking him, offering suggestions. Could he play the Spring Song next Saturday? Would the boys please sing I Love You Truly?

"Gradually the thing grew," related Dr. Conrad. "One of the boys I appointed announcer. Another boy was the son of a phonograph dealer. As new records were issued he would borrow them, and in broadcasting these selections we would announce that they were provided through the courtesy of the Brunswick Shop. I suppose that was the first radio advertising."

SOMETHING FOR NOTHING AT LAST!

Many times before this the human voice had been vibrated into space on radio waves. As early as 1906 Reginald A. Fessenden transmitted a musical program. But these occasional performances were in the nature of scientific tests or demonstrations. Conrad's performances were unique in that they were offered as a regular scheduled service for the entertainment of the public.

There were some who smiled at the naïvety of this twice-a-week free entertainment. What was the object? How long could he keep it up? Something for nothing was strange business. But these after-hours activities of their engineer were followed with the keenest interest by executives of the Westinghouse company—and especially by vice-president Harry P. Davis.

Davis had been in close touch with Conrad's radio research from the beginning. "But it was more than a merely personal interest and curiosity," says Mr. Davis. "Our company had just bought the International Radio Telegraph Company in order to get control of certain patents. It made this purchase on my recommendation, paying $2,500,000 —which loomed as big in 1920 as $20,000,000 does today—and now the problem was how to turn this new property to profitable account. And since I was responsible for the purchase, I felt responsible for making it pay.

"One Sunday morning, in October of 1920, I picked up a Pittsburgh newspaper, and my eye chanced to fall on an advertisement. A department store was featuring certain wares, and an item down in one corner caught my attention." It read:

A special line of radio receiving sets suitable for listening to Dr. Conrad's concerts.

"The instant I read that paragraph my mind clicked," went on Mr. Davis. "If a retail store saw enough in radio to set up a department to sell goods on the strength of this twice-a-week entertainment, then there must be something in it for a radio manufacturer. Suppose the entertainment were provided daily? Suppose it were broadcast on greater power? Suppose a variety of features were provided? Would not great numbers of people become interested, and buy radio sets in order to listen? If so, here was the solution of our problem. We could manufacture for the multitude instead of for the few wireless telegraph stations."

Next morning Davis sent for Conrad. "Frank, we want you to close down that radio station of yours." Conrad was plainly surprised. "Because," explained the vice-president, "I have an idea that the company ought to get into this broadcasting business." He outlined his plan, and Conrad fell in with the idea at once.

It was decided to launch the new station on the night of November second by broadcasting the election returns. Cox and Harding were contending for the Presidency, and this provided the big national event that was wanted to attract attention to the broadcast. But it made hectic work for Mr. Davis and his associates; for the election was only two weeks off.

Meanwhile, down in Washington, government officials were rather flabbergasted by this strange request for a "broadcasting license." There was no such animal. Finally the Department of Commerce decided that this broadcasting project was something of an experiment, so they licensed it as experimental station 8ZZ.

At 8:30 o'clock on election night Station 8ZZ began its historic broadcast on a wave of 330 meters. A telephone line from the news room of the Pittsburgh Post brought the election items to the hastily built studio on top of a factory building. Conrad went home to his backyard station and stood by, in readiness to take up the broadcast in case anything happened to 8ZZ. A telephone connection between the two stations awaited this emergency use, but there was no need for it. The program went over as planned. It was heard as far north as Manchester, N. H., as far south as New Orleans, La.

KDKA, BROADCASTING'S PIONEER

It was the birth of a new industry. The Radio Division in Washington soon recognized that this new use of wireless was more than an experiment; it granted the first broadcasting license and assigned the call letters KDKA to the Pittsburgh station. For the first ten months of its life KDKA had the radio audience all to itself, and the only interference it knew was that of amateur "sparks."

Competition began in the fall of 1921. Three new stations took to the air in September, one in October, one in November, twenty-three in December. Most of them were small, but each added fuel to a flame that was sweeping the country. Radio shops sprang up in the cities; mail-order stores carried the business into the small towns. The radio craze was on.

By the end of 1922 there were 508 stations broadcasting in the United States. By the fall of 1926 the number had risen to more than seven hundred, and there was pandemonium!

Some stations had deliberately jumped their assignments and appropriated the frequencies of others. Some had increased their transmission power. New stations had popped up demanding time and space in channels already crowded to overflowing. And the law gave the government no power to deny a license nor to regulate a station. On the face of it, one might suppose that no business asset could be of more doubtful value than a broadcasting license; yet, when this chaos was at its height, in November of 1926, the Radio Corporation of America paid the American Telephone & Telegraph Company $1,000,000 for station WEAF and incorporated it as the National Broadcasting Company.

THE GOVERNMENT STEPS IN

It would take many millions to buy WEAF today. Under the present law, broadcasting licenses are granted for ninety days only, and confer on their holder no vested rights; yet the goodwill value of some of the large stations is prodigious. The National Broadcasting Company, with 75 transmitters in its hook-up, and the Columbia Broadcasting System, with 72, have demonstrated that radio entertainment may be operated as a nation-wide business. And now plans are drawn for a "city of radio" to be built on three square blocks facing Fifth Avenue, New York, at a cost of $250,000,000—more physical evidence of the importance of radio as a business.

Of course, the basis of its prosperity is the willingness of the invisible audience to listen. In a recent survey of San Francisco, made public by the Federal Radio Commission, 5 per cent of those interviewed said they were "tired of radio" and 53 per cent said they were "annoyed" by radio advertising. Perhaps these reactions are representative; but, in spite of the banalties and the advertising, the American people continue to buy radio apparatus. They paid $850,000,000 for receiving sets and parts in 1929. Last July, when lay-offs and salary cuts were affecting many industries, a radio manufacturer announced that his company was putting on seven thousand workers in addition to its regular force of thirteen thousand.

Two factors contributed to the stabilizing of the industry. First, the Federal regulation of broadcasting—a measure forced by the lawless competition of 1926. Before this, all efforts to place broadcasting under government control had been defeated in Congress, but now many of the suffering broadcasters themselves cried for relief from chaos. The radio law of 1927 was enacted, creating a Federal Radio Commission with power to license and to withhold or withdraw licenses and empowering the Radio Division of the Department of Commerce to police the broadcasters.

TIME—A MARKETABLE COMMODITY

Today this police function is administered by a staff of more than one hundred inspectors and technicians, working through sixteen district and branch monitor stations scattered over the country. In September of 1930 the effectiveness of the service was greatly enhanced by the opening of the central monitor station. Here—near Grand Island, Nebraska, midway between the two oceans—is installed the most powerful and sensitive detecting apparatus ever assembled. With it the radio police will be able to pick up broadcasts from every American station, to check frequencies, transmitter power, time—all the minutiæ on which a broadcaster must keep within the law.

Radio law is by no means a finished instrument. There are still too many American stations—six hundred in the summer of 1930. But the improvement over conditions four years ago is enormous.

The second factor which has prospered the broadcasting industry is the rise of radio advertising. The purpose of broadcasting ten years ago was frankly to boost the radio business. Eventually the broadcasters discovered that they could also boost the automobile business or the ginger ale business, and time on the air became a marketable commodity.

For an hour on the "blue network" reaching eleven of the largest cities, an advertiser pays $3,350; for the same time on the "red network" of twenty cities, he pays $4,980; and for a nation-wide hook-up of forty-seven cities, $10,180. The National Broadcasting Company reports for 1929 a gross income of $150,000,000, most of it receipts from advertisers.

Advertising has made broadcasting an industry, but from the ranks of radio itself, from no less a personage than Dr. Lee De Forest, comes this frank warning: "The present tendency of the broadcast chain and many individual stations to lower their bars to the greed of direct advertising will rapidly sap the lifeblood and destroy the usefulness of this magnificent new means of contact."

Broadcasting is possible without advertising. In the British Isles and in most of the countries of Europe radio programs carry no paid advertising. "Our American system is better," answered Mr. H. P. Davis, when I brought up this point. "If every owner of a receiving set had to pay an annual license fee of $2.50, as is the rule in England, there would be far fewer sets.

"From the very beginning of broadcasting the question as to who is to pay has been repeatedly raised, and one plan after another has been proposed—and abandoned in favor of the present system. Radio advertising requires a special technique, and objectionable advertising tends to eliminate itself. The individual or firm that can bring the subject of its activities to the listening millions in an adroit and satisfying way is employing a means of great commercial possibilities, and it can justify the expenditure of large sums of money."

No doubt the radio advertiser can justify any expenditure. Amos and Andy receive a salary of $100,000 a year, but the toothpaste company which is advertised by their foolery has sold ever so many hundreds of thousands of tubes and reports a 300 per cent increase in business. However, there remain some who resent the intrusion of even adroit advertising.

The future of radio entertainment focuses on this question. Television is just around the corner; in another ten years it will be in the home. Will it bring into the home visual announcements of cigarettes and soap, thus adding to the ear appeal of the announcer the eye appeal of the screen?

Perhaps the engineers will contribute. It may be possible to devise a radio filter which one may buy or rent, as one buys a season ticket to the symphony or the opera, and by means of which entertainment may be brought into the homes of those—and only those—who pay for it.

Or it may be that in the future radio stations will be endowed for the entertainment and education of the public, as orchestras and universities are endowed.

In another ten years the billion-dollar baby will have grown up. Perhaps it will be a very different thing. But it can hardly have any more romantic and exciting history than it experienced in its first ten years.

● ● ● ● ●

This extract is from an article by Wilson J. Weatherbee, an early station operator. "Good Evening Everybody," *The American Magazine,* March 1924, p. 60.

EARLY IN OUR OWN BROADCASTING EXPERIENCE WE CASUALLY ANNOUNCED one evening that we hoped the audience was enjoying the program, and we added that we should be glad to have people telephone in and tell us what selections they would like played or sung. We gave our telephone numbers. Instantly we were swamped! It was night, and we had just three telephone lines in service. For four hours we didn't get a chance to hang up the receiver. The operator would say:

"Just a minute: here's another call for you!"

The next day the telephone company officials told us they had calls at the rate of *one thousand an hour* for each of our three lines. Of course not more than a few hundred could be put through, for it was physically impossible to complete the others.

We had to stop that kind of communication! Now we have a private telegraph wire direct to the studio. An operator is on duty while we are giving programs, and we invite people to send in their requests that way.

One of our entertainers called himself Professor "Radio" Wheeler, and broadcast several talks on astrology. Mentioning the date, he proceeded to give the signs of the zodiac for people whose birthday it was, and told them what would probably happen to them, if it hadn't already occurred!

He did it in a chaffing way; but in an audience of probably hundreds of thousands, naturally he had a good many listeners whose birthdays actually came on that date. In closing his first talk, he made what he meant to be taken as a farcical offer.

"If you're in trouble or need advice," he announced, "let me know and I'll help you out!"

Then he put on his hat and coat and started to leave the studio. He was not out of the room, however, before the telephone rang.

"Is Professor Wheeler still there?" a woman asked.

"Yes."

"Could he help me, if I gave him the information about myself over the telephone?"

"Tell her I can!" Wheeler laughed.

So we asked her to give the year, the day, and the hour of her birth, together with all the other facts the professor claimed he needed. He pondered a minute, then walked to the telephone.

"You are contemplating a change, madam," he said to her; " a business change for your husband—is that right?"

"Yes," she replied.

"Well," he said, "the signs are unfavorable for his making the change."

"Good!" she said; "that's just what we think, too!"

The professor had satisfied one customer. But he was not through! The telephone kept ringing for an hour or more, and other eager people sought the advice of this man who had never seen them and whom they had never seen. He was quick of wit, he had studied his subject, he knew people, and he evidently satisfied a majority of them.

12. MUSIC FOR EVERYONE

Unquestionably the radio played an important part in introducing both classical and popular music to millions of Americans. But even without radio, jazz music and the dancing craze of the Twenties would probably have been popular. Jazz has been called the folk music of the industrial city and social dancing the standard exercise of the young urbanite. According to the authority below, jazz was also an instrument of revolt against convention and custom. In any event, it took the country by storm during the Twenties, hailed alike by the populace and the musical literate. In the article below, the author also finds it a cultural expression of the rising masses. J. A. Rogers, "Jazz at Home," *Survey,* March 1, 1925, p. 665.

WHAT AFTER ALL IS THIS TAKING NEW THING, THAT, CONDEMNED IN CERTAIN quarters, enthusiastically welcomed in others, has nonchalantly gone on until it ranks with the movie and the dollar as the foremost exponent of modern Americanism? Jazz isn't music merely, it is a spirit that can express itself in almost anything. The true spirit of jazz is a joyous revolt from convention, custom, authority, boredom, even sorrow—from everything that would confine the soul of man and hinder its riding free on the air. The Negroes who invented it called their songs the "Blues," and they weren't capable of satire or deception. Jazz was their explosive attempt to cast off the blues and be happy, carefree happy even in the midst of sordidness and sorrow. And that is why it has been such a balm for modern ennui, and has become a safety valve for modern machine-ridden and convention-bound society. It is the revolt of the emotions against repression.

In its elementals, jazz has always existed. It is in the Indian war-dance, the Highland fling, the Irish jig, the Cossack dance, the Spanish fandango, the Brazilian *maxixe,* the dance of the whirling dervish, the hula hula of the South Seas, the *danse du ventre* of the Orient, the *carmagnole* of the French Revolution, the strains of Gypsy music, and the ragtime of the Negro. Jazz proper, however, is something more than all these. It is a release of all the suppressed emotions at once, a blowing off of the lid, as it were. It is hilarity expressing itself through pandemonium; musical fireworks.

The direct predecessor of jazz is ragtime. That both are atavistically African there is little doubt, but to what extent it is difficult to determine. In its barbaric rhythm and exuberance there is something of the bamboula, a wild, abandoned dance of the West African and the Haitian Negro, so stirringly described by the anonymous author of Untrodden Fields of Anthropology, or of the *ganza* ceremony so brilliantly depicted in Maran's Batouala. But jazz time is faster and more complex than African music. With its cowbells, auto horns, calliopes, rattles, dinner gongs, kitchen utensils, cymbals, screams, crashes, clankings and monotonous rhythm it bears all the marks of a nerve-strung, strident, mechanized civilization. It is a thing of the jungles—modern man-made jungles.

Musically jazz has a great future. It is rapidly being sublimated. In the more famous jazz orchestras like those of Will Marion Cook, Paul Whiteman, Sissle and Blake, Sam Stewart, Fletcher Henderson, Vincent Lopez and the Clef Club units, there are none of the vulgarities and crudities of the lowly origin or the only too prevalent cheap imitations. The pioneer work in the artistic development of jazz was done by Negro artists; it was the lead of the so-called "syncopated orchestras" of Tyers and Will Marion Cook, the former playing for the Castles of dancing fame, and the latter touring as a concertizing orchestra in the great American centers and abroad. Because of the difficulties of financial backing, these expert combinations have had to yield ground to white orchestras of the type of the Paul Whiteman and Vincent Lopez organizations that are now demonstrating the finer possibilities of jazz music. "Jazz," says Sergei Koussevitzky, the new conductor of the Boston Symphony, "is an important contribution to modern musical literature. It has an epochal significance—it is not superficial, it is fundamental. Jazz comes from the soil, where all music has its beginning." And Stokowski says more extendedly of it:

> Jazz has come to stay because it is an expression of the times, of the breathless, energetic, superactive times in which we are living; it is useless to fight against it. Already its new vigor, its new vitality is beginning to manifest itself. . . . America's contribution to the music of the past will have the same revivifying effect as the injection of new, and in the larger sense, vulgar blood into dying aristocracy. Music will then be vulgarized in the best sense of the word, and enter more and more into the daily lives of people. . . . The Negro musicians of America are playing a great part in this change. They have an open mind, and unbiassed outlook. They are not hampered by conventions or traditions, and with their new ideas, their constant experiment, they are causing new blood to flow in the veins of music. The jazz players make their instruments do entirely new things, things finished musicians are taught to avoid. They are pathfinders into new realms.

Yet in spite of its present vices and vulgarizations, its sex informalities, its morally anarchic spirit, jazz has a popular mission to perform. Joy, after all, has a physical basis. Those who laugh and dance and sing are better off even in their vices than those who do not. Moreover jazz with its mocking disregard for formality is a leveler and makes for democracy.

The jazz spirit, being primitive, demands more frankness and sincerity. Just as it already has done in art and music, so eventually in human relations and social manners, it will no doubt have the effect of putting more reality in life by taking some of the needless artificiality out. . . . Naturalness finds the artificial in conduct ridiculous. "Cervantes smiled Spain's chivalry away," said Byron. And so this new spirit of joy and spontaneity may itself play the role of reformer. Where at present it vulgarizes, with more wholesome growth in the future, it may on the contrary truly democratize. At all events jazz is rejuvenation, a recharging of the batteries of civilization with primitive new vigor. It has come to stay, and they are wise, who instead of protesting against it, try to lift and divert it into nobler channels.

13. MAH JONG, CROSSWORDS, AND FLAGPOLE SITTERS

Undoubtedly popular amusement fads had stormed across the country before the Twenties, although it is relatively difficult to think of one during the period from 1900-1920 that had the acceptance of any number of curious public crazes in the next ten years. During the decade, the crossword puzzle craze followed hard on a national devotion to the Chinese game of Mah Jong, played with colored tiles, accompanied by exotic terms such as "the four winds," and even oriental decor and costumes. Later flagpole sitting replaced the marathon dance fad of 1928.

With the exception of the crossword puzzle, most of these amusement innovations disappeared as rapidly as they had been taken up. The ephemeral character of the fads caught the attention of the nation's editorial writers who warned the country in solemn homiletics that the rising taste for the transient and superficial signified an end to the stable and law-abiding Republic. Looking back, the historian is not so worried about the Republic; the fads of the Twenties were as harmless and as worthless to society as most such things are. But the student is interested in how they originated and why they spread across the country with such rapidity. The three following selections illustrate the varying origins and the fueling forces for such social phenomena. The first, dealing with Mah Jong, indicates that social snobbery and self-gain, together with the new national media of publicity, were the most important forces in building up public interest in the popularity of games. Crossword puzzles, however, seemed to be of a non-synthetic character, a fact that may explain the persistence of this amusement. But the flagpole sitting fad seemed to be the product of pure press agent ballyhoo, supported by advertising. Whatever the origins of the fads, their almost simultaneous public acceptance in every section of the country indicated that public opinion could be mobilized within a few hours by the modern techniques of information and publicity. The first article below, "The Rise and Present Peril of Mah Jong," August 10, 1924, is reprinted by permission of *The New York Times.*

THE WAVE OF THE MAH JONG CRAZE HAS ADMITTEDLY PASSED ITS CREST. Yet there are more people playing Mah Jong today than there were a year ago, when the rage was the hottest. . . .

This year those who do not want to play Mah Jong no longer have to play to keep up Mah Jong appearances. It is no longer the "thing to do." Instead, it is now the thing one does, if one wants to do it. . . . It has definitely passed beyond its bijou period.

Witness the 10-cent decks of Mah Jong to be had at Woolworth's. So are $4.98 near-ivory sets prevalent at department stores. Two-dollar-and-a-half sets are syndicated in chain drug stores. There, alone, is indication enough that the purely fashionable period of Mah Jong has passed. Therein lies its present strength. Therein, too, lies the peril, which the commercial interests behind the game have brought upon it. . . .

Smart San Francisco had not discovered Mah Jong. The $100 and $200 English-speaking sets on the market were just what the commercial impetus needed. From the Golden Gate Mah Jong jumped the continent at one leap and established itself on the Eastern seaboard.

From this point on—sinister isn't exactly the right word, "Synthetic," that's it—influences behind the game began to be realized. Society editors of the metropolitan sheets say that social pressure began to be felt from a dozen sources. . . .

So, too, were the serious "authorities" on auction bridge on the job. They straightway set themselves the task of becoming authorities on Mah Jong, and then issued their own "authoritative" textbooks on the subject. . . .

Nor were these the only commercial by-products of the game. Teachers with social backing sprang up over night, as did the tango and the turkey-trot teachers twelve years ago in our early Vernon Castle period. Each of these teachers, whether in New York or Washington or San Francisco society, promptly began teaching her own private method—one she might have "developed" the night before. After five lessons each pupil of each teacher was ready in turn to hang out her own shingle. . . .

Thus boomed the by-product business throughout 1922 and 1923, stimulating things socially wherever it could get a hook in.

All this while the actual industrial forces were gathering. . . .

All in all, the capital invested in this fad runs high into the millions. . . . Where the vogue for auction bridge had been the product of a slow, unstimulated evolution, the craze for Mah Jong has certainly occurred more in accordance with Mr. Bryan's ideas on biology.

● ● ● ● ●

The origins of the Crossword puzzle craze are discussed in the extracts from an article by Allan Harding, "Why We Have Gone Mad Over Crossword Puzzles," *The American Magazine,* March 1925, p. 28.

. . . ON JANUARY 1ST, 1924, TWO YOUNG MEN, NAMED RICHARD L. SIMON and Max Lincoln Schuster, started in business for themselves as the Plaza Publishing Company—a name which was changed later to Simon and Schuster, Inc. They had an unpretentious office in West Fifty-seventh St., New York, and had hired one girl as their entire staff.

Little did they dream that inside of a year they would be occupying half a dozen offices, directing a score of employees, and having several of their books on the list of best sellers. That such a state of affairs did come about is due to the fact that young Mr. Simon made a New Year's call on his aunt! Which may or may not be proof that aspiring young men should not neglect their female relatives.

It seems that the aunt in question had a daughter; and that the daughter had become addicted to the crossword puzzles which the New York "World" printed regularly on the puzzle page of its Sunday Magazine Supplement.

"It occurred to me," said Mr. Simon's aunt to Mr. Simon, "that my daughter would like to have a book of these crossword puzzles. I would give it to her as a present, if I knew where to find one."

Whereupon, Mr. Simon—being a model nephew—said he would make inquiries concerning such a book. What is even greater proof of his model character, he did make inquiries; only to discover that there was no such book in existence.

This sounded like a funeral knell to Auntie's hopes; but to the alert ears of Mr. Simon it sounded also like a distinct knock on the Door of Opportunity! Hurrying back to the new office, he said to his partner:

"I've a great idea! Let's publish a crossword puzzle book!"

This was on the second day of January. On the third day, for these young men certainly were fast workers, they took up the matter with Prosper Buranelli, F. Gregory Hartswick, and Margaret Petherbridge, puzzle editors of the New York "World." This trio of confirmed crossword caterers agreed to aid and abet the new scheme.

No one concerned had the faintest suspicion that they were launching something over which the country would go mad. When Mr. Simon, for instance, asked various booksellers how they thought a volume of crossword puzzles would succeed, the idea simply didn't register at all.

"No, no!" said the dealers with gloomy certainty. "People aren't interested in puzzle books."

In spite of this pessimistic note, the two young men stuck to their plan. But as they didn't want to get in too deep, they decided to bring out a small edition—only 3,600 copies. This first edition was published the middle of April.

Meanwhile, Mr. Simon had been going around to the dealers, trying to get advance orders for the book. One of the largest he obtained was an order for twenty-five copies from the buyer in a very important New York book store. This buyer, who was a personal acquaintance of Mr. Simon's, told him later that he ordered those twenty-five copies merely out of friendship. He *hoped* he might "work off" three of them, although he wasn't very sanguine.

But the experts can make some pretty big blunders in sizing up you and me and the rest of the great public. Instead of "working off" only three crossword books, that store alone has sold thousands and thousands of copies.

Inside of a month the demand began to grow. New editions of the first book came out in rapid succession. A second one followed and sold like hot cakes. When the third book was published, it *started* with an edition of forty thousand copies! Approximately three quarters of a million of these books have been sold, and still the demand keeps up.

Other publishers have followed suit. There are all kinds of crossword puzzle books, including several for children. There is a Biblical one, containing only words which are found in the Scriptures. There is a "celebrity" book, made up of crossword puzzles which have been constructed by famous people. There are Yiddish puzzles for the Jews; and so on almost without end.

I have seen letters from professors in the leading American and English universities, telling how they use the crossword puzzles in their classrooms. Some of these professors are employing the puzzles in connection with intelligence tests. They say that these two methods of checking up our mental alertness corroborate each other. If you are a good puzzler you also get a good rating in the intelligence tests.

One interesting result of the mania has been reported by the publishers of dictionaries. They declare that their sales, since the crossword furor started, have been unprecedented.

As for Roget's Thesaurus, a good many people didn't know, a year ago, whether it was a prehistoric animal or a disease. Those same people, today, turn feverishly to a book of synonyms, as if it were a long-lost friend.

In the good old pre-crossword days, folks used to lay in a supply of novels when starting for Europe. Now they have sent to the steamer a set of puzzle books, one for each member of the party! a dictionary, a thesaurus, an atlas, and perhaps also a French and a Spanish dictionary.

This is no exaggeration of the truth. Ocean voyages have become protracted crossword orgies. The Simon and Schuster office receives hectic telegrams, directing that the puzzle books, with the sets of answers, be sent *without fail* to departing steamers. . . .

● ● ● ● ●

The finer as well as the more gross points of the "sport" of flagpole sitting are discussed in the following article by Frederick Nelson, "The Child Stylites of Baltimore," *The New Republic,* August 28, 1929, p. 37.

. . . It all started when, a few weeks ago, a curious fellow known as Shipwreck Kelly, who goes about from city to city demonstrating the hardihood of the American posterior by sitting for extended periods on flagpoles, visited the conservative city of Baltimore and "put on a sitting." During his protracted stay aloft, which was long enough to break the world's record for this particular form of virtuosity, Shipwreck attracted large crowds to the park which was the scene of his effort, and the celebration attending his eventual descent was a demonstration of the ease with which almost any form of imbecility becomes important in these States. Inevitably there was a juvenile aspirant to Shipwreck's fame. Boys from time immemorial have wanted to be locomotive engineers, bareback riders, and major generals. Their heroes are, quite naturally, those who cause the most excitement. It was no great surprise, therefore, when one read in the Baltimore newspapers the modest announcement that Avon Foreman, fifteen, had mounted a flagpole and would sit there until he had broken what might be considered the "juvenile record." When he had sat for ten days, ten hours, ten minutes and ten seconds, he decided that the "juvenile record" in this field had been broken, and he came down.

That might have ended the matter had not various people, no longer accounted children, behaved so preposterously. "The older Baltimore" could hardly believe its ears when it learned the details of the hullabaloo following Avon's descent. For days before this amazing event crowds had gathered nightly to see him perched on his platform upon which bright searchlights had been trained by his father, who is an electrician. When Avon decided that his "record" was safe, there was a neighborhood celebration at which Mayor Broening, for whom no occasion lacks its oratorical opportunities, made an address and presented to Avon an autographed testimonial bearing the great seal of Baltimore City. In the course of his remarks the Mayor described Avon's achievement as an exemplification of "the pioneer spirit of early America." It is quite likely His Honor believed it, but it is equally possible that he was merely making a speech. When two or three people are gathered together Mayor Broening makes a speech, and most of his speeches are much the same.

Whatever these occasional remarks meant to the Mayor, they were a Challenge to the Youth of Baltimore. From that moment Baltimore was dotted with boys and girls ranging from eight to thirteen years of age who were determined to upset Avon Foreman's record as a flagpole sitter. Some of them came down as soon as Father got home, but since the ceremonies attending the Avon Foreman descent from a flagpole, there has been an average of some fifteen children roosting in various contrivances atop "flagpoles" ranging from ten to twenty feet high. Two of them have broken legs and one an arm, and one little girl was ill for days from the effects of her experience, but others mount poles to replace the casualties and the sittings go on. Parents, who at first were inclined to forbid their youngsters to enter the lists, lend their aid and provide their offspring with such comforts as are possible on top of a pole. It is difficult to make out a case against a practice which the Mayor of a city of 750,000 people has sanctioned as an exhibition of "grit and stamina so essential to success in the great struggle of life."

Editors in Baltimore and elsewhere promptly suggested a quick mobilization of shingles, hairbrushes, straps, and slippers as a means of breaking this children's crusade under the banner of St. Simon Stylites. As a matter of fact, however, the children seem sages in comparison with the imbecility of their elders. When a boy, through the simple expedient of installing himself in a coop at the end of a pole can bring the Mayor to call on him, cause a minister of the Gospel to hold services with sermon at the foot of the pole and be the central occasion for a brass band, scores of popcorn vendors, offers of free dentistry for a year and a "write-up" in the newspapers, parental authority—in the class mainly afflicted with this mania—avails very little. Indeed, the parents of most of these children exhibit a distinct pride in the performance, protected by ignorance and stupidity from appreciating the possible consequences, physical and otherwise, of these idiotic vigils. They rival one another in fitting out the child's flagpole equipment with electric lights and, occasionally, a radio set! The corner druggist pays a dollar or two for the right to advertise his business on the sacred totem and the city officials, perhaps in an effort to restrain the epidemic, add importance to flagpole sitting by solemnly issuing specifications for flagpoles for this use and charging a license fee of one dollar! If stripes could cure this malady, other backs than those of the children might appropriately receive them.

A NEED FOR HEROES

The Twenties had an obvious need for heroes. The abounding materialism, the new wealth, the luxury, the indulgent living, and the rapidly changing moral standards may have made Americans feel uneasy and a bit guilty as they looked back over their shoulders to their more sober past. Just as public heroes endowed with the old virtues of strength, courage, and probity once acted as surrogates in penitential rites, the prim and parsimonious Coolidge in the White House sat silently doing nothing as the nation indulged itself in an orgy of wealth-making and wealth-spending.

Charles A. Lindbergh was the decade's unchallenged hero not only because he had daringly flown the Atlantic by himself in a single-engine plane, but also because of his modesty and restraint once the spectacular deed was accomplished, because he refused to "cash in" on his reputation, and because he would not sell himself. Lindbergh represented so much that America was not. So did other folk heroes of the decade, and by function, at least, so did the sporting heroes.

Mass spectator sports boomed during the Twenties. It was the age of the million-dollar gate, of the million-dollar personality, who often in a few minutes in the ring, on the ball field, or in the stadium was paid more than was the President of the United States for a year. Explanations abound for the spectacular rise of professional sports, among them the new leisure time of the masses, increased living standards, and especially the new means for the creation of synthetic reputations as often based upon "ballyhoo"—a word that gained currency during the decade —as upon fact. But perhaps as important as all of these other factors was the instinctive need of a rapidly growing collectivized society for individual expression. On the battlefield, in the factory production line, at home in a city apartment, and increasingly even in the business world the individual was becoming lost in a welter of the hive. The sporting field was one of the few remaining areas of pure individual expression where success or failure depended precisely upon individual physical and intellectual prowess. And if the masses themselves could not or would not participate directly they could at least, by a process of identification, salute the old virtues. The following documents indicate the hero worship of the age and perhaps also the deeply felt need for it.

14. CHARLES A. LINDBERGH

Few men have ever been given such public adulation as was Charles A. Lindbergh after his epoch-making flight from New York to Paris alone in a single-engine plane. His reception in Europe had been a succession of triumphs, but America went completely overboard in its enthusiasm when he returned to this country. For days domestic troubles and foreign affairs were almost eliminated from the front pages of the newspapers to make way for accounts of Lindbergh's progress. The radio, newsreels, and magazines were full of his exploits. Not the least interesting to the historian are the many comments printed upon the significance of Lindbergh's accomplishments and deportment as tokens of the fundamental soundness of American youth and American character. Seemingly a good many people had serious doubts about both during the jazz age and were seeking reassurance that the old prized traits of courage, self-reliance, modesty, and dignity still existed. The following four extracts indicate something of the public interest in and adoration of this new hero of the air age. The first, "The Start for Paris" is from *The New York Times,* May 21, 1927. Reprinted by permission of *The New York Times.*

"SO LONG," HE SAID, AS IF HE WERE STARTING OFF ON AN AUTOMOBILE TRIP. The blocks were pulled from beneath the wheels, the motor roared and the heavy plane lumbered forward.

It moved with disheartening slowness. The field was wet and the wheels sank in deeply. A harder stretch was reached and the plane suddenly moved ahead and began to gather speed. And then a soft spot was struck and the speed dropped again.

Halfway down the runway went the lumbering plane, its wing lurching a little as it met bumps in the ground. It did not seem to get anywhere near flying speed, and those watching it groaned inwardly. Lindbergh was holding the tail down, as the plane was slightly nose heavy and he did not want to take the chance of letting her nose over and upsetting her. He was hoping she would get speed enough to lift of her own accord.

Still the motor roared and he lurched onward, hitting more rough spots, and still the plane did not get up flying speed. He had passed the point of safety, the point where he could stop his motor and try over again. Now he must either lift the plane or pile up in a gully at the end of the runway which he was approaching more and more rapidly.

Suddenly the plane jumped into the air. It had hit a bump which threw it upward, and apparently Lindbergh helped it go, in order to get rid of the sticky soil which clung to his wheels. The slight leap gave him a little more speed. But how quickly he came down, in a sort of leap-frogging jump!

Again the plane left the ground, sailed a little further and again came down. It did not have flying speed yet, and the end of the runway was just ahead of him. Commander Byrd, standing in front of his big machine, Bert Acosta in the cockpit, others near the end of the runway, looked on in fearful fascination. The boy had to do it or die.

It did not seem possible that he could get off. And then, at the last moment, the plane began to go up. Those on the field felt as if Lindbergh, with his great courage, was lifting it from the ground, making it take the air. Defeat and death stared him in the face and he gazed at it unafraid, intent only on the task which he had set himself.

A few feet in the air he sailed by a little group of men. They saw his face for a moment outlined by the little window of the cabin. His head was slightly bent forward, eyes fastened on the dial which showed the revolutions of his motor. His jaw was set, his whole face grim with determination. The boyish lines had vanished in the terrific moment. Only the man of the lion heart was left, using his brain and the instinct of the trained flier to avoid destruction:

The wheels of the plane cleared by a bare ten feet a tractor which lay directly in his path. A gully was ahead into which he might have plunged, but which he left safely below. Over the telephone lines he passed with a scant twenty feet to spare.

Ahead was the rolling, open country of a golf course. A line of trees on a slight slope lay beyond, a mile or two away. The silver plane dropped a little as if to gather speed and then lifted upward again, but so slowly! It could hardly be seen to rise, and men watched it with anguish in their gaze.

The plane turned a little to the right and then swung back again toward the lowest point in the tree line against the sky, as if Lindbergh had been sweeping it with his periscope, looking for an opening. And then, very gradually but surely, the wide silver wing lifted toward the skyline at the tree tops, over it, and a space of pale sky showed between it and the green line beneath.

A soft glow came above the clouds, the first of the sun breaking through. Far off above the trees the silver wing dipped and was gone.

● ● ● ● ●

The following, abstracted from an account of the historic flight by Lindbergh himself, appeared in *The New York Times*, May 23, 1927, and is reprinted by permission of *The New York Times*.

WELL, HERE I AM IN THE HANDS OF AMERICAN AMBASSADOR HERRICK. From what I have seen of it, I am sure I am going to like Paris. . . .

That reception I got was the most dangerous part of the whole flight. If wind and storm had handled me as vigorously as that Reception Committee of Fifty Thousand I would never have reached Paris and wouldn't be eating a three-o'clock-in-the-afternoon breakfast here in Uncle Sam's Embassy.

There's one thing I wish to get straight about this flight. They call me "Lucky," but luck isn't enough. As a matter of fact, I had what I regarded and still regard as the best existing plane to make the flight from New York to Paris. . . .

All in all, I couldn't complain of the weather. It wasn't what was predicted. It was worse in some places and better in others. In fact, it was so bad once that for a moment there came over me the temptation to turn back. But then I figured it was probably just as bad behind me as in front of me, so I kept on toward Paris. . . .

Actually it was comparatively easy to get to Newfoundland, but real bad weather began just about dark, after leaving Newfoundland, and continued until about four hours after daybreak. We [his ship and himself] hadn't expected that at all, and it sort of took us by surprise, morally and physically. That was when I began to think about turning back. . . .

I had made preparations before I started for a forced landing if it became necessary, but after I started I never thought much about the possibility of such a landing. I was ready for it, but I saw no use in thinking about it, inasmuch as one place would have been about as good or as bad as another. . . .

The only real danger I had was at night. In daytime I knew where I was going, but in the evening and at night it was largely a matter of guesswork. . . . All in all, the trip over the Atlantic, especially the latter half, was much better than I expected. . . .

Fairly early in the afternoon I saw a fleet of fishing boats. On some of them I could see no one, but on one of them I saw some men and flew down, almost touching the craft and yelled at them, asking if I was on the right road to Ireland.

They just stared. Maybe they didn't hear me. Maybe I didn't hear them. Or maybe they thought I was just a crazy fool.

An hour later I saw land. I have forgotten just what time it was. It must have been shortly before 4 o'clock. It was rocky land and all my study told me it was Ireland. And it was Ireland!

After I had made up my mind that it was Ireland, the right place for me to strike rather than Spain or some other country, the rest was child's play. . . .

I noticed it gets dark much later over here than in New York and I was thankful for that. . . .

When I was about half an hour away from Paris I began to see rockets and lights sent up from the air field, and I knew I was all right. . . .

I circled Paris once and immediately saw Le Bourget [the aviation field], although I didn't know at first what it was. I saw a lot of lights, but in the dark I couldn't make out any hangars. I sent Morse signals as I flew over the field, but no one appears to have seen them. The only mistake in all my calculations was that I thought Le Bourget was northeast rather than east of Paris.

Fearing for a moment that the field I had seen—remember, I couldn't see the crowd—was some other airfield than Le Bourget, I flew back over Paris to the northwest, looking for Le Bourget. . . .

I was anxious to land where I was being awaited. So, when I didn't find another airfield, I flew back towards the first lights I had seen, and flying low I saw the lights of numberless automobiles. I decided that was the right place, and I landed.

That reception was the most dangerous part of the trip. Never in my life have I seen anything like that human sea. It isn't clear to me yet just what happened. Before I knew it I had been hoisted out of the cockpit, and was on the shoulders of some men and the next moment on the ground.

It seemed to be even more dangerous for my plane than for me. I saw one man tear away the switch and another took something out of the cockpit. Then, when they started cutting pieces of cloth from the wings, I struggled to get back to the plane, but it was impossible. . . .

It isn't true that I was exhausted. I was tired, but I wasn't exhausted.

Several French officers asked me to come away with them and I went, casting anxious glances at my ship. I haven't seen it since, but I am afraid it suffered. I would regret that very much because I want to use it again. . . .

I have been asked if I intend to fly back to New York. I don't think I shall try that. . . .

But I do want to do a little flying over here.

● ● ● ● ●

The following is an account of Lindbergh's welcome home. *The New York Times,* June 11, 1927, reprinted by permission of *The New York Times.*

LINDBERGH'S HOME-COMING MAY BEST BE DESCRIBED IN HIS OWN WORDS: "MY mind is ablaze with noise, terrific noise, oceans of upturned friendly faces and an electric sort of something that can hardly be described." His reception both in Washington and New York was an unprecedented triumph. His ship, the Memphis, arrived on June 10. America's first greeting to the triumphant flier was delivered a hundred miles out at sea by four destroyers, and the Memphis was escorted up Chesapeake Bay by a convoy of four destroyers, two army blimps and forty airplanes. The Memphis arrived off Piney Point, Md., at 9 P.M. (June 10) and anchored over night. Lindbergh was received on the morning of June 11 at the Navy Yard pier, by Secretaries Wilbur, Davis, New, and former Secretary Hughes, Admiral Eberle, and Major Gen. Patrick and Rear Admiral Moffett, heads of the Army and Navy air services, and Commander Byrd, his mother being the first to greet him. They then drove in parade down Pennsylvania Avenue to the Washington Monument where he was welcomed by President Coolidge. In his speech the President voiced "the gratitude of the republic" referring to Lindbergh as "our ambassador without portfolio" and "a messenger of peace and good will" whose achievement had "broken down the barriers of time and space and brought two great peoples into closer communion." He then awarded the Distinguished Flying Cross and a commission as Colonel in the Officer's Reserve Corps. Colonel Lindbergh replied that he brought from Europe the following message:

"You have seen the affection of the people of France for the people of America demonstrated to you. When you return to America take back that message to the people of the United States from the people of France and of Europe."

After the ceremonies Colonel Lindbergh had dinner with the President and attended the National Press Club reception at which various tributes were presented, including the Langley Medal of the Smithsonian Institute.

NEW YORK'S WELCOME

Lindbergh carried out his plan of flying from Washington to New York, but not, to his great regret, in his now famous airship, "The Spirit of St. Louis," the motor of which proved to have been temporarily damaged by salt moisture during the trip from Cherbourg to New York. He was given an army pursuit plane of the P-1 class, in which he made the flight (June 13.) He took off from Bolling Field at Washington at 9:54 A.M. The flight from Washington to Mitchel Field occupied exactly two hours and 4 minutes. At Mitchel Field he at once transferred to an Amphibian plane, in which he flew to the Narrows. There he descended and taxied toward the marine guard of honor awaiting him amid the wild tumult of a harbor that seemed to have gone mad with joy over his arrival. There were 400 ships in that guard, led by the municipal reception boat Macom, on which was Grover A. Whalen, Chairman of the Mayor's Reception Committee.

Lindbergh was at once transhipped by a police launch to the Macom. Amidst the cheering of a great throng, he landed at the Battery and after greeting his mother, was transferred to the automobile that brought him to the Mayor's stand at City Hall. There the Mayor expressed to him New York's welcome, telling him how highly the city regarded him and his epochal achievement, presented to him the City's Scroll of Honor and decorated him with the Medal of Valor of New York State. A great parade the length of Fifth Avenue amid a vast and continuous roar of applause from a surging ocean of people and beneath a storm of fluttering white paper, completed Lindbergh's public reception in New York.

● ● ● ● ●

The following, taken from an article by Mary B. Mullett, "The Biggest Thing That Lindbergh Has Done," *The American Magazine,* October 1927, p. 106, expresses thoughts repeated many times in the summer of 1927.

. . . EVER SINCE THE WAR THERE HAS BEEN AN OUTCRY AGAINST "MODERN" character, ideals, and morals; especially against those of the younger generation. Most of us have contributed our share to this chorus of denunciation. All of us have had to listen to it.

You hear it in every stratum of society. The high-brows talk of the "moral degeneration of the age." The low-brows say: "Ain't it perfectly awful!" The old folks raise their eyebrows in horror—and the young folks defiantly raise Cain! The professional reformers bewail the passing of "the good old days." The professional cynics shrug their shoulders and reply: "*Autres temps, autres mœurs.*" Or, if they don't speak French, they say: "Get it into your bean that times have changed, old thing!"

And this is the big thing Lindbergh has done: He has shown us that this talk was nothing *but* talk! He has shown us that we are *not* rotten at the core, but morally sound and sweet and good!

At the time Lindbergh made his flight, a particularly atrocious murder was the leading front-page story in the New York newspapers. They were giving columns to it every day. There were other crimes and scandals on the front pages.

Lindbergh banished these to almost complete oblivion. Not exactly that, either. We ourselves banished them! For if it had not been for the things *we* did, the Lindbergh news would not have demanded much space.

There wouldn't have been much to write about, if there had been no public demonstrations; no parades, dinners, receptions; no tidal wave of letters and telegrams; no truck-loads of gifts; no reams of poetry; no songs; no cheers and shouts; no smiles of pride; no tears of joy; no thrill of possessing, in him, our dream of what *we* really and truly want to be!

When, because of what we believe him to be, we gave Lindbergh the greatest ovation in history, we convicted ourselves of having told a lie *about* ourselves. For we proved that the "things of good report" are the same today as they were nineteen hundred years ago.

We shouted ourselves hoarse. Not because a man had flown across the Atlantic! Not even because he was an American! But because he was as clean in character as he was strong and fine in body; because he put "ethics" above any desire for wealth; because he was as modest as he was courageous; and because—as we now know, beyond any shadow of doubt—*these are the things which we honor most* in life.

To have shown us this truth about ourselves is the biggest thing that Lindbergh has done.

15. SPORTS: THE NEW BRONZED GODS

One of the most interesting phenomena of the decade was the rise of mass spectator sports, and the virtual, if temporary, enshrinement in the national pantheon of the sporting heroes of the day. Newspapers and the radio unquestionably had much to do with this process. Scarcely ever *n*as prose been more purple than in the sporting pages of even the more dignified newspapers. Nor were statements rarely more unqualified than those uttered by the nationally known radio sportscasters. But beyond all the hyperbole and, occasionally, downright dishonesty, beyond all the hullabaloo and salesmanship which the sports promoters employed, the vast crowds that attended the sporting events of the Twenties were probably responding to something deeper than to the blandishments of the professional pitchmen. The following four articles deal with the exploits of four of the more venerated sports characters of the decade as seen through the eyes of the sports writers. The first concerns the famous national singles tennis match in which William Tilden beat William Johnston. Appearing in *The New York Times,* September 7, 1920, the account is noteworthy for its lack of restraint and suggests what passed for accurate reportage of such events. Reprinted by permission of *The New York Times.*

WILLIAM T. TILDEN, 2ND, OF PHILADELPHIA, IS THE TENNIS CHAMPION OF the United States and of the world in general. His victory over William M. Johnston, the former national title holder, at the Westside Country Club, Forest Hills, yesterday afternoon, stamps him as not only the greatest of all living tennis players but, perhaps, the greatest of all time. It was a victory, however, completed only after five of the most terrific sets ever staged on a turf court, scored at 6-1, 1-6, 7-5, 5-7, 6-3. To what was probably the most dramatic scene in the history of lawn tennis was added the excitement of an airplane tragedy, in which Lieutenant J. M. Grier of the U. S. Navy and Sergeant Saxe of the army lost their lives in full view of the spectators, narrowly escaping a far more disastrous fall into the crowded stands themselves. . . .

The Tilden-Johnston struggle will go down on the records as the most astounding exhibition of tennis, the most nervewracking battle that the courts have ever seen. It is not often that such a climax of competition lives up to every preliminary expectation. Yesterday, however, the wildest expectations were surpassed. . . . Tilden and Johnston played five acts of incredible melodrama, with a thrill in every scene, with horrible errors leading suddenly to glorious achievements, with skill and courage and good and evil fortune inextricably mingled, and with a constant stimulus to cheers, groans, and actual hysteria, so far as the spectators were concerned. . . .

Praise for the two contenders for the American championship of 1920 may be equally divided. There is plenty for both. Tilden's victory was a triumph of supertennis, a vindication of the game which the best judges have for some time considered invincible. But, if Tilden is the greatest tennis player that ever lived, Johnston is the gamest man that ever trod a court. . . .

It is by his service that the Tilden of yesterday will chiefly be remembered, for time and again it came to his rescue when all else had failed. But he had also a marvel of a backhand drive, a newly developed asset to his game, an offensive not a defensive stroke, and one which scored equally well across the court or straight down the line. Johnston's backhand, except for its accuracy of placement, was largely a defensive weapon. . . .

In the last analysis, however, it was the edge on service that told the story, and it was this tremendous difference that made Johnston's fight such an astonishing one. . . . The tennis that he offered yesterday would have annihilated anyone but a Tilden, and a super-Tilden, at that. . . .

But if Tilden showed courage and a commendable control of his nerves in these situations the tennis that he exhibited in the opening set was something that stood on the pinnacle of supremacy, overwhelming in its magnificence, a unique display of matchless strength and skill that permitted no resistance, and took thought of nothing but his own perfection. . . .

It was a glorious victory.

●　●　●　●　●

Of the many football heroes of these years Red Grange was the most widely known. The following account in *The New York Times,* October

19, 1924, is of the classic struggle between Michigan and Illinois. Reprinted by permission of *The New York Times*.

A FLASHING, RED-HAIRED YOUNGSTER, RUNNING AND DODGING WITH THE SPEED of a deer, gave 67,000 spectators jammed into the new $1,700,000 Illinois Memorial Stadium the thrill of their lives today, when Illinois vanquished Michigan, 39-14, in what probably will be the outstanding game of the 1924 gridiron season in the West.

Harold (Red) Grange, Illinois phenomenon, all-American halfback, who attained gridiron honors of the nation last season, was the dynamo that furnished the thrills. Grange doubled and redoubled his football glory in the most remarkable exhibition of running, dodging, and passing seen on any gridiron in years—an exhibition that set the dumbfounded spectators screaming with excitement.

Individually Grange scored five of Illinois' six touchdowns in a manner that left no doubt as to his ability to break through the most perfect defense. He furnished one thrill after another. On the very first kick-off Grange scooped up the ball bounding toward him on the Illinois five-yard line and raced ninety yards through the Michigan eleven for a touchdown in less than ten seconds after the starting whistle blew.

Before the Michigan team could recover from its shock, Grange had scored three more touchdowns in rapid succession, running sixty-five, fifty-five, and forty-five yards, respectively, for his next three scores. Coach Zuppke took him out of the line-up before the first quarter ended. He returned later to heave several successful passes and score a fifth touchdown in the last half. . . .

Grange surpassed all of his former exploits in every department. He handled the ball twenty-one times, gained 402 yards and scored five touchdowns. Unbiased experts agree that his performance was among the greatest ever seen on an American gridiron. . . .

The game was won and lost in the first thrill-packed moment when Grange, extricating himself repeatedly from seemingly hopeless tangles of tacklers, crossed the goal line and permanently shook the Wolverine morale. . . .

● ● ● ● ●

The following account covers a World Series game between the New York Yankees and the Pittsburgh Pirates. *The New York Times* report of September 8, 1927, plays down Babe Ruth's part in the game. But it does underline what so many of the crowd had come to see. Reprinted by permission of *The New York Times*.

It won't be long now.

The 1927 world's series is rapidly tottering to a lopsided finish, for yesterday George Herman Ruth hit a home run at the stadium and Herb Pennock blotted out the Pirates with three hits and the Yankees surged up the trail again to win their third straight victory before the biggest money crowd in the history of the title series.

. . . The ancient Herb Pennock was pitching the best seven innings we have ever seen in a world's series—seven-and-one-third innings in which twenty-two Pirate batters marched up to the plate and marched right back again.

Seven and one-third innings of faultless, masterful, inspired pitching with not a Pirate getting to first base. And just a few minutes before, his majesty the Babe had sent 64,000 folks in a paroxysm of glee by clubbing a screaming liner into the right field bleachers. . . .

From the moment in the first inning that Gehrig drove in two runs with a mammoth triple to the moment that Babe finished the happy cannonading with a homer in the seventh, the Pirates were outclassed—fighting hard, but with the dull stubbornness of men who realize that they have met their master. . . .

It was Pennock who broke the Pirates' hearts. With a lefthander in the box this was to have been the Pirates' big day. They were going to murder him. But the lefthander turned in an exhibition that made George Henry Pipgras' efforts look puny and puerile. George Henry was great, but Pennock was simply superb. . . .

Only five batters stood between Pennock and a place in the ranks of baseball's immortals.

. . . The big time came in the seventh. The Yanks had the game safely stowed away and the suspense was over after six innings of sturdy batting, but the fans still stood up and demanded that Mr. Ruth get busy and do something for home and country. . . .

"A homer, Babe! Give us a homer!" ran the burden of the plea, and the big fellow pulled his cap on tighter, took a reef in his belt, dug spikes into the ground and grimly faced little Mike Cvengros, the southpaw, who had just relieved Lee Meadows.

. . . Upward and onward, gaining speed and height with every foot, the little white ball winged with terrific speed until it dashed itself against the seats of the right-field bleachers, more than a quarter of the way up the peopled slope.

And now the populace had its homer and it stood up and gave the glad, joyous howl that must have rang out in the Roman arenas of old. . . .

Suddenly the Pirates looked very old and weary and oppressed, and life seemed to lean very heavily on their shoulders. . . .

● ● ● ● ●

It is doubtful whether any President of the United States was known by so many Americans as was Jack Dempsey, the reigning heavyweight champion. But the following account of Dempsey's fight with the Frenchman Georges Carpentier, *The New York Times*, July 3, 1921, by one of the more restrained and realistic writers of the age, Irvin S. Cobb, indicates just what obstacles the sports pitchmen had to overcome before they made Dempsey one of the mass heroes. Reprinted by permission of *The New York Times*.

IT IS RECORDED THAT, ONCE UPON A TIME, AARON BURR, BEING CHALLENGED by Alexander Hamilton, bade Hamilton to meet him over in Jersey and there destroyed his enemy. Yesterday afternoon, New Jersey history, in a way of speaking, repeated itself, which is a habit to which history is addicted. Challenger and challenged met, and again the challenger lost the issue.

Posterity has appraised the loser of that first duel as of more value than the winner who survived. One is moved, to wonder whether in the present instance the analogy will continue. Carpentier, an alien, a man who does not speak our language, was the favorite of the crowd before the fight started and while it progressed, and, if I am one to judge, was still its favorite when he came out of it summarily defeated though he was. Dempsey, a native born, will never forget, I am sure, the vast roar of approbation which arose from thirty acres of close-packed humanity about him when for a half-minute it seemed that he was slipping toward defeat. The thing never happened before when an American champion fought before an American audience. But then we never had for a champion a man whose war record—his lack of one rather—was stained with a taint.

Even so, and to the contrary notwithstanding, he showed himself a better man, as a fighter, than the Dempsey who whipped Willard two years ago at Toledo. Carpentier was the soul of the fight, but Dempsey was the body of it. . . .

It was that drum-fire on his body which wasted Carpentier's substance of resistance. . . . He fought fairly, did Carpentier, and like a gentleman he was licked fairly and like a gentleman. As a gentleman and a fighter he bulks tonight as the man the majority of the audience hoped to win and for whom, as a gallant soldier and a brave man, they wish good luck through all his days.

As for Dempsey, unless this country should go to war again, it seems probable that he will continue to be our leading fighter for quite some time to come. . . .

Through a hundred entrances the multitude flows in steadily, smoothly, without jamming or confusion. The trickling streams run down the aisles and are absorbed by capillary action in the seats. If it takes all sorts of people to make up the world then all the world must be here already. That modest hero of the cinemas, Tom Mix, known amongst his friends as the Shrinking Violet of Death Valley, starts a furor by his appearance at 12:15, just as the first of the preliminary bouts is getting under way. His dress proclaims that he has recently suffered a personal bereavement. He is in mourning. He wears a sea-green sport suit, a purple neckerchief, a pair of solid-gold-filled glasses and a cowboy hat the size of a six-furlong track. . . .

A calling over of the names of the occupants of the more highly priced reservations would sound like a reading of the first hundred pages of Who's Ballyhoo in America. . . .

Bout after bout is staged, is fought out, is finished. Few know who the fighters are and nobody particularly cares. . . .

Governor Edwards of New Jersey comes at one-thirty; the first good solid knockdown in the ring at one-thirty-six. Both are heartily approved with loud thunders of applause. Not everyone can be the anti-dry, sport-loving Governor of a great commonwealth, but a veritable nobody can win popular approval on a day like this by shoving his jaw in front of a winged fist. There are short cuts to fame though painful. . . .

At intervals a zealous member of Governor Edwards' staff rises up, majestic in his indignation, and demands to know why some presumptuous commoner is permitted to stand or stoop in front of his Excellency. . . .

It's 3 o'clock. (Prompt on the appointed hour, for once in the history of championship goes,) the men are brought forth on time. . . . Dempsey sitting there makes me think of a smoke-stained Japanese war idol; Carpentier, by contrast, suggests an Olympian runner carved out of fine-grained white ivory. Partisans howl their approval at the champion. He refuses to acknowledge these. One figures that he has suddenly grown sulky because his reception was no greater than it was. . . .

Dempsey keeps his eyes fixed on his fists. Carpentier studies him closely across the eighteen feet which separate them. The Gaul is losing his nervous air. He is living proof to give the lie to the old fable that all Frenchmen are excitable. . . .

The first round is Dempsey's all the way. He has flung Carpentier aside with thrusts of his shoulders. He has shoved him about almost at will. . . . The third round is Dempsey's from bell to bell. . . .

In the fourth round, after one minute and sixteen seconds of hard fighting—fighting which on Carpentier's part is defensive—comes the foreordained and predestined finishment. . . . Dempsey's right arm swings upward with the flailing emphasis of an oak cudgel and the muffed fist at the end of it lands again on its favorite target—the Frenchman's jaw. . . .

In a hush which instantaneously descends and as instantaneously is ended, the referee swings his arm down like a semaphore and chants out "ten."

The rest is a muddle and a mass of confusion. . . .

As I settle back to watch now with languid interest this anti-climax, three things stand out in my memory as the high points of the big fight, so far as I am personally concerned.

The first is that Carpentier never had a chance. . . .

The second is that vision of him, doubled up on his side, like a frightened hurt boy, and yet striving to heave himself up and take added punishment from a foe against whom he had no shadow of hope.

The third—and the most outstanding—will be my recollection of that look in Dempsey's lowering front when realization came to him that a majority of the tremendous audience were partisans of the foreigner.

THE DRY CRUSADE

The dramatic struggle to enforce Prohibition was in a way a national conflict between two groups. Supporting the dry crusade was, roughly, the small town, farming, middle-class tradition infused with the radical Protestant ethic that sought to make men better by legislation. The opposition to the Volstead Act drew much of its strength from the newer urban groups, mixed in religious affiliation or secular-minded and devoted to a much freer, tolerant, and often sybaritic way of life.

Immediately after the passage of the Volstead Act it became apparent that many otherwise good citizens did not intend to abide by the law, and a colorful battle for enforcement started between the always too few federal agents, often unaided in the large cities by the local police, and a host of lawbreakers ranging from the solitary maker of bathtub gin to the well-organized and heavily financed wholesale bootlegger. Supporting the entire structure, of course, were the otherwise law abiding citizens who en masse purchased the illegal liquor.

The fundamental indictment of Prohibition rested on the fact that a large minority or even a majority of citizens refused to obey the Volstead Act. From that sentiment many of the other evils followed: a growing willingness to condone lawlessness, the serious invasion of personal rights by overzealous federal enforcement agents, the corruption of government officials with the ample funds provided by the illegal traffic, and the veritable choking of the federal courts with liquor cases. But perhaps more serious than any of these factors was the growth of organized gangsterism financed by the immense profits from bootlegging. Enforcing their mandates with hired gunmen, the gangs soon took on the attributes of illegal governments and ultimately reached up into city politics, legitimate business, and labor unions. The resulting struggle between the gangsters and the law enforcement agencies was one of the most colorful in American history, supplying endless material for movies, television, and detective stories. But upon its outcome also rested the fate of an ordered and a secure American society. The following documents illustrate various phases of the "dry crusade."

16. THE CRUSADE STARTS

From the very first hours of the attempted enforcement of the Volstead Act it was apparent that almost insurmountable difficulties lay ahead. Significantly, the first raids of the federal agents took place in two northern cities rather than against the traditional "moonshiners" of the southern mountains. The following extract from "The Crusade Starts" by Charles Merz, *Outlook and Independent,* October 15, 1930, p. 278, is a running record of the first six months of the struggle between the bootleggers and the Federal agents, as well as a commentary upon the all but insuperable obstacles to enforcement. Reprinted by the kind permission of the author, whose book, *The Dry Decade* (1931) is still the best on the subject.

. . . IT WAS AT MIDNIGHT ON JANUARY 16 THAT THE LAW TOOK EFFECT and twenty-four hours later that the public received its first enforcement news. "Four stills, two in Detroit and two in Hammond, Indiana, were raided yesterday in the government's crusade against violators of the Volstead Act," said an Associated Press dispatch from Chicago on January 17. "The raided stills, according to A. V. Dalrymple, head of the Central West prohibition forces, were operating on a major scale."

The country was dry. Prohibition had come. The Constitution itself forbade the manufacture of intoxicating liquor. It seems clear, however, that there was no sharp break between the old and new, in the sense that manufacture ceased abruptly for a time and only at a later date did illicit stills begin to flourish. The stills were present from the start, not only in the hill country of the border states, where they had always flourished, but in the Middle West, the East and South: obviously prepared to carry on the business of manufacture without interruption.

On January 26, the tenth day of national prohibition, a moonshine plant with a daily capacity of 500 gallons was raided by prohibition agents near the town of Pelham, twenty miles from Birmingham, Alabama. Here was one extreme, a suggestion of the possibilities latent in large-scale manufacture with a nearby city as the convenient market for a product which could be sold at an attractive profit. At the opposite extreme from large commercial operations was the one-gallon still, designed to cheat the law through a process of home manufacture.

On January 28, the twelfth day of national prohibition, a force of federal agents set out from the Customs House in New York City in what was described as "the greatest campaign ever conducted against violators of the prohibition law," a phrase which was destined to become familiar. The goal of this drive was a round-up of one-gallon stills which, even as early as the second week of national prohibition, were thought to be in wide use throughout the city.

"Any person caught with one of these stills in his possession will be proceeded against at once," said the Federal Prohibition Administrator in New York. "I advise everybody who has one to bring it to my office immediately." On the following day, no stills having been surrendered, the Federal Administrator announced that his men would promptly begin to search the city for them. For this purpose he had at his disposal a staff of 178 agents to distribute among 1,278,431 homes.

Both the commercial still and its small compatriot for kitchen use thus made their appearance promptly, in the first two weeks of prohibition. From the point of view of effective enforcement of the law, the obvious problem which they presented was the difficulty of detecting and destroying an illicit source of liquor when it was hidden away in miniature form in a city home or in its commercial form concealed in some thicket or some hollow so inaccessibly placed that even the owner of the land on which it stood might be unaware of its existence. A case in point occurred during these early months when a still with a capacity of 130 gallons was found operating at full blast five miles north of Austin, Texas, on the farm of Senator Morris Sheppard, author of the Eighteenth Amendment.

If the question of illicit stills raised a problem for the government, there is nothing in the record to suggest that the prompt appearance of this problem tempered the optimism shown by enforcement officials in their early statements to the press.

The Treasury Department had brought to Washington, as the first Prohibition Commissioner in the history of the United States, an Ohio lawyer and a former member of the Ohio Legislature—John F. Kramer, a devoted dry.

This man was not a party boss. He controlled no votes. He had no experience in the business of party plunder. He was an unknown in Washington, a disinterested outsider, a lifelong friend of prohibition and a champion whose first announcement to the press breathed confidence and fire: "This law will be obeyed in cities, large and small, and in villages, and where it is not obeyed it will be enforced. . . . The law says that liquor to be used as a beverage must not be manufactured. We shall see that it is not manufactured. Nor sold, nor given away, nor hauled in anything on the surface of the earth or under the earth or in the air."

Nevertheless, despite the finality of this statement and the confidence with which it bristled, it rapidly became apparent that the law would encounter a variety of problems which had not been anticipated by its authors. Illicit distilling was one of these problems. Others cropped up with a disconcerting promptness which is evident in the calendar of the first official efforts at enforcement.

January 16: The law took effect.

January 30: Three members of the Internal Revenue Department engaged in prohibition work were indicted at Chicago on charges of corruption.

January 31: Congress was informed that wholesale smuggling of liquor was in progress on the borders. In a letter to the Appropriations Committee of the House of Representatives, George W. Ashworth, Director of the Customs Service, reported that only "an infinitesimal quantity" of this liquor was being seized, advised Congress that it had not adequately prepared to meet the problem and asked for the immediate appropriation of an additional $2,000,000.

February 19: Two agents of the Internal Revenue Department engaged in prohibition work were arrested at Baltimore on charges of corruption.

February 28: Two carloads of patent medicine containing fifty-five per cent of alcohol were seized in Chicago by government officials.

March 11: Federal agents in Brooklyn began a round-up of druggists accused of selling whisky without a prescription from a doctor.

March 19: The lower House of the Mississippi legislature voted down a bill proposing to appropriate state funds to aid the federal government in suppressing stills. Major W. Calvin Wells, Federal Prohibition Commissioner for the state, urged the members of the legislature to reveal the sources of liquor which he said was being sold to state officials "openly and brazenly."

May 8: The federal prohibition office in New York City complained that it was not receiving the support of the New York police. "We are making a great many arrests, but the co-operation of the local authorities is absolutely necessary. We don't get that co-operation."

May 24: Dr. Charles W. Eliot of Harvard University declared in an address at Boston that people with money and social position were helping to defeat the law. "These so-called 'best people,' who are doing so much to interfere with prohibition enforcement, are causing a great deal of trouble in nearly all parts of the country and they are teaching lawlessness, especially to the young men of the country."

June 2: Captain Hubert Howard, Federal Prohibition Administrator for Illinois, estimated that 300,000 spurious prescriptions had been issued by Chicago physicians since the law became effective.

June 6: The special train of the Massachusetts delegation to the Republican National Convention was raided by prohibition agents who seized half its stock of liquor.

June 17: District Attorney Clyne reported that the dockets of the federal courts in Chicago were congested with prohibition cases. "Between five hundred and six hundred cases are now awaiting trial."

June 18: The Department of Justice announced that it would be unable to employ special attorneys to handle prohibition cases because of the failure of Congress to provide the necessary funds.

June 30: San Francisco was reported to be wide open in honor of the Democratic National Convention. Acting Mayor McLernan later said:

"Everybody knew it. The roof of the house was off and San Francisco was entertaining."

July 2: Jail sentences aggregating fifty-nine months and fines totaling $85,000 were imposed on officials of two companies in New York City manufacturing flavoring extracts and hair tonics. Officials of the two companies were found guilty of withdrawing from bond 25,000 gallons of alcohol which were diverted to beverage purposes.

July 25: A Washington dispatch to the New York *Times* reported: "Federal authorities are greatly concerned over the failure of state and city law officers to co-operate with prohibition agents. The fact that the anti-liquor laws are being flouted in many of the greatest cities of the country causes chagrin and disappointment to the government."

Here is a page from the record of the first six months of prohibition. One point it shows clearly. Even within so brief a time as half a year every major question which is now prominent in the problem of enforcement had already raised its head. . . .

17. THE BOOTLEGGER

With the advent of the Volstead Act a new occupation or "profession" opened for thousands of Americans, that of bootlegging, a term which apparently originated in the southern hills from the practice of illegal still operators carrying their goods to consumers in the top of their boots. But bootlegging in the Twenties was a much more complex industry running from a one-man manufacturing operation to those headed by an organization worthy of a large legitimate corporation. An assistant District Attorney of Philadelphia, Joseph K. Willing, discusses the new profession in its many aspects. The extract is from "Profession of Bootlegging," *Annals of the American Academy of Political and Social Science,* May 1926. Reprinted by permission of the Academy.

THE SPECIFIC SUBJECT WHICH I HAVE BEEN ASKED TO DISCUSS IS THE "PROfession of bootlegging." When my mind first attacked this subtitle it asked itself, what is a profession? I resorted immediately to the dictionaries and found it to be generally described as a phase of human endeavor, openly avowed by one who has become expert by reason of special scholastic training. The latest Funk & Wagnalls' Dictionary is the only one which seems to know anything about bootlegging. Whatever is said about it there implies that there is a sort of antinomy between the word "profession" as defined above and "bootlegging" as it is generally practiced and known. Bootlegging has none of the characteristics of the definition, except that it seems to be a new line of human endeavor. It is, however, not openly avowed and requires no scholastic education nor academic sanction.

It is presumed that the word "bootlegging" comes from a practice in some of the southern states where the "moonshiner" sought to avoid the payment of the Federal tax on manufactured distilled spirits. The moonshiner would deliver his pint or half-pint in the leg of his boot and this article of wearing apparel may be described as the first vehicle used in the transportation of intoxicating liquor, even antedating the hippocket. Whatever be the historical antinomy inherent in the title chosen, it seems that the public at large is prepared to recognize a new profession, and to require no academic degrees for its candidates. This new profession wrings from the bosom of Mammon many more shekels than its legitimate brethren. Let us now turn to a consideration of its characteristics.

Like all professions in this modern age, it has become specialized, and the specialties arrange themselves in the following categories:

      I. Smuggling and transportation
     II. Redistillation or recooking
   III. Doctor and druggist complex
   IV. Brewing of high power beer
    V. Home brew and accessory stores
   VI. Homemade wine, ciders and cordials

To state the divisions of the profession is to say almost all that need be said about them. They have become so well known that the public can be said to take judicial notice of their content.

SMUGGLING AND TRANSPORTATION

Under the heading of "smuggling and transportation" we include that individual, corporation, ring or gang whose primary business is to import intoxicating liquors into the United States. This specialty divides itself into two classes: trans-oceanic traffic, and trans-continental traffic. Considering first trans-oceanic traffic: it is important to recognize that most of the details incident upon a legitimate shipment of merchandise are incident in the smuggling of intoxicating liquors. Ships must be chartered, crews must be employed, finances must be arranged, insurance policies must be obtained or a reserve fund set aside to cover risks, and the hazards of the ocean encountered, with the additional hazard inherent in the occupation, namely, detection. In spite of all these commercial details, it needs no argument to convince the public at large that large quantities of foreign liquors find their way into the United States day after day. Once a shipment is landed the next link in the chain is soldered, the transportation link. Motor trucks meet the shipment and distribute it to the wholsale bootleggers, who in turn sell the liquor in small case lots to the retailer, who in turn transports the same in ordinary automobiles and vehicles to the consumer. One can buy everything from the rarest of French wines and Russian Kümmel to Scotch whiskey. Ships have been known to leave Vancouver chartered for Mexico with a load of liquor, and return to Vancouver having delivered their cargo, in twenty-four hours. Are Portland and Seattle in Mexico or in the United States?

Collaterally with the smuggling of liquor, which is illegal, there has developed the so-called legitimate import trade of essences. In a first-class grocery store one can buy the essence of crème de menthe, benedictine, crème de cocoa, vermouth, scotch mash, chartreuse, sloe gin, etc. A few drops of essence, a little grain of sugar, a dash of pure ethyl alcohol, and the monks of Pavia would marvel at American chartreuse and benedictine. Practically all liquors from Martini to Kümmel are imported into the United States after they have been dealcoholized. When landed from Italy, Spain or France they contain one-tenth of one per cent by volume of ethyl alcohol. Of course one is not supposed to add alcohol and serve —if one does, that's not the importer's concern!

There are imported also quantities of foreign grape juices. France, or Spain, or Italy will drop into your cellar a cask of genuine grape juice of its finest quality and all you need to do is to let a little air into the cask if you like a kick in your grape juice. Is aërating grape juice a crime? I do not know.

The same procedure, with the exception of the ship, is followed in smuggling across the border of Canada and Mexico. For traffic between Canada and the United States, and Mexico and the United States, every possible conveyance is used by the smugglers, from the saddle bags and diamondhitch of the ranchman to specially built automobiles. The liquor thus imported into the United States is commonly designated as "good liquor." That is to say, it was manufactured from genuine materials and intended at the time of manufacture to be used for beverage purposes. It contains no latent, deleterious substances. It is often fresh and raw, particularly the Scotch.

At this point it might be well to know what is defined as "good liquor." We use "liquor" here as synonymous with whiskey. Genuine whiskey is a spirit distilled from a grain mash and aged at least three or four years in charred oak barrels, containing from forty-seven to fifty per cent by volume of ethyl alcohol. There are some slight modifications of this definition, but they have to do more with the barrels used for ageing and the special ways of rectification than with the substance used or its alcoholic content. The important thing to note is the period of ageing and the alcoholic content by volume. The word "whiskey" comes from the Celtic *uisgebeatha* which later became *usquebaugh* and means "water of life." At the Feast of Cana the water became wine. Nineteen hundred years later, the "water of life" became the "Block—and—Fall" of the bootlegger. Legitimate whiskies contained from forty-five to sixty per cent by volume of ethyl alcohol, and before prohibition they were frequently reduced so as to contain from seventeen to twenty-four per cent.

The persons engaged in this specialty of the bootlegging profession have the greatest contempt for the redistiller or "recooker" as he is commonly known. He is a pariah in their eyes. Not because he makes a competitive product but for alleged humanitarian reasons. The smuggler considers himself a benefactor to society for he assumes that people will drink, and that he is the only purveyor of "good liquor," and therefore saves society from what is commonly called "poison liquor."

REDISTILLATION

It is not unlawful in the United States to manufacture, possess or deal in grain alcohol or denatured alcohol for manufacturing and industrial purposes, provided one has a permit to do so. The Volstead Act sets up in addition to the basic permit or license a withdrawal permit system whereby permittees can withdraw a given quantity of pure alcohol on each withdrawal permit. The total amount withdrawn by any permittee varies with the size of the bond he has given to the Federal Government pledging its legitimate use. While tremendous quantities of pure grain alcohol are thus withdrawn, the cumbersomeness of obtaining it and its cost drives most bootleggers out of this class into the denatured alcohol field. Anyone can secure a permit to use denatured alcohol.

There are two kinds of denatured alcohols—completely denatured and partially denatured or "specially" denatured alcohol. We need pay little or no attention to completely denatured alcohol. Denatured alcohol is ordinary grain alcohol denatured by adding certain foreign substances in accordance with government formulae. Completely denatured alcohol is rarely used in the bootlegging industry because it is so difficult to extract the denaturant. The so-called "specially" denatured alcohols are the ones that are most frequently used. Experience has shown that the denaturants most commonly used are isopropyl, quinine, brucine, diethylphthalate and or nicotine and methylene blue. Alcohol denatured with any one of these, with the exception of isopropyl, which is in itself a higher form of alcohol, is easily distilled off. One has simply to boil the denatured alcohol and condense the vapor passing over and one gets a more or less pure grain alcohol. To this is usually added caramel or prune juice for coloring purposes.

To make rye whiskey a greater amount of caramel is added than to make Scotch, for the larger the amount of caramel the deeper the color. It is then necessary to add flavor because whiskey, in addition to alcohol and coloring, has an unique flavor and bouquet. This in legitimate whiskey comes from the storing and ageing of whiskey in what is commonly known as "the wood." In the wood a certain amount of genuine amyl alcohol or fusel oil is generated and this adds flavor to the spirits. The charred oak barrels give the woody taste to Scotch and some rye whiskies. The redistiller or "recooker" cannot wait two or three years for genuine fusel oil to be generated or for a genuine wood flavor to be added. He gets the flavor by charring wood and, if unscrupulous enough, adds a drop of fusel oil. There are other flavoring materials used. What they are it is often impossible to detect.

The redistiller works as quickly as possible, both for the reason of making a profit and avoiding detection. Often in one night the denatured alcohol is redistilled, colored, flavored, bottled, labelled and shipped. May I at this point call your attention to the definition given above of legitimate whiskey. Age is an important factor in the making of genuine whiskies. Speed is the *sina qua non* of bootleg whiskey. Even if chemically pure they are often crude combinations of alcohol and the other materials mentioned, but the alcoholic content ranges up to ninety-seven per cent by volume. This amounts to drinking practically pure grain alcohol.

The Federal Government has eighty special denaturing formulae, and six complete denaturing formulae. The bootlegger uses specially denatured alcohol, and the chief formulae which are abused are the so-called formula No. 4, nicotine and methylene blue; formula No. 39, isopropyl in combination with alkaloid salts, quinine and brucine; formula No. 39-B, diethylphthalate, and formula No. 40, brucine. If you have been asking yourself the question why denatured alcohol is used for bootlegging purposes rather than grain alcohol, the answer is the government tax of $4.18 per gallon on grain alcohol. The present market price of grain alcohol at the distillery is $4.60 per gallon, and the price of specially denatured alcohol at the distillery is fifty cents to ninety cents per gallon. Have you been asking yourself another question: Can anyone buy denatured alcohol? The answer is yes if he has a permit. Permits are not difficult to obtain from the Federal Government, provided the applicant shows a use requiring denatured alcohol. This has given rise in large cities to many new barber supply houses, cigar and cigarette makers, perfume and lotion manufactures, soap makers, varnish and furniture polish makers, extract makers, and what not.

Very often the redistiller or "recooker" does not get behind the camouflage of a legitimate industry. It is much cheaper and easier to rent a garage or a small private dwelling, and for a few thousand dollars set up a complete redistillation plant without disguise. Such persons are known in this state as "cookers." They do practically nothing but recook the alcohol and deliver it to shopkeepers of such places as saloons, restaurants, cigar stores, lunch counters, lunch wagons, etc. The shopkeeper gets the recooked alcohol and flavors and colors it in accordance with his own prescription. Frequently he adds only a little prune juice or a few spoons full of good whiskey. Good whiskey to-day is used more as an essence than as a beverage. The product is then ready for sale to the consumer in pints, half-pints, quarts or simply a drink.

From the sociological or physiological point of view this is the worst phase of the bootlegging profession. It is by all odds the most extensive and it distributes to the consuming public a vastly inferior and deleterious product. The persons who practice in this specialty of the bootlegging profession are even harder to reach than the smuggler. Of course it is easy to arrest the common laborer tending that boiler attached to a still, or the janitor caring for the building, but the aim of society should be the apprehension of the "higher-ups." It is often impossible to catch the "higher-ups" because the permits are taken out in the name of some company or other, and the permittee does not take delivery of the product, but by a special *arrangement* with the "bonded" drayman or his own drayman, has the product delivered from the denaturing plant to the re-cooking plant without ever touching the alcohol. Consequently when the police raid the establishment there is frequently no one around, and if there is someone around, he is usually seated at a corner window or back door and makes his escape. The garages and dwellings are rented under fictitious names and little or no clues can be gathered from the leases. Much has been said about poison liquor. That there is some there can be no doubt, but it is a rare case where metallic or alkaloidal poisons are found in solution upon analysis.

Whiskey is not the only liquor manufactured by redistillation. I know of one redistilling plant that was equipped to supply every form of liquor and cordial. I believe the owner is now resting quietly in jail.

Denatured alcohol, recooked, colored and flavored as above described and bottled in the bathtub is not fit in my opinion for beverage purposes Is there much of this going on? Let a government expert testify. He says 87,000,000 gallons of grain alcohol were distilled in 1925. Six million gallons went to physicians and hospitals, and the government takes credit for 100 per cent on that item. Eighty-one million gallons are supposed to have been denatured for industrial purposes. But between the consumption for industrial purposes and the release, the government loses at least ten million gallons. What happens to this alcohol? Guess!

THE DOCTOR AND DRUGGIST COMPLEX

Under the third heading we shall consider the doctor and druggist complex. The Volstead Act and Liquor Enforcement Acts do not prohibit the prescribing of intoxicating liquor for medical purposes. Doctors are permitted to withdraw six quarts of whiskey and five gallons of alcohol per year for laboratory purposes. In addition, every physician who has a permit is given a pad of blank prescriptions numbered from one to one hundred. He can use the entire pad in ninety days, but must not prescribe more than one pint of whiskey, or one quart of wine to any one person every ten (10) days. When the emergency for prescribing intoxicating liquor arises, is left to the integrity of the physician. How often the physician is his own doctor and patient is difficult to ascertain. I have heard it said that if one suffers from a chronic "thirstitis" there is no friend like a doctor. There have been a few cases where the ethics of that noble profession have been violated, but no indictment can be drawn against the profession. Druggists have gone a little further. They have frequently sold liquor without any prescriptions or on fake prescriptions knowing them to be so. The liquor thus sold to the consuming public is usually "good liquor." Those who can afford to pay the price buy the liquor as it comes from the government bonded warehouses; others who cannot afford to pay the price buy it as diluted by the bootlegging druggist.

BREWING HIGH POWER BEER

The brewing and distillation of malt liquors containing more than one-half of one per cent by volume of ethyl or grain alcohol is also another special field. The manufacture of malt liquor on any scale requires a large investment of capital and a large plant. This business is facilitated by the fact that the Volstead Act and many other state acts provide that it shall not be unlawful to have in one's possession beer of a higher alcoholic content than one-half of one per cent during the process of manufacture. During the trial of cases of this character it is often found impossible to determine when the process of manufacture ceases. Usually, when the raid is made on a brewery, the beer is in the process of manufacture and when it is about to be distributed as a completed product the raiders are not present, or in some cases they have eyes but they see not. The same problem of distribution of high power beer arises as in all other cases and the subterfuges are many. The barrels are frequently labeled with large labels reading: *"Cereal Beverage, less than one-half of one per cent."* This satisfies the conscience of the drayman. An analysis shows very often that the beer contains from a fraction of a per cent to about six per cent by volume of ethyl alcohol. Bottles of beer are delivered in sugar barrels, paper cartons, rag bags and market baskets. When carload lots of beer are shipped it is often necessary to bring into the conspiracy train crews, switchmen and locomotive engineers. In some cases the last mentioned are innocent victims of the plan.

The brewers feel that they have been discriminated against and they have at last found a champion. In fact the goddess Ceres is in the fray. Why should it be lawful to make non-intoxicating fruit juices and not non-intoxicating cereal juices? If the Federal and state governments are prepared to say that whether or not a fruit juice is intoxicating is a question of fact, why be arbitrary about cereal juices? This, of course, makes martyrs out of the brewers and bolsters their consciences. They consider themselves as benefactors of society for the same reasons as the smugglers.

ACCESSORY STORES

There are some crimes that make accessories before and after the crime subject to punishment. The liquor laws provide no such crimes and penalties. In many sections of large cities there are those whose business consists entirely of selling apparatus and material for home brewing. One can buy very openly everything from mash to bottle stoppers and caps. It is an education in the art of making liquor to look into the windows of such a store. It contains every conceivable object that might be employed in the manufacture, distillation, brewing, bottling, barrelling and preserving of intoxicating liquors. Ostensibly the object of these stores is to enable the housewife to make catsup or rootbeer. If sometimes the catsup turns to brandy and the "root" drops out of the beer, that's a happy accident.

HOMEMADE BREWS

This leads us to our last specialty—homemade wines, cider and cordials. It is not unlawful to possess intoxicating liquors in one's *bona fide* private dwelling, used as such, provided it has been lawfully acquired before prohibition. It is not unlawful to make non-intoxicating fruit juices in one's private dwelling, used as such. The so-called "private dwelling" has become a haven for private bootlegging. It is true that a man's home is and should be his castle. In the trial of these cases it often becomes necessary to determine what is a private dwelling, and what is a non-intoxicating fruit juice. Is an ordinary six-rooms-and-bath-house, in which liquor is stored in close proximity to a saloon, and from which liquor in small quantities is drawn off for sale in the saloon, a private dwelling? If a man is engaged in a restaurant business and leases a dwelling several blocks away from the business and stores wine and liquor in the cellar, and puts a table and bed in the other parts of the house, is that a private dwelling? Does a person who resides in a private dwelling and who presses grapes and lets nature do the rest, occupy a winery or a dwelling, or both? As was stated above, it is not unlawful to manufacture grape juice, but is it unlawful to permit grape juice to become a wine? There is a great diversity of opinion about this. It is not unlawful for a person legally in the possession of intoxicating liquor in his private dwelling to give it to his *bona fide* guests. If a man occupies a store and dwelling and a customer drops in to buy a cigar, and the proprietor invites him into the kitchen for a glass of wine, is the customer a *bona fide* guest? These are some of the questions that arise in the homemade wine and cordial violations. Wines are made from grapefruit, dandelion, rhubarb, elderberries, blackberries, cherries and pineapple; and brandies are made from cherries, peaches and apricots. It takes the skill of a botanist to determine what is a fruit and what is not. Must persons, who before prohibition never violated any law, be classed in the criminal class if they make any of the foregoing products? It seems to me that if America is returning at any point to home industry it is in the field of intoxicating liquor.

I have said nothing about the seepage of sacramental wines into non-sacramental uses. That some of it escapes can be easily demonstrated, but fortunately it cannot yet be dignified as a specialty in the profession of bootlegging.

SCOPE OF BOOTLEGGING

At this point it might be interesting to consider the scope of the profession of bootlegging in a community such as Philadelphia. Beginning with the year 1919, the era of prohibition, the Police Department of the City of Philadelphia made the following number of arrests for intoxication, intoxication and disorderly conduct, and habitual drunkenness. Intoxication and disorderly conduct are very closely allied. There seems to be an ancient historical precedent for this crime. In Genesis IX:20, 21, we read the following:

> And Noah began to be an husbandman, and he planted a vineyard;
> And he drank of the wine, and was drunken; and he was uncovered within his tent.

This might also be classed as the first case of drunkenness and indecent exposure.

It is interesting to note that all this occurred after a sea voyage, and perhaps the sailor lad comes by his land spree through heredity.

The statistics of the Police Department, beginning with the year 1919, follow:

1919		*Total*	*1921*		
Intoxication	16,819		Intoxication	21,850	
Intoxication and disorderly conduct	6,794		Intoxication and disorderly conduct	5,232	
Habitual drunkards	127		Intoxicated drivers*	494	
		23,740	Habitual drunkards	33	
1920					27,609
Intoxication	14,313		*1922*		
Intoxication and disorderly conduct	6,097		Intoxication	36,299	
Habitual drunkards	33		Intoxication and disorderly conduct	7,925	
		20,443	Intoxicated drivers	472	
			Habitual drunkards	50	
					44,746

* Not classified previous to year 1921.

		Total			
1923			*1925*		
Intoxication	45,226		Intoxication	51,361	
Intoxication and disorderly conduct	8,076		Intoxication and disorderly conduct	5,522	
Intoxicated drivers	645		Intoxicated drivers	820	
Habitual drunkards	177		Habitual drunkards	814	
		54,124			58,517
1924					
Intoxication	47,805				
Intoxication and disorderly conduct	6,404				
Intoxicated drivers	683				
Habitual drunkards	874				
		55,766			

It is hard to believe that during the year of 1925 there were more than a thousand arrests per week in Philadelphia for the above described offenses. For the month of January, 1926, there were the following number of arrests for the aforementioned crimes:

1926		
Intoxication	3,466	
Intoxication and disorderly conduct	362	
Habitual drunkards	14	
Intoxicated automobile drivers	39	
		3,881

The District Attorney's office of Philadelphia County has statistics of the seizures of intoxicating liquors and property used in the manufacture and transportation of liquor from November and December, 1923, and for the years 1924 and 1925. From November 1, 1923, to December 31, 1924, the Police Department of the City of Philadelphia made and delivered to the District Attorney 6308 seizures of liquor and property used in the manufacture and transportation of liquor. When I tell you that these seizures vary from a milk bottle to a freight car or cars, you will have some idea of the complexity of handling the situation. For the same period of time the Police Department seized 538 vehicles, or a total of 6846 seizures.

For the year 1925, the police made and delivered to the District Attorney 8146 seizures of liquor and property, and seized 323 vehicles, or a total of 8469 seizures.

For the year 1926, up to February 15, the police seized and delivered to the District Attorney 1224 seizures of liquor and property, and seized twenty-five vehicles, or a total of 1249 seizures.

The District Attorney has been forced to rent a five-story concrete building—a garage and warehouse—containing approximately 600,000 cubic feet. The liquor staff handling only the condemnation of liquor, etc., is more than twice the staff doing all other kinds of work.

18. POISONED HOOCH

Each of the following three documents illustrates a phase of the Prohibition era. The first by the U. S. Prohibition Commissioner, Roy A. Haynes, is mainly concerned with the manufacturing methods of the small "moonshiner," the low quality of his product, and the danger it carried to the imbiber. The second is an account of a trip with the wholesale smugglers of illegal liquor from Canada across the border from Detroit. The third article concerns a day's activity in the life of Izzy Einstein, perhaps the most famous of all the Federal Prohibition agents. "Izzy" and his partner "Moe" were almost national figures in the early days of Prohibition enforcement, their methods exciting both strenuous protests and lavish praise from the press, depending upon the wet or dry attitudes of the individual newspapers. The first article, by Roy A. Haynes, is reprinted by permission of *The New York Times,* July 26, 1923.

IT IS A COMMON PRACTICE AMONG MOONSHINERS TO PLACE THEIR LIQUOR in old-fashioned fruit jars with zinc tops. The acids corrode the zinc, which goes into the liquor in the form of zinc salts. Cases of acute gastritis and other fatal ailments undoubtedly are caused by drinking that sort of moonshine.

The moonshiners' greed for profits adds still other poisons. The mountain moonshiner of the old days, though he was illiterate, knew that the "heads" or "first shots" of the distillation and the "tails"—the scum and the dregs—should be thrown away. He knew, also, that the middle run must be redistilled to make it passable. He did not know that the "heads" were high in aldehydes and the "tails" high in fusel oil, nor did he know that redistilling helped to eliminate them, but he did know that unless these things were done even the strong men of the mountains could not safely drink his product.

The modern moonshiner neither knows nor cares. His interest is to get every penny his "run" will bring, and with as little work as possible. Neither "heads" nor "tails" are thrown away.

One of the worst features of moonshine liquor, however, is not that it is filthy, not that it contains metallic poisons, but that it is raw spirits— new liquor not properly aged in wood—and that it contains all the poisons incidental to such liquor. . . .

One thing, however, is known: the harmful constituents of new whiskey can be removed in only two ways. One is by fractionating in an alcohol column. The other is by aging in a wooden barrel. The first of these methods is not practicable for the present day moonshiner to adopt. The other he does not practice; often he sells his wares warm from the still. . . .

Next to that kind of moonshine, the liquor most commonly dealt in by bootleggers is made from denatured alcohol, a non-beverage liquor intended for industrial uses. Denatured alcohol originally was pure grain alcohol. . . .

Theoretically it is possible to recover pure grain alcohol from the denatured product. That is what many illicit manufacturers attempt to do, either by redistillation or by neutralizing the poisons. Almost without exception such a manufacturer is without chemical knowledge or training. The delicate and complicated process by which pure grain alcohol may be recovered is beyond his powers. He succeeds in distilling a liquor from which most of the disagreeable taste has been removed, so that when it is combined with flavoring and coloring substances the buyer will accept it as real liquor. But it still contains quantities of the poisons used in the denaturing process. . . .

Poisons are sometimes added for the purpose of giving a "kick" to the liquor, but practically all the samples coming into the laboratories have such a powerful and immediate intoxicating effect that the addition of such poisons is unnecessary. . . .

Wood alcohol's toll of death and blindness is ghastly. The cases come in seeming epidemics. Apparently they are the product, not of deliberate intent to murder, but of ignorance on the part of the compounder. . . .

Many cases of wood alcohol poisoning probably have been due to the fact that a bootlegger or manufacturer of synthetic liquor used wood alcohol by mistake. His victims die more quickly and more violently than those of the moonshiner or the redistiller of denatured alcohol. . . .

Home brewing appears to be dying a natural death. Many persons who have tried it have found that, without adequate brewery equipment, they cannot make anything fit to drink. . . .

Delirium tremens was the aftermath of real liquor in its day. The aftermath of bootleg liquor often is a stupefaction following hard on the heels of frenzy. It may bring loss of sensation even while consciousness remains. . . .

From all parts of the country have come reports of after-effects of bootleg liquor more weird than delirium tremens. Sometimes the victim prefers death to the agony and, with closing consciousness, takes his own life. A young actress, for instance, who killed herself in her dressing room in a Washington theatre, lived long enough to say that the effects of the liquor drunk at the party had caused her to seek death as a relief. Again, there was the case of a young woman on a Hoboken ferryboat who took a drink from a flask carried in the pocket of her escort. Almost immediately, she staggered to the stern, plunged into the Hudson and was drowned.

Who drinks bootleg drinks with Death.

●   ●   ●   ●   ●

Charles A Selden, "Rum Row in the Middle West," *The New York Times,* May 27, 1928. Reprinted by permission of *The New York Times.*

SIX HUNDRED MILES FROM THE ATLANTIC SEABOARD, THE CITY OF DETROIT makes a convincing bid for the title of the liquor capital of the United States. It is the automobile capital of the world, but there are imposing and reasonably reliable figures to support the statement that the illegal liquor business is Detroit's second largest industry. The manufacture and sale of automobiles in Detroit involves nearly $2,000,000,000 annually and the chemical industry about $90,000,000. Between the two stands Detroit's illegal liquor traffic, estimated at $215,000,000. . . . shrewd guesswork analyses of some of the major items make it seem plausible.

These major items are the smuggling of liquor into the city from Canadian towns on the other side of the mile-wide Detroit River; its manufacture in Detroit; its consumption in that city, and its distribution to other parts of the United States from Detroit as the port of illegal entry. . . .

The Mayor neither apologized for his city nor boasted of it. He just took the liquor situation as a matter of course without attempting to measure it. . . . After his election Mayor Lodge said there should be no fanaticism in the running of the city. Regardless of what the Mayor may have had in mind, the popular translation of the word "fanaticism" in Detroit is enforcement of the prohibition law. And the city is not "fanatic." . . .

All cities have their clubs in which drinks may be had and bootleg delivery systems for homes, offices and hotels. But it is along her waterfront and the river itself that Detroit has her distinctive features as a rum-smuggling city. It is the largest border community in the country and nowhere else is the water boundary between the Dominion and the States so narrow and so easily navigable.

On the Canadian side the manufacture, sale and export of liquor is a legal industry. Opposite the city of Detroit, with its 1,500,000 people, are the seven so-called border cities of Canada, with an aggregate population of 110,000. . . . In these communities are breweries, distilleries, and Government liquor stores. All along their waterfronts are export docks from which liquor cargoes may legally be cleared through Canadian customs for export to Detroit; which, for a speedboat, is a three-minute voyage to the westward. . . .

When the joint boundary commissioners, after the War of 1812, determined the line between Canada and the United States in this region, they drew their line down the middle of the Detroit River, swerving, however, first one way and then the other to avoid the several small islands in that river. So instead of both countries having joint ownership of mid-stream islands, these islands were distributed alternately—the first one going to Canada, the next to the United States and so on all the way downstream. The very best possible arrangement to make rum-running simple and easy by furnishing many hiding places and points of departures where the United States border patrol has no right to go.

So much for the geographical and political aspects of the river on which the two Detroit officials embarked with the man from New York to give a speedboat demonstration of the liquor business. . . . The speedboat party went through all the legal rigmarole of clearing through the customs (at the border), declaring no cargo.

The brewers were most hospitable. . . .

The output of this place is 2,500 cases, or 60,000 pint bottles a day. Eighty per cent of this is shipped to Detroit. . . .

From Riverside the speedboat voyage proceeded down to another Canadian point opposite Fighting Island, where there was ample proof that even on the Dominion side, with its laws permitting manufacture and sale, there is plenty of violation. Drinks were freely sold here over a bar in the old American manner, despite the law against consumption in public.

All this visiting of breweries and liquor resorts and inspection of docks where many loaded boats were tied up waiting for darkness was preliminary to seeing the American end of the transaction, the illegal ending of a trade with a legal beginning. . . .

It was after dark when the return trip was undertaken. As we sped upstream my attention was called to an occasional lantern being swung from the end of a wharf or the roof of a warehouse, and electric lights being flashed on and off from high windows in waterfront buildings. They were signals that were alleged to indicate the whereabouts of the customs officers. Several swift boats crossed our bow or wake and disappeared into the darkness along the Detroit shore. As a rule these boats carried only their own loads, but several had good-sized barges in tow. . . .

Another means of smuggling is by means of freight cars which come into Detroit after liquor has been substituted for or included with their legitimate cargo somewhere along the line in Canada. Cars thus tampered with are resealed with bogus seals and sent on to the United States. . . .

The wide discrepancy between the amount smuggled and the amount captured is not due to lack of zeal, energy, or honesty on the part of the

American customs men. Now and then there may be a case of collusion between rum-runner and rum-chaser; but it is not necessary to seek in such corruption, if it exists, an explanation of the situation. The American border patrol is hopelessly overmatched by the liquor people.

The customs collector at Detroit has a force of only ninety men for his patrol. To have continuous service he has to work them in three shifts, so there are never more than thirty men on duty at one time to cover the various land jobs and to man both the picket and patrol boats. . . .

● ● ● ● ●

"Einstein, Rum Sleuth," *The New York Times,* March 26, 1922. Reprinted by permission of *The New York Times.*

IN RUM-RUNNING CIRCLES THE NAME OF IZZY EINSTEIN HAS BECOME A CURSE; among rum-consuming elements, an epithet; in rum-chasing quarters, an "ideal." Next to Volstead himself, Izzy Einstein represents all that is good or bad, depending upon your point of view, in the matter of prohibition. . . .

Izzy Einstein stands forth with his trusty lieutenant Moe Smith as the master hooch-hound, alongside whom all the rest of the pack are but pups. . . .

The Izzy Einstein theory is as simple as it is effective, and in its simplicity and its effectiveness it is bewildering. It would seem to be predicated, first, on the fairly well substantiated belief that the desire to buy and consume liquor is general among all walks and classes of people and, second, upon the not illogical assumption that the inclination of those who have the liquor to dispense are willing to sell it to all those walks and classes, with one exception—those who walk in a class by themselves and are known as prohibition agents. Izzy pondered this simple problem and decided the way to catch the rum sellers was to look and dress and act the part of any and all walks and classes except the unwelcome one. . . .

A day with Izzy would make a chameleon blush for lack of variations. Up with the milk strikers and car crews, along the docks in the morning hours of ship-to-truck loading, in and out of the best and worst of noon-hour lunch bars, on one or more of any number of special coups in the afternoon, to the restaurants in and near New York for dinner and an evening devoted to social and semi-social events where flask, private stock, and cellar contribute to the festivity—his day is just one booze complex after another. . . .

One of his earliest exploits in which he takes pride, even though the haul was small, occurred last Fourth of July, when the great "wet" parade was held. Not only did he march with the "wets," but he followed some of them into the bypaths, with devastating effect on the unsuspecting dealers in the very article for which the demonstrators were perspiringly parading. In one of the drug stores at which he stopped he asked for a half-pint. He stuck it in his pocket and sauntered leisurely toward the door. Some wares caught his eye. He casually looked them over. Nothing precipitate about Izzy. A minute or two elapsed after the purchase of the flask, and to all intents and purposes the purchaser was about to go on his way. The cautious druggist called to him as his hand was on the door. "Come back, friend, and I'll sell you some real stuff," the druggist called out. Izzy turned. "I wasn't sure who you were when you came in and I gave you colored water. You might have been a prohibition agent, and I have to be careful. But you haven't tried to pinch me, so I guess you're all right."

Whereupon the druggist took back the decoy bottle and gave the "all right" customer its equivalent in real whiskey. Then Izzy arrested him. . . .

And just to show his range, Izzy one evening walked into the Yorkville Casino with a trombone under his arm. The false-front shirt, Ascot tie and other infallible markings of the orchestra musician were upon him. He could play the trombone, too, just as on a similar occasion in Brooklyn he utilized a violin to win over the restaurant management. A good fellow, in each instance the charm of his music brought proffers of drinks, which he accepted, and then displayed his gratitude by distributing summonses. . . .

Izzy can drive a truck as well as he can guide a push cart. And trucks bear a definite relation to bootlegging. The average truck driver knows enough about the illicit liquor trade to hang many men. Ergo, Izzy mastered trucking and on occasions too numerous to recount he has in his capacity of chauffeur driven many a load of his unsuspecting employer's booze straight to a Government warehouse. And not only the immediate load, but all the rest of the supply from which it came. The avenues for learning the liquor traffic's routes are limitless for the truck driver, and the evidence gained on any one such sally is sufficient to last an agent of Einstein's caliber many a day. . . .

As a pickle salesman, Izzy trapped many a saloon owner and grocer who thought the drummer's reasonable prices warranted a return favor. In one instance Izzy's low pickle prices prompted the trusting grocer to offer him a drink of his best Scotch, also at a price correspondingly reduced—and the grocer at once suffered the consequences. . . .

Izzy doesn't crowd his victim. He doesn't beg for a drink. . . .

"It takes a little finesse," Izzy admitted, in recounting the incidents of his exciting year or more of prohibition work. "The main thing, it seems to me, is that you have to be natural. The hardest thing an agent has to do is to really act as if he wanted and needed a drink. That doesn't mean you can walk in with the stock excuse of a toothache. They've got stung on that story so many times a man could roll over and die of it on the saloon floor and never get a drop.

"But maybe I'd better not tell you exactly how it's done—it's pretty dangerous information these days."

19. NIGHT CLUBS

The following two articles examine the rise of retail establishments for the illegal liquor trade, the vice that inevitably clustered around them, and the resulting corruption of the local police. A few night clubs existed in the larger cities well before Prohibition, but they came into full flower with the combination of liquor and jazz music. Since most of them were engaged in illegal liquor traffic, they operated behind relatively closed doors and inevitably became a center for other illegal activities. Ranging from the most luxurious establishments down to the "speakeasies" and the "blind pigs," the night clubs also ran the gamut from places of relatively innocent amusement to centers of depravity, a New York investigating Committee of Fourteen reported in 1925. Since most were technically illegal establishments it became customary for them to make payments to the police for "protection," a procedure that led to the wholesale corruption of city governments. The following article, "The Night Clubs of New York," by George E. Worthington, *Survey*, January 1929, p. 413, rested heavily upon the committee's investigations.

EAST SIDE, WEST SIDE AND ALL AROUND THE TOWN, ALIKE BEHIND THE WHITE lights of Broadway and the somber brownstone fronts in quiet side streets, night clubs have been springing up in New York as suddenly and unexpectedly as mushrooms in rainy weather. A line of limousines and taxicabs parked in front of a dark house may be the only outward and visible sign. You ring a bell and a wary eye surveys you through a peephole; then, if the omens are good (that is, if you resemble neither a policeman nor a federal officer), the door is opened a crack for further enquiry, which may include the demand for a password or a "membership card," and finally you are admitted. What goes on inside?

Popularly it has been supposed that the night club, like the mushroom, is a symptom of wetness, in other words, by-product of the prohibition act. The outstanding characteristic that the clandestine places have in common is that they sell liquor. But last summer even those fairly well informed in New York's vagaries were amazed by a report from the Committee of Fourteen, giving the preliminary findings of a study of night clubs, in which it was shown beyond dispute that the cover of secrecy necessary in dispensing synthetic gin or bootleg whiskey is cloaking still less reputable activities.

For the past fifteen years New York has justified the claim of being the cleanest metropolis in the United States, if not in the world, so far as commercialized prostitution is concerned. Until 1923 there was a steady decline, and even then there was but a very slight and inconsiderable increase until 1926. But now for three years, with the rise of the speakeasy and the night club, the swing is in the other direction. Apparently illicit liquor is not enough to keep many of these enterprises going in fierce competition with each other, and still more primitive entertainment is provided on demand or almost forced on their patrons. In the completed study, from which the data of this article is taken, the Committee of Fourteen reports the investigation of 373 night clubs and speakeasies in the past eighteen months. Of these, 52 are beliveed to be "respectable." From the remaining 321, there are reports on 806 hostesses and other women employes, of whom 487 acknowledged that they were prostitutes. In addition, there are reports on 418 other prostitutes who were permitted to solicit customers and 260 procurers, connected with the business of commercialized prostitution, who were found in these clubs.

"Night club" is a term popularly used to cover many varieties of enterprises, some of which may not even operate at night. It does not accurately describe the place which is open from 11 A.M. till 6 P.M.; nor can it be correctly applied to the public cabaret whose patrons are not required to be members, even though many such places incorporate the word "club" in their names. While all of the clandestine "clubs" are speakeasies, not all speakeasies are clubs.

The clubs, accurately speaking, require some form of membership. A prospective patron is introduced by a "club member," or by a taxi driver, or by a tout or runner, the three latter receiving a percentage of the expenditures of each new prospect on his first visit. Frequently strangers are admitted with no introduction at all, if they have something to identify them as ordinary citizens. The only persons who are prima facie ineligible to membership are those who are known to be federal revenue officers or policemen.

Every person not recognized as an officer of the law who enters the place is given a "membership card" and thenceforth is a full-fledged member with all the rights and privileges thereunto appertaining. Registration of name and address in a registry book is sometimes required. In reality membership has no technical significance. The so-called "members" are persons believed to be bona-fide customers. Patronage is stimulated by circularizing selected lists, such as the Social Register, social clubs, and the like, and enclosing an application for a "membership card." The following invitation was received by the writer through the mails:

Dear Sir:

Kindly fill in your name and address and return to us, we will be pleased to mail you a membership card of our exclusive .... Club, ... West 56th Street, New York. Telephone Circle ....
Name .... Address ....

Some of these "clubs" have actually incorporated under the state Membership Corporation Act, since certain magistrates have ruled that clubs thus incorporated are not subject to the provisions of the city curfew ordinance which requires night clubs and cabarets to close at 3 A.M.

Of course it is obvious that these places are, in reality, not clubs at all. They are places which were originated to thwart the prohibition act and are still popularly considered only as violators of that law. It is difficult to place them under one general classification, because they shade up into the realm of the respectable cabaret and they shade down to the prostitution dive, with many on the border-line.

In this fact lies the distinction between the disreputable night club and its forerunners in the long history of *maisons de tolerance*. To it come all classes and conditions of people. The place may have every outward earmark of respectability, and those of its customers who are not obvious easy marks will never suspect what is going on, unless under the genial influence of drinks and the charm of the "hostesses" they can be led to seek entertainment beyond that which they originally intended. . . .

● ● ● ● ●

The following extract is from the article "Detroit Sets a Bad Example," by Ernest W. Mandeville, *The Outlook*, August 22, 1925, p. 612. It examines the retailing of illegal liquor in Detroit with particular reference to the corruption of the local police.

DETROIT, MICHIGAN, IS A FLAGRANT EXAMPLE OF A WIDE-OPEN BOOZE TOWN. The time limits of my stay in town prevented me from visiting all of the reputed twenty thousand "blind pigs." I think I did my duty as an investigator by going to a dozen or more. Any one who would run the risks of a greater number of these places would have to be more of a hero than I am.

The "blind pig" conditions are worse in every way than in any other town I visited, and the liquor sold is of a ruinous quality. The profits here on "needle beer" are one thousand per cent. Moonshine profits are slightly over that. "Moon" (as it is called) can be bought for $2.50 a gallon and redistilled denatured alcohol for about $3 a gallon. Both of these retail in the "blind pigs" for 25 cents an ounce, which would bring in $32 a gallon. "Blind pig" owners are without scruple, and you can be sure of being served whatever will bring them in the largest profits.

These booze-selling "blind pigs" are scattered all over the town. I was in the company of men who were well informed on the question, and they pointed out several large apartment houses which, they said, were given over almost entirely to this trade. I saw enough indications in the ones I visited to lead me to believe this statement. The Super-intendent of Police has since stated publicly: "If a policeman goes into an apartment building containing thirty-six apartments, he may find five or six bootlegging places, but it would be impossible for him to stand on the sidewalk and estimate how many there were inside. It is just as hard to estimate the number of these places in the city, but there are easily fifteen thousand."

A request of a taxi driver, to whom I was a stranger, took me on a tour of "blind pigs"—a tour which I gathered could last as long as I wished it.

A good many of these places are run by women, and there seems to be some sort of co-operation between them whereby they summon extra women from one another to entertain their guests. The fact is that they are centers of immorality as well as of illicit liquor selling.

Most of the vices of Detroit are said to center around these "blind pigs." Narcotics are said to be distributed through them, crime plots are hatched there, and there among criminals mingle the members of respected families. I doubt if the influence of one class on the other, in this case, is an uplifting one.

In the downtown section every manner of store-front is used to disguise the "blind pigs." I went to a radio sales store which seemed well equipped and had several salesmen and clerks in attendance. A very suave, respectable-looking gentleman nodded recognition to my com-panion, and we walked through the railing gate, back through the stockroom, into a completely furnished barroom with easy-chairs, a white-coated bartender, and several people sitting around nonchalantly sipping their drinks. This same experience was repeated in a trunk store and a laundry. I was told of an undertaker's shop which served as a "blind pig" and stored its liquor in caskets. Lack of time prevented me from visiting it.

I did visit several saloons which were very crowded and very remi-niscent of the old-time barrooms. The only difference seemed to be the shabbiness and temporary fixtures in contrast to the old gilded splendor. They appeared to be selling to everyone, and a fairly constant stream of men pushed in and out for their drinks. I noticed a very old man hobble into one saloon and put down his quarter on the bar. The bartender drew a glass of beer and placed it directly on top of the coin. The old man emptied the glass and put the quarter back in his purse. My neighbor told me that the old man was a local character whom all the bartenders served free of charge. It was always the same quarter, and always the same performance of putting it on the bar and pocketing it again. . . .

I talked to one saloon owner (a former army lieutenant) who complained of the high graft he had to pay. Others told me, however, that from a roving ne'er-do-well he has through bootlegging become a wealthy man. Another saloonkeeper said, "Yesterday I gave away forty-three dollars' worth of booze (wholesale prices) to a policeman."

I was told of still another saloonkeeper, that he passes in society as a gentleman, that his daughter attends a fashionable finishing school (which was named to me), that his wife drives a high-powered car and always refuses to drink at social functions.

Detroit a while ago enacted a "tip-over" order which allowed a policeman to enter a saloon or "blind pig" without a warrant and to tip over or rip out all the paraphernalia. He could use an ax on the furnishings and confiscate the liquor. (Since my trip to Detroit this "tip-over" raid order has been rescinded because the method proved a failure.)

This "tip-over" ruling put a great weapon for loot in the hands of the police and elevated the honor of the bartender. Saloon-owners had to employ bartenders whom they could trust with money payments. If the saloon was entered and about to be "tipped over," the bartender had to act quickly and supply cash from the cash register for the raiders, if they were bribable. Therefore, on the check up of receipts with the owner, the bartender's word had to be taken for the various hundred-dollar items missing from the cash register accounting. The bartender also took the risk of being arrested.

A wage standard for a bartender seems to have been fixed as follows: $75 a week and $50 extra for every time he is arrested. If the arrest is made at a time when bail is unavailable and the bartender has to remain in jail over Sunday, the bonus is raised to $75.

Statistics in the Detroit Police Court for 1924 show 7,391 arrests for violations of the Prohibition Law, but only 458 convictions. In 1920 there were 1,952 arrests and 555 convictions.

As far as I could learn, one cannot buy liquor in the prominent Detroit cabarets, but one sees many bringing their own liquor with them.

Prices in Detroit average about as follows: Highballs, 50 cents; beer, 25 cents by the glass and 50 cents by the bottle; whisky by the quart, $8 or $9. The beer is said to be made locally and the hard liquor to come from two sources—Canada and the eastern coast. . . .

"Ten years ago a dishonest policeman was a rarity and was pointed out and 'put on the tape.' Now the honest ones are pointed out as rarities.

"The result is that the law is, I should say, ninety per cent controlled. The policeman who is a dry at heart is called down for interfering with those higher up. He is shifted around and his work made unpleasant for him.

"A good share of the policemen are Poles, and drinking liquor to them is a tradition. They can't understand why liquor should be prohibited and think of prohibition as an affront. It strikes them as a prohibition of sugar for our coffee would strike us.

"Their relationships with the bootleggers are perfectly friendly. They have to pinch two out of every five every once in a while, but they choose the ones who are the least agreeable about paying graft. The jails are full of bootleggers, but they are mostly foreigners—little fellows, suckers, who have been making booze in their kitchens.

"The booze pay-off doesn't go very high up. The Police Commissioner makes a persistent and conscientious effort to enforce the law.

"But the lower officers make a business of dealing with the bootleggers. As soon as any saloon or 'blind pig' opens the proprietor is 'propositioned,' then they 'handle him,' then everything is 'all set.' These are the terms they use.

"Seven policemen have just been dismissed for ignoring the recent mandate 'not to frequent blind pigs while on duty.' There might have been many times that number dismissed. These seven say they were framed by the rum interests, who have a grip on the police officials and wanted to get rid of them. Think of it! having to issue an order to policemen not to commit an illegal act while on duty.

"Inspectors sometimes find a plant of liquor, collect one hundred dollars apiece, and then tip off the hijackers as to the location of the liquor. Then in turn they pinch the hijackers and take half of the loot. Double-cross methods have become the reigning ethics.

"The result is that there are about eight saloons in every downtown block. William Rutledge, Superintendent of Police, says that there were 1,500 saloons in the city when prohibition went into effect, and that now there are at least 15,000 places in Detroit selling liquor."

20. RACKETEERING

Once well-organized with political protection, many of the more powerful liquor-running gangs turned to preying on legitimate business. Racketeering reached its zenith in Chicago. In the article below, "The High Cost of Hoodlums," *Harper's Monthly Magazine,* October 1929, p. 529, John Gunther discusses the development of this sinister activity and its meaning for business labor unions and for the private citizen. Reprinted by permission of Harold Ober and Associates

. . . CRIME IS AFFECTING THE CHICAGO CITIZEN IN A NEW FASHION. A system of criminal exploitation, based on extortion, controlled by hoodlums, and decorated with icy-cold murder, has arisen in the past five or six years, to seize the ordinary Chicagoan, you and me and the man across the street, by the pocket-book if not the throat. Crime is costing me money. It is costing money to the taxi-driver who took me to the office this morning, the elevator boy who lifted me ten stories through the steel stratifications of a great skyscraper, the waiter who served me my luncheon, the suburban business man who sat at the next table. Very few persons, in Chicago or out of it, realize how this criminal system works. Very few persons, in Chicago or out of it, realize that the ordinary citizen is paying literal tribute to racketeers. This tribute is levied in many ways. The ordinary citizen pays it, like as not, whenever he has a suit pressed and every time he gets a haircut; he may pay it in the plumbing in his house and the garaging of his car; the very garbage behind his back door may perhaps mean spoils for someone.

II

A racket may be defined as any scheme of exploitation by which criminal conspirators live upon the industry of others, maintaining their hold by intimidation, terrorism, or political favoritism. The word "racket" has come to be loosely synonymous, on the one hand, with any scheme for making easy money, whether illegal or not; on the other, as a blanket definition of organized crime. All gangsters, without discrimination, have come to be called racketeers. Beer and alcohol running or, for that matter, bank robbery and white slavery, are rackets from this point of view. But in this article I hope to avoid stereotyped discussion of the beer wars and the booze gangs, and confine myself to the less-known activities of business racketeers.

What, in a paragraph, does a racketeer do? How does a racket work?

Suppose I happen to be a hoodlum, and suppose I want some easy money. I have friends among crooked labor leaders and perhaps among politicians. I am in a position to hire thugs and gunmen. I form an organization and I choose a field. Suppose I choose pretzels as a field. I then "invite" the pretzel dealers in Chicago to "join" me. From each of them I demand, say, one hundred dollars per month. For this sum my men will "protect" them from competition, since they must raise their prices to pay my one hundred dollars. If any pretzel man refuses to join me I bomb him. I slug his drivers. I cut off his supply. Meantime I delimit the pretzel market among my dealers, and make anyone who wants to enter the pretzel business pay me handsomely first. I extend my pretzel monopoly in one direction to the big wholesalers (since I control the dealers), and in another direction to the small shopkeepers (since I control the jobbers). And from all of them I exact tribute. The price of pretzels meantime goes up. Simply because I say so, the pretzel people pay a levy to me, and the consumer pays the levy. This is the essence of racketeering—simple extortion based on simple threat.

The word "racket" originated in Chicago six or seven years ago. In the neighborhood of 12th and Halsted Streets, in the district of "alky" peddlers, thugs, and hoodlums, a group of satellites grew up, hanging on the outskirts of the great "mobs"—the O'Banion "mob," the Genna "mob," the Capone "mob." These satellites were not often actual killers. They were parasites. With gangster protection, they went into "business." At first the word describing them was "racketer." In newspaper stories during 1923 and 1924 the word grew to "racketeer." Probably it first referred to the hullabaloo in the "joints" where gangsters assembled. "How's the racket?" became "What's your racket?"

Rackets are, of course, old as the hills. This decade holds no monopoly on extortion. But extortion has rarely reached such a point of development as distinguishes the Chicago rackets today. It would be difficult to trace the exact causes of this efflorescence. Prohibition was certainly one cause. Traffic in beer and whisky enormously increased the amount of easy money in circulation among hoodlums. Gangsters became elaborate spendthrifts. Silver coffins decorated funerals. Politics bought into gangs. Meantime the booze traffic increased the number of professional criminals at large, and their power, ruthlessness, and immunity to law.

So the rackets began, out of criminality begat by alcohol and easy money. The success of racketeering was immense. It existed through contempt of law and, as success increased, contempt increased, to give way to more success. Gangsters saw that there was almost as much money in coats and suits as there was in alcohol; gangsters "muscled in" to various rackets. Politicians saw the enormous sums being made and took their share of this citizens' tribute.

Since racketeering is based on business, it came into early contact with labor. Racketeering sucked into labor, living like a leech on its own wound. The argument of the racketeer to the business man was simple: "Look here. We'll stabilize prices. Today you get $1.00 a bundle for your (for example) laundry. We'll organize the laundry business and raise the price to $1.50. We'll eliminate competition. Meantime you pay us $20 per month." And if a thousand laundrymen joined the "association," the racket was worth, at the outset, $20,000 per month. If anyone withstood the racket arson was his lot or bombs.

Now, in most businesses associations already existed, namely, labor unions; so it saved a good deal of trouble to the racketeer to organize his racket directly through the union. The American Federation of Labor has, of course, fought racketeering bitterly; not two per cent of legitimate union men are racketeers. But the A. F. of L. is an enormously widespread organization, and racketeers did get control of some unions, by criminal subversion of unscrupulous labor leaders.

There are 91 rackets in Chicago today, according to the state's attorney's office, all but 25 of them active. Some few are "dormant," it being a characteristic of rackets that they lie low periodically; often when a racket "disappears" the leader has simply shifted his activity to another racket. So the number is always variable.

But it is a fair guess that 60 odd rackets are in fairly active operation. The cost of these 60 to the people of Chicago is estimated by the Employer's Association of Chicago, an anti-racketeer organization, at $136,-000,000 per year, or approximately $45 for every man, woman, and child in the city. This is direct cost. It is a levy, a tribute—no less. The indirect cost may be as much again. . . .

Since racketeering is predicated on the concept of threat, and the concept of threat predicated in turn on the concept of force, the items by which the racketeer makes use of force are important. Witness buying is one, so is jury tampering, so are acid throwing, window smashing, tire cutting, slugging, arson, and bombs. And so is murder. Most of the more exciting of the recent Chicago murders have been caused by alcohol wars, with which this article is not concerned; but the racketeer too has murder in his pay.

But first as to bombs. The current "quotations" by manufacturers of bombs are as follows: black-powder bombs, $100; dynamite bombs, $500 to $1,000 (depending on the risk involved); "guaranteed" jobs, $1,000 and up. Cash in full is generally paid for bombs, two days before delivery.

The following bombings have taken place in Chicago in the last few years, most of them by-products of racketeering:

1920	51
1921	60
1922	69
1923	55
1924	92
1925	113
1926	89
1927	108
1928	116

Murder generally is a bit more expensive; and maybe this is the reason, what with the American fetish for price as an index of value, that murder is more common. Following is the murder roll:

1926 366
1927 379
1928 ....: . 399
1929 (to June 1) 147

These are all murders for which an actual verdict of murder was brought by a coroner's jury. There may have been others too. Not all of these murders were caused by racketeering, by any means. But some of them were. As to the number of convictions gained, and murderers sentenced to the penitentiary or executed, the statistics are so shameful that they scarcely may be printed. In 1926, 70 murderers (out of 366) were convicted and 8 executed; in 1927, 87 and 3; in 1928, 77 and 0. Most of those executed were what might be called individual murderers, stickup men so ill-advised as to shoot policemen, drunken friends who unfortunately quarreled—small fry. Members of organized "mobs" are arrested often enough, but very rarely convicted. Since 1922 not one single racketeer murderer has been hanged.

Murder in Chicago costs from $50 up. If someone wants to put our friend Angelo "on the spot," or "take for a ride" a victim equally poor and obscure, the job can be done for less than $100. The racketeer telephones a "friend." The victim is described—his name, abode, habits, and so on. The "friend" gets in touch with a professional killer. Like as not, the killer sees the victim for the first and last time when he drills him full of lead. For big jobs the killers are usually imported from out of town, Detroit say, or New York.

It is almost literally true, then, that every man in Chicago has his price—if a gangster wants to get him. The more important the victim, the steeper the price. To kill me, a newspaper man, would probably cost $1,000. To kill a prominent business man might cost $5,000, a prominent city official, $10,000. To kill the president of a large corporation, or a great power magnate, would cost a great deal more, probably $50,000 or $100,000.

Just as it costs money for murder, so it costs money to get a murderer out, should he happen—which would be remarkable—to be caught and indicted. The "defense fund" is usually $25,000 or more. This amount is distributed to defense lawyers, private detectives, witnesses, or, in some cases, even jurors. But $25,000 is a lot of money. So usually your racketeer takes pretty good care not to be caught—and seldom is. . . .

The racket in the cleaners and dyers business deserves a special word. This is the most famous of Chicago rackets, and probably the most typical. It has made enormous profits, and almost every type of crime has been laid against its door. Pieces of dynamite are sewn into the seams of clothing—and the clothing sent to the cleaner. Drivers for "opposition" trucks are beaten to such a pulp that in their faces only the eyes remain intact. The cleaners and dyers racket is even said—on interesting if not convincing authority—to have had a good deal to do with the St. Valentine's Day massacre, in which seven gangsters were shot against a wall by other gangsters. Finally, this racket is of really intimate interest to every Chicagoan, because for a considerable interval every Chicagoan who wanted to have his trousers pressed paid fifty cents to the racket for the privilege.

The cleaners and dyers racket is a complicated business. Controlling it is the Master Cleaners and Dyers Association, which is supposed (a) to collect 2 per cent of the gross annual business of each master, (b) to control the Cleaners, Dyers, and Pressers Union, which collects clothing from the thousands of shops in the city, and the Laundry and Dye House Chauffeurs, Drivers, and Helpers Union, which delivers it, and to exact tribute from both, and (c) to collect from the retail shops, organized into the Retail Cleaners and Dyers Union, a further tribute from the source. The small shopkeepers pay dues of $2 per month plus a general fee of $10 per year—$340,000 annually—for the privilege of collecting from the public the business that the Association controls.

It should be obvious what enormous leverage the association can bring to bear on any independent master who would dare to cut prices, solicit business in someone else's "territory," or otherwise fight the racket— not to mention any small-shop owner who tried the same thing. It was easy to "discipline" the masters—via strikes. It was even easier to "discipline" the small folk—-through simple terrorism.

Business was routed among "loyal" members of the association like pawns on a checkerboard. Shop owners were instructed what master to patronize. Truck drivers were told what cleaning to pick up. Small-shop owners were told what prices to charge—and the prices went up. The normal price for cleaning and pressing a suit of clothes was $1, or at most $1.25. This gave the shopkeeper in the old days a decent profit. The price for cleaning and pressing a woman's dress was $2 or $2.25. Through the racket, the prices went up to $1.75 and $2.75 respectively.

It should be obvious, too, what enormous wealth the association came to command. A "treasury" existed for a time calculated at $700,000. So naturally hi-jackers arose. "Big Tim" Murphy was one of the most picturesque criminals Chicago has ever produced, a sort of independent freebooter racketeer from the time he left the penitentiary to which he had been sentenced for mail robbery. Big Tim "muscled" in on these gaudy spoils. He was shot, "executed," in June, 1928. A few months later, John G. Clay, secretary-treasurer of the Laundry and Dye House Organization, was shot and killed.

An independent cleaner and dyer named John Becker revolted against the racket ring. He made a fight. He succeeded in getting indictments returned against several masters in the association, before the Cook

County Grand Jury. But when time came to testify, Becker and his son were the only witnesses there. When (it is said) he asked the prosecuting attorney where the other witnesses were, he was told, "Go out and get your own witnesses—I'm a prosecutor, not a process-server."

Meanwhile other independents had broken away. A group of little fellows started an insurrection with a cleaning establishment of their own, known as the Central Cleaners and Dyers. This revolt caused the real entrance of hoodlumry into racketeering. The gangs had been busy with beer, alcohol, booze, vice, gambling. They now discovered cleaning and dyeing. In some cases they "muscled in"; in others the struggling independents hired them, to fight terrorism with terrorism.

Becker went straight to the top. He went to Scarface Al Capone. So the citizenry of Chicago witnessed strange ironical conditions. With a few friends, in May, 1928, Capone incorporated the "Sanitary Cleaning Shops, Inc." and went into the business. Defiantly, his shops dropped their prices. The association fought back. But there was little it could do—against Mr. Capone. Becker obtained immunity practically through the use of Capone's name. The association knew that for every bomb it could throw, Mr. Capone could throw two.

And so the price of getting my suit pressed, and yours, came down, first to $1.25 (from $1.75), then to $1 even—thanks to Mr. Capone. The civic spirit of Mr. Capone triumphed. What the police could not do, what the state's attorney's office did not do, Mr. Capone did. The old racket is probably smashed to bits. It is the first of the great, toprank rackets to get smashed. And it was Mr. Capone who did much to smash it.

Out of the old racket, once the present chaotic interregnum passes, will a new racket come?

INTOLERANCE

The intolerance American society showed during the Twenties to minority groups, aliens of various types, and to all varieties of radicalism has often been explained as an inheritance of World War I, and as a product of the political conservatives who had been victorious in 1920 in most of the states as well as in Washington. But perhaps a better and more inclusive explanation can be found in the rather frightened determination of the old and essentially rural-minded majority to maintain its supremacy over rapidly increasing urban groups professing other social and religious faiths. The conflict was in some degree waged between an older North European American stock devoted to the Protestant ethic, with its emphasis upon individualism, hard work, sobriety, and frugality, and the newer immigrant folk crowding the cities, by origin from Southern and Eastern Europe, by religion Catholic and Jewish, and by temperament devoted to more personal indulgence and to paternalistic ways of thought inspired by either political or religious consideration. On another level the conflict was simply one between sophisticated urbanites of whatever racial origins and religious beliefs and rural folk—the first group devoted to the cosmopolitan and hedonistic ends of the new mass consumption economy, the second to the older parochial, economic, and social dogma.

In its wider dimensions, skirmishes of this cultural conflict can be seen in numerous episodes of the decade: in the debate over the immigration acts, in the Sacco-Vanzetti case, in the Scopes "monkey trial," and in the Democratic Party Convention of 1924 and the election of 1928. But for the purposes of this section the articles chosen are confined to just four subjects, the topic of religion being left for the following section.

21. SHIP OR SHOOT

The wave of post-war strikes, many of which resulted in violence, the repeated terroristic incidents, including the most famous, that of the 1919 Wall Street bombing outrage, and the founding of the Communist Party triggered a wave of anti-radicalism in the country that was to last most of the decade. Imputing much of the domestic troubles to the Communist leader Trotsky's call for world revolution and to its dissemination in the United States by the swarm of immigrants fleeing from a war-torn Europe, Wilson's Attorney General Mitchell A. Palmer led a national drive to wipe out radicalism by the wholesale deportation of aliens. In the following article the Attorney General obviously made little attempt to discriminate between communists, anarchists, "radical union agitators, and socialists, to say nothing of moral perverts and hysterical women." It is small wonder then that the crusade was rapidly turned against all forms of political and social heterodoxy. The mood of the defenders of the status quo as the decade opened is well brought out in the Attorney General's "The Case Against the Reds," *The Forum,* February 1920, p. 63.

IN THIS BRIEF REVIEW OF THE WORK WHICH THE DEPARTMENT OF JUSTICE has undertaken, to tear out the radical seeds that have entangled American ideas in their poisonous theories, I desire not merely to explain what the real menace of communism is, but also to tell how we have been compelled to clean up the country almost unaided by any virile legislation. Though I have not been embarrassed by political opposition, I have been materially delayed because the present sweeping processes of arrests and deportation of seditious aliens should have been vigorously pushed by Congress last spring. The failure of this is a matter of record in the Congressional files.

The anxiety of that period in our responsibility when Congress, ignoring the seriousness of these vast organizations that were plotting to overthrow the Government, failed to act, has passed. The time came when it was obviously hopeless to expect the hearty co-operation of Congress, in the only way to stamp out these seditious societies in their open defiance of law by various forms of propaganda.

Like a prairie-fire, the blaze of revolution was sweeping over every American institution of law and order a year ago. It was eating its way into the homes of the American workman, its sharp tongues of revolutionary heat were licking the altars of the churches, leaping into the belfry of the school bell, crawling into the sacred corners of American homes, seeking to replace marriage vows with libertine laws, burning up the foundations of society.

Robbery, not war, is the ideal of communism. This has been demonstrated in Russia, Germany, and in America. As a foe, the anarchist is fearless of his own life, for his creed is a fanaticism that admits no respect of any other creed. Obviously it is the creed of any criminal mind, which reasons always from motives impossible to clean thought. Crime is the degenerate factor in society.

Upon these two basic certainties, first that the "Reds" were criminal aliens, and secondly that the American Government must prevent crime, it was decided that there could be no nice distinctions drawn between the theoretical ideals of the radicals and their actual violations of our national laws. An assassin may have brilliant intellectuality, he may be able to excuse his murder or robbery with fine oratory, but any theory which excuses crime is not wanted in America. This is no place for the criminal to flourish, nor will he do so, so long as the rights of common citizenship can be exerted to prevent him.

OUR GOVERNMENT IN JEOPARDY

It has always been plain to me that when American citizens unite upon any national issue, they are generally right, but it is sometimes difficult to make the issue clear to them. If the Department of Justice could succeed in attracting the attention of our optimistic citizens to the issue of internal revolution in this country, we felt sure there would be no revolution. The Government was in jeopardy. My private information of what was being done by the organization known as the Communist Party of America, with headquarters in Chicago, of what was being done by the Communist Internationale under their manifesto planned at Moscow last March by Trotzky, Lenin, and others, addressed "To the Proletariats of All Countries," of what strides the Communist Labor Party was making, removed all doubt. In this conclusion we did not ignore the definite standards of personal liberty, of free speech, which is the very temperament and heart of the people. The evidence was examined with the utmost care, with a personal leaning toward freedom of thought and word on all questions.

The whole mass of evidence, accumulated from all parts of the country, was scrupulously scanned, not merely for the written or spoken difference of viewpoint as to the Government of the United States, but, in spite of these things, to see if the hostile declarations might not be sincere in their announced motive to improve our social order. There was no hope of such a thing.

By stealing, murder and lies, Bolshevism has looted Russia not only of its material strength, but of its moral force. A small clique of outcasts from the East Side of New York has attempted this, with what success we all know. Because a disreputable alien—Leon Bronstein, the man who now calls himself Trotzky—can inaugurate a reign of terror from his throne room in the Kremlin; because this lowest of all types known to New York can sleep in the Czar's bed, while hundreds of thousands in Russia are without food or shelter, should Americans be swayed by such doctrines?

Such a question, it would seem, should receive but one answer from America.

My information showed that communism in this country was an organization of thousands of aliens, who were direct allies of Trotzky. Aliens of the same misshapen caste of mind and indecencies of character, and it showed that they were making the same glittering promises of lawlessness, of criminal autocracy to Americans, that they had made to the

Russian peasants. How the Department of Justice discovered upwards of 60,000 of these organized agitators of the Trotzky doctrine in the United States, is the confidential information upon which the Government is now sweeping the nation clean of such alien filth. . . . In my testimony before the sub-committee of the Judiciary Committee of the Senate on July 14, 1919, at its request, I had fully outlined the conditions threatening internal revolution in the nation that confronted us. Legislation which I then recommended to meet this great menace has not been enacted. This is not my fault, for I knew that Congress was fully aware of the "Reds'" activities in this country.

Many States passed certain acts which embodied the basis of my request to Congress for national legislation bearing upon radicalism. California, Indiana, Michigan, New York, Ohio, Pennsylvania, Washington and West Virginia have passed State laws governing the rebellious acts of the "Reds" in their separate territories. These States have infinitely greater legal force at their command against the revolutionary element than the United States Government, for detecting and punishing seditious acts. In their equipment of men to carry out their laws, they far surpass the facilities of the Department of Justice. New York City alone has 12,000 policemen charged with the duty of investigation, and the District Attorney of New York County has a force of over fifty prosecuting attorneys.

Under the appropriations granted by Congress to the Department of Justice, the maximum number of men engaged in the preparation of the violation of all United States laws is limited to about 500 for the entire country. Startling as this fact may seem to the reader who discovers it for the first time, it is the highest testimony to the services of these men, that the Department of Justice of the United States, is today, a human net that no outlaw can escape. It has been netted together in spite of Congressional indifference, intensified by the individual patriotism of its personnel aroused to the menace of revolution, inspired to superlative action above and beyond private interests.

One of the chief incentives for the present activity of the Department of Justice against the "Reds" has been the hope that American citizens will, themselves, become voluntary agents for us, in a vast organization for mutual defense against the sinister agitation of men and women aliens, who appear to be either in the pay or under the criminal spell of Trotzky and Lenin.

DEPORTATIONS UNDER IMMIGRATION LAWS

Temporary failure to seize the alien criminals in this country who are directly responsible for spreading the unclean doctrines of Bolshevism here, only increased the determination to get rid of them. Obviously, their offenses were related to our immigration laws, and it was finally decided to act upon that principle. Those sections of the Immigration Law applicable to the deportation of aliens committing acts enumerated in the Senate Resolution of October 14, 1919, above quoted, were found in the Act of Congress, approved October 16, 1918, amending the immigration laws of the United States.

Although this law is entirely under the jurisdiction of the Department of Labor, it seemed to be the only means at my disposal of attacking the radical movement. To further this plan, as Congress had seen fit to refuse appropriations to the Department of Labor which might have enabled it to act vigorously against the "Reds," I offered to co-operate with the immigration officials to the fullest extent. My appropriation became available July 19, 1919. I then organized what is known as the Radical Division.

Briefly this is a circumstantial statement of the present activities of the Department of Justice, co-operating with the Department of Labor, against the "Reds." They require no defense, nor can I accept as true the counter claims of the "Reds" themselves, who, apparently indifferent to their disgrace, violent in their threats against the United States Government, until they are out of sight and sound of it, betray the characterless ideas and purposes that Trotzky has impressed upon the criminal classes which constitute communism.

WILL DEPORTATIONS CHECK BOLSHEVISM?

Behind, and underneath, my own determination to drive from our midst the agents of Bolshevism with increasing vigor and with greater speed, until there are no more of them left among us, so long as I have the responsible duty of that task, I have discovered the hysterical methods of these revolutionary humans with increasing amazement and suspicion. In the confused information that sometimes reaches the people, they are compelled to ask questions which involve the reasons for my acts against the "Reds." I have been asked, for instance, to what extent deportation will check radicalism in this country. Why not ask what will become of the United States Government if these alien radicals are permitted to carry out the principles of the Communist Party as embodied in its so-called laws, aims and regulations?

There wouldn't be any such thing left. In place of the United States Government we should have the horror and terrorism of bolsheviki tyranny such as is destroying Russia now. Every scrap of radical literature demands the overthrow of our existing government. All of it demands obedience to the instincts of criminal minds, that is, to the lower appetites, material and moral. The whole purpose of communism appears to be a mass formation of the criminals of the world to overthrow the decencies of private life, to usurp property that they have not earned, to disrupt the present order of life regardless of health, sex or religiou rights. By a literature that promises the wildest dreams of such low aspirations, that can occur to only the criminal minds, communism distorts our social law.

The chief appeal communism makes is to "The Worker." If they can lure the wage-earner to join their own gang of thieves, if they can show him that he will be rich if he steals, so far they have succeeded in betraying him to their own criminal course.

These are the revolutionary tenets of Trotzky and the Communist Internationale. Their manifesto further embraces the various organizations in this country of men and women obsessed with discontent, having disorganized relations to American society. These include the I. W. W.'s, the most radical socialists, the misguided anarchists, the agitators who oppose the limitations of unionism, the moral perverts and the hysterical neurasthenic women who abound in communism. The phraseology of their manifesto is practically the same wording as was used by the Bolsheviks for their International Communist Congress.

22. THE CHICAGO RACE RIOT

Throughout World War I, easy employment and high pay brought the first great mass Negro migration to the northern cities. During the war there was little tension because the Negro most often took the menial jobs which the whites did not want—in the packing houses, laundries, and especially as servants. But with the return of normal conditions trouble soon occurred over jobs, mostly in and around the growing Negro housing sections. Riots attended by destruction of property and death took place in many northern cities, but the great Chicago Race Riot of the summer of 1919 outdid all others in producing violence and hatred. The account below by Charles W. Holman, "Race Riots in Chicago," appeared in *The Outlook,* August 13, 1919, p. 566.

CHICAGO HAS JUST FINISHED HER FIRST WEEK OF RIOTING BETWEEN WHITES and Negroes. Already thirty-three people have lost their lives and more than three hundred have been injured. The death toll was slightly greater among the blacks, on Tuesday there being fifteen of them dead as against eleven whites. During this wild week mobs of whites pursued and beat and killed Negroes. Other mobs of Negroes pursued and beat and killed whites. From the upper windows of tenements, when darkness came, snipers picked off pedestrians or fired into squads of police and soldiers sent to bring order to the Black Belt. Armed bands in motor trucks dashed wildly up and down the streets, firing into houses. It required the combined efforts of three thousand regular policemen and six thousand State militia to bring the people back to the verge of common sense and establish a condition even remotely resembling order.

Even then, if rain had not come, it is doubtful if the armed forces could have stemmed the emotional tide that was inflaming Chicago's citizens. The week ended with a wholesale attempt to fire the city, more than one hundred dwellings being burned and three thousand people rendered homeless.

Complications, such as refusal of the icemen's union and the milk-drivers' union to deliver their commodities into the Black Belt and fear of delivery-men moving groceries that they would be assaulted and robbed, quickly reduced the Negro population to the verge of starvation and produced a ghastly condition in respect to infant feeding.

It became necessary to establish a dead line around the Black Belt, where 125,000 Negroes live, and prohibit movements in and out of either race, except under guard. Even then patrolling was unable to prevent mob action from breaking out, and at times the Loop, Chicago's main business district, was the scene of actions that disgraced the community. A mob of five hundred white men stormed the Palmer House, the oldest first-class hotel in the city, where Negroes have been employed for generations; Negroes going about their work were beaten and killed, and it finally became necessary for the owners of buildings either to discontinue elevator service or arrange for the quartering of their attendants under guard in the Loop.

The trouble broke out, as all such troubles do, with an incident of minor importance. It began at the Twenty-sixth Street bathing beach which until two years ago was patronized almost entirely by white people. With the advent of a great Negro population, brought in by the packers and other large producers, the Negro, in seeking recreation, began to flock to some of the South Side swimming places. At this particular beach there is a rope which extends into the water for some distance, and by common consent the whites bathed on one side of the rope while the Negroes bathed on the other. Yet it was only an agreement made effective by the fact that it might become unhealthy for a Negro to wander across the line.

On Sunday afternoon, July 27, a Negro boy swam beyond the line and climbed upon a raft from which the whites were accustomed to dive. A white man threw a stone which knocked the Negro off the raft, and he drowned. It is said that a policeman in the neighborhood of the scene failed to do his duty and make an immediate arrest of the white man. The occurrence made a profound impression upon the blacks, who went away to their own neighborhoods and a few hours later began retaliating by attacking individual whites. The situation quickly took on the aspect of armed mobs fighting each other in the open streets, and soon got beyond police control.

On Monday rioting reached its height, and before noon twenty-four known dead had been taken to the morgue. On Tuesday a mob of four thousand Negroes at Fifty-first and Federal Streets attacked small groups of individuals until dispersed. That same day the bodies of four Negroes were taken from "Bubbly Creek," the refuse canal of the stockyards, made famous by Upton Sinclair in his novel "The Jungle."

In their rioting neither whites nor blacks discriminated between women and men or youth and age. To each any person of the opposite color was hateful and must die.

The confusion of the city as a whole was heightened by a strike of surface and elevated street car employees which paralyzed traffic, not a single car being in operation from midnight Sunday until the early hours of the following Saturday. During this time the people adopted any method of conveyance possible, and many of them got into trouble by being forced to walk through the districts where rioting was in progress.

The trouble in Chicago in no way resembled outbreaks which have taken place in other cities, such as those in Washington and St. Louis. The Chicago situation arose primarily out of the housing situation and racial antipathy. There was no question of the Negroes taking white men's jobs, as the Negroes were brought up to Chicago to fill positions in which there was a great scarcity of available labor. The packers were primarily responsible for importing them, and it became necessary for the Negroes to live within walking or short traveling distance of their work. Accordingly, they filled up the South Side between Forty-third Street and Seventeenth Street, taking over almost entirely the section formerly occupied by Chicago's notorious "red light" district. The high wages which they received produced an immediate reaction upon them and made them ambitious to improve their standards of living. Accordingly, they began to spread out into the more select residential districts and produced consternation among the white people.

Troubled relations were first noticed two years ago, when the Negroes began to compose an important part of the street car and elevated railway traffic. It was noticed that they strung themselves through the trains or cars in such a way that it appeared to the white people as if they did it on purpose to force the whites to sit down beside them. This was the cause of much resentment, and it became apparent that trouble was not far distant. It is also said that many apartments were rented to Negroes by whites for "spite reasons."

It has been remarked time and again that certain classes of white people have not hesitated to grant the Negroes absolute social equality. In the Negro section white girls walked with Negro men and white men paraded the streets with Negro women. They even intermarried. There were a few notorious dance-halls operated by Negroes to which white men and women came and where mixed dancing was the rule. Also, for the first time in the Negroes' lives, they were catered to in a political way, and they became a powerful element in municipal politics. They elected to the City Council two of their own race.

This treatment gave the Negro population of Chicago an extraordinary opinion of its own importance and led it to claim more than the Northern people were willing to give.

Since the rioting, Negroes have been fleeing the city. Many have bought tickets for their old homes in the South; others have gone to Wisconsin and near-by cities to wait until the trouble blows over. Real estate dealers and rental agents have also reported that hundreds of cancellations by Negroes in select residential districts have been made, and that the blacks are recongregating within the Black Belt. Refusal of packing-house white operatives to work with the colored people has brought about a serious labor situation which Governor Frank O. Lowden and the packers have been trying to solve. Curtailment of packing-house operations, as the result of quarantining of the Negroes in their homes, has had an important bearing on the local market and made it necessary to restrict receipts of live stock at the yards.

23. BLACK ZIONIST

As the racial conflict between white and Negro mounted during the early years of the 1920's, various radical Negro movements both in the North and the South grew rapidly. One of the more interesting was that led by Marcus Garvey which sought to shepherd the American Negro back to Africa. Foreshadowing the Black Muslim movement of a later date, Garveyism was just one expression during the Twenties of the growing group consciousness of the nation's minorities. Rather than producing solidarity, the post-war crusade for 100 per cent Americanism instead created among Negroes, Jews, and Catholics alike an insistent particularism.

The following account of Garveyism, "Imperator Africanus, Marcus Garvey: Menace or Promise?" by Eric D. Walrond appeared in *The Independent*, January 3, 1925, p. 8.

ONE OF THE EFFECTS OF THE WORLD WAR WAS THE QUICKENING OF RACIAL consciousness among the negroes of the Western Hemisphere, the group to which, because of its industrial, economic, and intellectual solidarity, the bulk of the blacks of the world look for leadership and guidance. Fresh from the war, from the bloodstained fields of France and Mesopotamia, the black troops, bitter, broken, disillusioned, stormed at the gates of the whites—pleaded for a share of that liberty and democracy which they were led to believe were the things for which they had fought. And it was of course a futile knocking. Hardened by the experience of the conflict, the negroes, drunk, stung, poisoned by the narcotics of white imperialism, rose in all their might to create for themselves those spoils of war and peace which they knew they could not hope for from the ruling whites.

In Egypt and Palestine and other parts of the war area the black troops of the Western Hemisphere met other blacks—native Africans. It was the first mass contact of the negro from the Old and the New Worlds. Here something which the white war lords had not bargained on resulted. The negroes met and exchanged and compounded their views on the whites, their civilization, and their masters. Here the policies of France and Britain and Belgium and the United States with regard to their black wards were put in the scales. And when the blacks rose from the resulting pyre of disillusionment a new light shone in their eyes—a new spirit, a burning ideal, to be men, to fight and conquer and actually wrest their heritage, their destiny from those who controlled it.

It was upon this ideal that the gospel of Marcus Garvey came into being. Garvey is a black native of one of a cluster of tropical isles ruled by Great Britain in the Caribbean. He is the head of an international movement of, he says, some 4,000,000 negroes. Known far and wide as the Garvey movement, its real name is the Universal Negro Improvement Association and African Communities League at 56 West 135th Street, New York. Its history is so inextricably bound up with the affairs of Marcus Garvey that to properly comprehend it and its racial significance one must need study the man's life and the forces that have governed it.

First, Garvey is of unmixed negro blood. On its surface this may not appear significant, but it is indispensable to any consideration of the man. Goaded on by the memory that the first slaves stolen from Africa were full-blooded negroes, Garvey and the gospel he preaches appeal particularly and not unexpectedly to the very black negro element. In the island of his birth, Jamaica, a land with as many color distinctions as there are eggs in a shad's roe, and all through his life, the fact that he was black was unerringly borne in upon him. Wherever he went, whether to Wolmer's, the college patronized by the upper-class mulattoes in Jamaica, or to Europe or Central America as student and journalist, he was continuously reminded that he was black and that it was futile for him to rise above the "hewer of wood and drawer of water."

In Jamaica, as elsewhere in the United Kingdom, England differentiates between the full bloods and the half bloods. In Garvey's Jamaica, the mulattoes are next in power to the whites. The blacks, who outnumber them three to one, have actually no voice politically or economically.

With such a background, no wonder Garvey, the "Moses of the Negroes,"—applying the law of compensation,—idealizes black. Coming into the emancipation of his spirit, it was inevitable. No wonder he talks glibly of a black state, a black empire, a black emperor. No wonder he is creating a black religion, a black deity, a black "Man of Sorrows." Who knows, he says, but that Jesus the Christ was not a black man? And, naturally, the hordes of black peasant folk flock to Garvey. They worship him. They feel that he is saying the things which they would utter were they articulate. They swarm to hear his fiery rhetoric. They pour their money into his coffers. They stand by him through thick and thin. They idolize him as if he were a black Demosthenes.

In turn, quite in keeping again with the law of compensation, but undoubtedly overdoing it, Garvey creates a fairy dream world for them which spiritedly makes up for the beauty and grandeur that are lacking in their drab, unorderly lives. Aping the English royalty, he manufactures out of black peasants of the lower domestic class dukes and duchesses, princes and princesses. Shall not, he quotes from the Bible, princes come out of Egypt, and Ethiopia stretch forth her hands unto God? An old white-haired negro, a veteran agitator, is made Duke of Uganda. A faithful ambassador just returned from a mission to the black Republic of Liberia is made Knight Commander of the Distinguished Order of the Nile. Out of the multitude of black stableboys, cooks and bottle washers, scullions and jim-swingers, is fashioned the timber of the crack African Legionnaires. Out of sombre-faced maidens from the French and Dutch and English colonies along the Spanish Main he creates "Black Cross Nurses." A black singer with the sacred eyes of a madonna becomes the "African Virgin Mary."

All the glamour, all the technique of delusion, is employed to satisfy the craving for this other thing which is missing in the lives of these long-repressed peasant folk. Essentially a movement of the black proletariat, Garveyism owes its strength largely to jangling swords and flaming helmets, titles and congeries of gold braid.

Arriving in the United States on March 23, 1916, Garvey, with a nucleus of thirteen, started in a Harlem hall bedroom the New York branch of the U. N. I. A. Briefly, the goal of the U. N. I. A. is the redemption of Africa—a black application of the Zionist principles. Afraid, according to its founder, that "if the negro is not careful he will drink in all the poison of modern civilization and die from the effects of it" and hearing the great cry of "Jerusalem for the Jews—Ireland for the Irish—India for the Indians"—the U. N. I. A. believes that it is about time for the negroes to raise the cry of "Africa for the Africans," at home and abroad.

In the United States Garveyism runs counter to the ideals governing most of the negro uplift movements. Garvey's reluctance, for example, to declare himself on the Ku-Klux Klan, with whose whole program he is said to be in perfect accord; his opposition to the negro middle and professional classes (in August, 1922, he issued a manifesto advising his followers not to invest their money in negro corporate enterprises other than his own) are indicative of two things: Garvey's slant on the black *bourgeoisie* and the pessimism with which he views the outlook for the negro in a hostile white world.

To get his ideas abroad Garvey started a weekly newspaper, the *Negro World*. Doubtless, it is the most bitterly racial newspaper published by negroes. Leading off with a full-page "message" weekly by Garvey, the journal is published in three sections—in Spanish, French, and English. It goes to every part of the world where there are black people. Numberless have been the times when it has been suppressed or otherwise debarred by the British and French authorities from entering their native Negroid possessions. As it is, the *bourgeois* colored people of the United States are ashamed to be seen with it. They do not care for it. It is too upstandingly, too sensationally, racial.

Yet it is through this medium of violence that Garvey hopes to unite the black people of the world. How successful he is in doing this is reflected again and again in the unswerving allegiance to the ideals set up by him no matter what the machinations of the enemy may do to throw him into disrepute.

Soon after he got his organization going Garvey conceived the idea of founding a steamship line to ply between North, Central, and South America, the West Indies, and Africa. And the name with which he christened it is illustrative of the spirit of the whole Garvey movement. He called it the "Black Star Line." Why not? Did not the whites have their "White Star Line?" And from all parts of the world the blacks bought stock in it. It found fertile soil in their repressed consciousness.

Now Garvey, a bewitching orator, a roof-raising propagandist, when it comes to actual comprehension of the forces governing the world of trade and commerce, is a hopeless nincompoop. He said it was not necessary for him to be an experienced seaman nor need he have a technical knowledge of shipping to direct a steamship line. Unwilling to relinquish the actual control of it, he said he'd get people, black people with the brains and experience, to run it. And here again, undoubtedly, Garvey was unconsciously drawing on his Jamaica experience. For back in his Jamaica days there were black pilots and engineers and captains of merchant vessels which traded along the Main. Garvey, his imagination leaping to the contemplation of boundless continents, staked all, some two or three million subscribed by the black folk, on the fulfillment of this exotic dream.

As the world knows, the "Black Star Line" failed, and for a moment Garvey's star took a downward plunge. Incompetency, dishonesty, mismanagement, fraud—these contributed to it. In his eagerness to put the project over, Garvey was a promiscuous chooser of men. He was bombarded on all sides by charlatans. Bogus engineers, unskilled experts, sloop masters all clamored for position and opportunity, and Garvey, blind to the things of the earth, fell prey to them—saw in them spirits hungry to show to the whites the oceanic genius of the blacks.

24. BIG BILL THOMPSON

The results of the 1927 Chicago mayoral election have been interpreted variously as a victory for 100 per cent Americanism, for the forces supporting censorship, and for the isolationist crusade against internationalism. The winning candidate, William Hale Thompson, campaigned mostly against the British influence in the United States and against high school and college textbooks which he deemed critical of American heroes. Often overlooked, however, was Thompson's positive appeal to the large minority groups in Chicago, the Irish, the Poles, the Italians. Thompson's opponent was of old patrician stock, and in a way the election was a contest between the old America with its cultural and religious ties to Britain and North Europe and the new urban America with its Catholic attachments to Central and Southern Europe as well as to Ireland. In some measure the election was a preview of the Presidential race of 1928. The following account, "Shall We Shatter the Nation's Idols in School Histories?" by the victorious Mayor William Hale Thompson is excerpted from *Current History*, February 1928, p. 619.

Treason-tainted school textbooks were a big issue in the Chicago mayoral campaign last Spring.

I exposed in speeches and campaign literature the vicious pro-British, un-American propaganda in the school histories which were in the Chicago public schools with the approval of Superintendent William McAndrew, who had been imported from New York by the Dever Administration through influences exerted by Professor Charles E. Merriam of the University of Chicago, and members of the English-Speaking Union. I showed how in many histories Revolutionary war heroes were defamed when mentioned, and how many were treated with the silence of contempt by being omitted entirely from the school histories. I revealed that League of Nations and World Court propaganda were distributed in the public schools under McAndrew; that the "Spirit of '76" and other patriotic pictures had been stripped from the school walls; that McAndrew had expressed satisfaction with this desecration in the educational magazine he edits; that McAndrew had denied the Chicago public school children the privilege of contributing their pennies and dimes to the fund for the restoration of the historic frigate Constitution ("Old Ironsides"), which collection and cause had been endorsed by President Coolidge.

To my meetings in the mayoral campaign I took a copy of Arthur Meier Schlesinger's history, *New Viewpoints in American History,* which history was the textbook in a history course conducted by the University of Chicago for Chicago school teachers, who sought advancement through extra credits in history. I read to my audiences the following among other passages from this infamous history, which was being taught to our school teachers to be taught by them in turn to the 550,000 school children of Chicago:

> When the representatives of George V rendered homage a few years ago at the tomb of the great disloyalist and rebel of a former century, George Washington, the minds of many Americans reverted with a sense of bewilderment to the time when another King George was guiding the destinies of the British nation. The fact is that the average American still accepts without qualification or question the partisan justifications of the struggle for independence which have come down from the actual participants in the affair on the American side.
>
> These accounts, colored by the emotions and misunderstandings of the times and designed to arouse the Colonists to a warlike pitch against the British Government, have formed the basis of the treatment in our school textbooks and have served to perpetuate judgments of the American Revolution which no fair-minded historian can accept today. (Page 160.)

I pledged the people of Chicago that if elected Mayor I would stop the teaching in the public schools that George Washington was "a rebel" and "a traitor"; that I would have recognition given to the heroes of Irish, Polish, German, Holland, Italian and other extractions who had been dropped from the histories; that I would stop the defamation of America's heroes; that I would see to it that the histories were brought back to the American viewpoint and American ideals that formerly prevailed.

This issue was accentuated and emphasized, coincident with the mayoral campaign, through the activity of a patriotic group of Chicagoans called the "Citizens' Committee for the investigation of History."

PRO-BRITISH ORGANIZATIONS

The Carnegie Foundation, Rhodes Scholarship Fund, English-speaking Union, Interdependence Day Association, and other pro-British and pacifist propaganda organizations have been shown to have direct connection with these alterations, their own officials having written several of the Anglicized textbooks. The flood of evidence in the McAndrew trial, to which no answer has been offered because it is unanswerable, overwhelmingly proves that organized foreign influences pervade the colleges and public schools of our country, and have caused these authors to re-write American school history from the British standpoint.

Pending the ousting of McAndrew and the restoration of real American histories to the public schools, I wrote the Board of Education on Nov. 22, to notify history teachers to give oral instruction with reference to the lives and achievements of the many heroes of many nationalities, now denied their proper places in the school histories. . . .

ATTITUDE OF FOREIGN ELEMENTS

Some critics scoff and say: "What's the School Board fight all about?" They know, but they do not want to admit they know. The people of Chicago know and understand. The Poles have held a great mass meeting, at which they indignantly protested against the dropping of the names of Kosciuszko and Pulaski from the school histories. Citizens of German and Irish extraction in mass meetings in Chicago and elsewhere have protested against the wrongs done heroes of those nationalities. Chicago citizens of Dutch descent have met and passed resolutions tendering me support and protesting because there has been eliminated from the school histories credit due to Holland in the cause of democracy and freedom and credit due to Dutch pioneers in America. Chicago citizens of Italian extraction have passed resolutions protesting against the teaching that "the spirit and institutions of our country are English"; declaring that the proposed English-speaking Union would "crowd to the background American citizens of other nationality origins"; pointing out that, because of the suspicion in Central and South America that we are tying up with England, our country has lost much of the friendship and confidence the Latin people of those countries formerly entertained for us. Other nationality groups have passed, or are now preparing to pass, similar resolutions. The Italians and others in their resolutions enthusiastically concur in the statement I made in my first letter last Fall to the Library Board:

> In truth, our national greatness was achieved, not by one but by many nationalities, and the present surpassing position of our country is due to the fact that here in America we have brought to the national surface the best in ideas and ideals of all nationalities, and the mingling of many strains has produced the highest type of civilization and the highest level of attainments in the world's history.

The Chicago case is not isolated. School books here are used in other cities. Some cities have thrown out propaganda-distorted books; most of them have not. The histories that the big cities use go to the small cities and to the crossroad schoolhouses of the country districts. So this matter of treason-tainted histories is not a Chicago local situation; it goes to the whole nation. The reading courses of the American Library Association are circulated in libraries generally throughout America. What Judge Bausman found in the Seattle Public Library, I found in the Chicago Public Library. What we here in Chicago have found in our perverted school histories, people of other cities have found or are finding in their histories. This is not the case of Thompson versus McAndrew. It is the case of patriotic Americans everywhere against those who defame our national heroes and make assaults on our national institutions.

The Christian church rests upon the divinity of Christ. To attack that is to assail the spiritual life of the Christian church. American patriotism rests upon the nobility of George Washington, father and founder of the nation, and the righteousness of the cause of freedom and independence that he led. Take that away and the patriotic structure falls, leaving but the shell of commercialism. The nobility of heroes, with belief in their cause and their ideals, is to the nation, what divinity is to religion. Freedom is in peril if the people turn from the ideals of the founders, because out of those ideals came the nation. Patriotism lives by the light of her heroes. Nations have their shrines of patriotism, as churches have their altars of divinity. The patriotic must guard the one, as the devout protect the other. Drop the heroes from the country's histories, and you take the stars out of the firmament of patriotism. . . .

25. KU KLUX KLAN

The Ku Klux Klan of the Twenties had no direct connection with the Reconstruction organization. But it did perpetuate the uniforms and paraphernalia of the older group, its spirit of intolerance, and its thirst for violence. What distinguished the newer Klan was its national basis and its inclusion of Catholics, Jews, radicals, and foreigners in general as objects of its intolerance. The Klan, then, almost ran the gamut of modern bigotry.

Any student of the Klan is immediately struck with its similarity in dogma to European Fascism. Both movements had their ideological roots deep in the country and village folk. Both stressed nationalism and racial purity, both seized upon so-called alien minority groups as objects for attack, and both were militantly opposed to many of the manifestations of the new urban culture of the western world. Both called for a return in almost mystical terms to the past, both attacked the new politics of the left, both decried what was described as the sensual and indulgent living of the city, both demanded a new discipline in order to return to the ancient verities. To such an extent the Ku Klux Klan was a counter-movement against the new urban civilization. The first of the following two articles on the Klan was written by Hiram Wesley Evans, the "Imperial Wizard" or boss of the Klan. Entitled "The Klan's Fight for

Americanism," *The North American Review,* March 1926, p. 33, it sums up the Klan's program. In the interest of brevity and clarity many of the succeeding passages have been transposed.

WE ARE A MOVEMENT OF THE PLAIN PEOPLE, VERY WEAK IN THE MATTER of culture, intellectual support, and trained leadership. We are demanding, and we expect to win, a return of power into the hands of the everyday, not highly cultured, not overly intellectualized, but entirely unspoiled and not de-Americanized, average citizen of the old stock. Our members and leaders are all of this class—the opposition of the intellectuals and liberals who held the leadership, betrayed Americanism, and from whom we expect to wrest control, is almost automatic.

This is undoubtedly a weakness. It lays us open to the charge of being "hicks" and "rubes" and "drivers of second hand Fords." We admit it. Far worse, it makes it hard for us to state our case and advocate our crusade in the most effective way, for most of us lack skill in language. Worst of all, the need of trained leaders constantly hampers our progress and leads to serious blunders and internal troubles. If the Klan ever should fail it would be from this cause. All this we on the inside know far better than our critics, and regret more. Our leadership is improving, but for many years the Klan will be seeking better leaders, and the leaders praying for greater wisdom. . . .

The Klan, therefore, has now come to speak for the great mass of Americans of the old pioneer stock. We believe that it does fairly and faithfully represent them, and our proof lies in their support. To understand the Klan, then, it is necessary to understand the character and present mind of the mass of old-stock Americans. The mass, it must be remembered, as distinguished from the intellectually mongrelized "Liberals."

These are, in the first place, a blend of various peoples of the so-called Nordic race, the race which, with all its faults, has given the world almost the whole of modern civilization. The Klan does not try to represent any people but these.

There is no need to recount the virtues of the American pioneers; but it is too often forgotten that in the pioneer period a selective process of intense rigor went on. From the first only hardy, adventurous and strong men and women dared the pioneer dangers; from among these all but the best died swiftly, so that the new Nordic blend which became the American race was bred up to a point probably the highest in history. This remarkable race character, along with the new-won continent and the new-created nation, made the inheritance of the old-stock Americans the richest ever given to a generation of men.

In spite of it, however, these Nordic Americans for the last generation have found themselves increasingly uncomfortable, and finally deeply distressed. There appeared first confusion in thought and opinion, a groping and hesitancy about national affairs and private life alike, in sharp contrast to the clear, straightforward purposes of our earlier years. There was futility in religion, too, which was in many ways even more distressing. Presently we began to find that we were dealing with strange ideas; policies that always sounded well, but somehow always made us still more uncomfortable.

Finally came the moral breakdown that has been going on for two decades. One by one all our traditional moral standards went by the boards, or were so disregarded that they ceased to be binding. The sacredness of our Sabbath, of our homes, of chastity, and finally even of our right to teach our own children in our own schools fundamental facts and truths were torn away from us. Those who maintained the old standards did so only in the face of constant ridicule.

Along with this went economic distress. The assurance for the future of our children dwindled. We found our great cities and the control of much of our industry and commerce taken over by strangers, who stacked the cards of success and prosperity against us. Shortly they came to dominate our government. The *bloc* system by which this was done is now familiar to all. Every kind of inhabitant except the Americans gathered in groups which operated as units in politics, under orders of corrupt, self-seeking and un-American leaders, who both by purchase and threat enforced their demands on politicians. Thus it came about that the interests of Americans were always the last to be considered by either national or city governments, and that the native Americans were constantly discriminated against, in business, in legislation, and in administrative government.

So the Nordic American today is a stranger in large parts of the land his fathers gave him. Moreover, he is a most unwelcome stranger, one much spit upon, and one to whom even the right to have his own opinions and to work for his own interests is now denied with jeers and revilings. "We must Americanize the Americans," a distinguished immigrant said recently. Can anything more clearly show the state to which the real American has fallen in this country which was once his own?

Our falling birth rate, the result of all this, is proof of our distress. We no longer feel that we can be fair to children we bring into the world, unless we can make sure from the start that they shall have capital or education or both, so that they need never compete with those who now fill the lower rungs of the ladder of success. We dare no longer risk letting our youth "make its own way" in the conditions under which we live. So even our unborn children are being crowded out of their birthright!

All this has been true for years, but it was the World War that gave us our first hint of the real cause of our troubles, and began to crystallize our ideas. The war revealed that millions whom we had allowed to share our heritage and prosperity, and whom we had assumed had become part of us, were in fact not wholly so. They had other loyalties: each was willing—anxious!—to sacrifice the interests of the country that had given him shelter to the interests of the one he was supposed to have cast off; each in fact did use the freedom and political power we had given him against ourselves whenever he could see any profit for his older loyalty.

This, of course, was chiefly in international affairs, and the excitement caused by the discovery of disloyalty subsided rapidly after the war ended. But it was not forgotten by the Nordic Americans. They had been awakened and alarmed; they began to suspect that the hyphenism which had been shown was only a part of what existed; their quiet was not that of renewed sleep, but of strong men waiting very watchfully. And presently they began to form decisions about all those aliens who were Americans for profit only.

They decided that even the crossing of salt water did not dim a single spot on a leopard; that an alien usually remains an alien no matter what is done to him, what veneer of education he gets, what oaths he takes, nor what public attitudes he adopts. They decided that the melting pot was a ghastly failure, and remembered that the very name was coined by a member of one of the races—the Jews—which most determinedly refuses to melt. They decided that in every way, as well as in politics, the alien in the vast majority of cases is unalterably fixed in his instincts, character, thought and interests by centuries of racial selection and development, that he thinks first for his own people, works only with and for them, cares entirely for their interests, considers himself always one of them, and never an American. They decided that in character, instincts, thought, and purposes—in his whole soul—an alien remains fixedly alien to America and all it means.

They saw, too, that the alien was tearing down the American standard of living, especially in the lower walks. It became clear that while the American can out-work the alien, the alien can so far under-live the American as to force him out of all competitive labor. So they came to realize that the Nordic can easily survive and rule and increase if he holds for himself the advantages won by strength and daring of his ancestors in times of stress and peril, but that if he surrenders those advantages to the peoples who could not share the stress, he will soon be driven below the level at which he can exist by their low standards, low living and fast breeding. And they saw that the low standard aliens of Eastern and Southern Europe were doing just that thing to us.

They learned, though more slowly, that alien ideas are just as dangerous to us as the aliens themselves, no matter how plausible such ideas may sound. With most of the plain people this conclusion is based simply on the fact that the alien ideas do not work well for them. Others went deeper and came to understand that the differences in racial background, in breeding, instinct, character and emotional point of view are more important than logic. So ideas which may be perfectly healthy for an alien may also be poisonous for Americans.

Finally they learned the great secret of the propagandists; that success in corrupting public opinion depends on putting out the subversive ideas without revealing their source. They came to suspect that "prejudice" against foreign ideas is really a protective device of nature against mental food that may be indigestible. They saw, finally, that the alien leaders in America act on this theory, and that there is a steady flood of alien ideas being spread over the country, always carefully disguised as American.

As they learned all this the Nordic Americans have been gradually arousing themselves to defend their homes and their own kind of civilization. They have not known just how to go about it; the idealist philanthropy and good-natured generosity which led to the philosophy of the melting pot have died hard. Resistance to the peaceful invasion of the immigrant is no such simple matter as snatching up weapons and defending frontiers, nor has it much spectacular emotionalism to draw men to the colors.

The old-stock Americans are learning, however. They have begun to arm themselves for this new type of warfare. Most important, they have broken away from the fetters of the false ideals and philanthropy which put aliens ahead of their own children and their own race.

To do this they have had to reject completely—and perhaps for the moment the rejection is a bit too complete—the whole body of "Liberal" ideas which they had followed with such simple, unquestioning faith. The first and immediate cause of the break with Liberalism was that it had provided no defense against the alien invasion, but instead had excused it—even defended it against Americanism. Liberalism is today charged in the mind of most Americans with nothing less than national, racial and spiritual treason.

But this is only the last of many causes of distrust. The plain people now see that Liberalism has come completely under the dominance of weaklings and parasites whose alien "idealism" reaches its logical peak in the Bolshevist platform of "produce as little as you can, beg or steal from those who do produce, and kill the producer for thinking he is better than you." Not that all Liberalism goes so far, but it all seems to be on that road. The average Liberal idea is apparently that those who can produce should carry the unfit, and let the unfit rule them.

. . . The Klan goes back to the American racial instincts, and to the common sense which is their first product, as the basis of its beliefs and methods. The fundamentals of our thought are convictions, not mere opinions. We are pleased that modern research is finding scientific backing for these convictions. We do not need them ourselves; we know that we are right in the same sense that a good Christian knows that he has been saved and that Christ lives—a thing which the intellectual can never understand. These convictions are no more to be argued about than is our love for our children; we are merely willing to state them for the enlightenment and conversion of others.

There are three of these great racial instincts, vital elements in both the historic and the present attempts to build an America which shall fulfill the aspirations and justify the heroism of the men who made the nation. These are the instincts of loyalty to the white race, to the traditions of America, and to the spirit of Protestantism, which has been an essential part of Americanism ever since the days of Roanoke and Plymouth Rock. They are condensed into the Klan slogan: "Native, white, Protestant supremacy."

First in the Klansman's mind is patriotism—America for Americans. He believes religiously that a betrayal of Americanism or the American race is treason to the most sacred of trusts, a trust from his fathers and a trust from God. He believes, too, that Americanism can only be achieved if the pioneer stock is kept pure. There is more than race pride in this. Mongrelization has been proven bad. It is only between closely related stocks of the same race that interbreeding has improved men; the kind of interbreeding that went on in the early days of America between English, Dutch, German, Hugenot, Irish and Scotch.

Racial integrity is a very definite thing to the Klansman. It means even more than good citizenship, for a man may be in all ways a good citizen and yet a poor American, unless he has racial understanding of Americanism, and instinctive loyalty to it. It is in no way a reflection on any man to say that he is un-American; it is merely a statement that he is not one of us. It is often not even wise to try to make an American of the best of aliens. What he is may be spoiled without his becoming American. The races and stocks of men are as distinct as breeds of animals, and every boy knows that if one tries to train a bulldog to herd sheep, he has in the end neither a good bulldog nor a good collie.

The Jew is a . . . complex problem. His abilities are great, he contributes much to any country where he lives. This is particularly true of the Western Jew, those of the stocks we have known so long. Their separation from us is more religious than racial. When freed from persecution these Jews have shown a tendency to disintegrate and amalgamate. We may hope that shortly, in the free atmosphere of America, Jews of this class will cease to be a problem. Quite different are the Eastern Jews of recent immigration, the Jews known as the Askhenasim. It is interesting to note that anthropologists now tell us that these are not true Jews, but only Judaized Mongols—Chazars. These, unlike the true Hebrew, show a divergence from the American type so great that there seems little hope of their assimilation.

The second word in the Klansman's trilogy is "white." The white race must be supreme, not only in America but in the world. This is equally undebatable, except on the ground that the races might live together, each with full regard for the rights and interests of others, and that those rights and interests would never conflict. Such an idea, of course, is absurd; the colored races today, such as Japan, are clamoring not for equality but for their supremacy. The whole history of the world, on its broader lines, has been one of race conflicts, wars, subjugation or extinction. This is not pretty, and certainly disagrees with the maudlin theories of cosmopolitanism, but it is truth. The world has been so made that each race must fight for its life, must conquer, accept slavery or die. The Klansman believes that the whites will not become slaves, and he does not intend to die before his time. . . .

The Negro, the Klan considers a special duty and problem of the white American. He is among us through no wish of his; we owe it to him and to ourselves to give him full protection and opportunity. But his limitations are evident; we will not permit him to gain sufficient power to control our civilization. Neither will we delude him with promises of social equality which we know can never be realized. The Klan looks forward to the day when the Negro problem will have been solved on some much saner basis than miscegenation, and when every State will enforce laws making any sex relations between a white and a colored person a crime.

For the alien in general we have sympathy, opportunity, justice, but no permanent welcome unless he becomes truly American. It is our duty to see that he has every chance for this, and we shall be glad to accept him if he does. We hold no rancor against him; his race, instincts, training, mentality and whole outlook of life are usually widely different from ours. We cannot blame him if he adheres to them and attempts to convert us to them, even by force. But we must see that he can never succeed. . . .

The third of the Klan principles is that Protestantism must be supreme; that Rome shall not rule America. The Klansman believes this not merely because he is a Protestant, nor even because the Colonies that are now our nation were settled for the purpose of wresting America from the control of Rome and establishing a land of free conscience. He believes it also because Protestantism is an essential part of Americanism; without it America could never have been created and without it she cannot go forward. Roman rule would kill it.

Protestantism contains more than religion. It is the expression in religion of the same spirit of independence, self-reliance and freedom which are the highest achievements of the Nordic race. It sprang into being automatically at the time of the great "upsurgence" of strength in the Nordic peoples that opened the spurt of civilization in the fifteenth century. It has been a distinctly Nordic religion, and it has been through this religion that the Nordics have found strength to take leadership of all whites and the supremacy of the earth. Its destruction is the deepest purpose of all other peoples, as that would mean the end of Nordic rule.

It is the only religion that permits the unhampered individual development and the unhampered conscience and action which were necessary in the settling of America. Our pioneers were all Protestants, except for an occasional Irishman—Protestants by nature if not by religion —for though French and Spanish dared and explored and showed great heroism, they made little of the land their own. America was Protestant from birth. . . .

The real indictment against the Roman Church is that it is, fundamentally and irredeemably, in its leadership, in politics, in thought, and largely in membership, actually and actively alien, un-American and usually anti-American. The old stock Americans, with the exception of the few such of Catholic faith—who are in a class by themselves, standing tragically torn between their faith and their racial and national patriotism—see in the Roman Church today the chief leader of alienism, and the most dangerous alien power with a foothold inside our boundaries. It is this and nothing else that has revived hostility to Catholicism. By no stretch of the imagination can it fairly be called religious prejudice, though, now that the hostility has become active, it does derive some strength from the religious schism.

We Americans see many evidences of Catholic alienism. We believe that its official position and its dogma, its theocratic autocracy and its claim to full authority in temporal as well as spiritual matters, all make it impossible for it as a church, or for its members if they obey it, to coöperate in a free democracy in which Church and State have been separated. It is true that in this country the Roman Church speaks very softly on these points, so that many Catholics do not know them. It is also true that the Roman priests preach Americanism, subject to their own conception of Americanism, of course. But the Roman Church itself makes a point of the divine and unalterable character of its dogma, it has never seen fit to abandon officially any of these un-American attitudes, and it still teaches them in other countries. Until its does renounce them, we cannot believe anything except that they all remain in force, ready to be called into action whenever feasible, and temporarily hushed up only for expediency.

The hierarchical government of the Roman Church is equally at odds with Americanism. The Pope and the whole hierarchy have been for centuries almost wholly Italian. It is nonsense to suppose that a man, by entering a church, loses his race or national loyalties. The Roman Church today, therefore, is just what its name says—Roman; and it is impossible for its hierarchy or the policies they dictate to be in real sympathy with Americanism. Worse, the Italians have proven to be one of the least assimilable of people. The autocratic nature of the Catholic Church organization, and its suppression of free conscience or free decision, need not be discussed; they are unquestioned. Thus it is fundamental to the Roman Church to demand a supreme loyalty, overshadowing national or race loyalty, to a power that is inevitably alien, and which at the best must inevitably inculcate ideals un-American if not actively anti-American.

We find, too, that even in America, the majority of the leaders and of the priests of the Roman Church are either foreign born, or of foreign parentage and training. They, like other aliens, are unable to teach Americanism if they wish, because both race and education prevent their understanding what it is. The service they give it, even if sincere, can at best produce only confusion of thought. Who would ask an American, for instance, to try to teach Italians their own language, history, and patriotism, even without the complication of religion?

Another difficulty is that the Catholic Church here constantly represents, speaks for and cares for the interests of a large body of alien peoples. Most immigration of recent years, so unassimilable and fundamentally un-American, has been Catholic. The Catholics of American stock have been submerged and almost lost; the aliens and their interests dictate all policies of the Roman Church which are not dictated from Rome itself.

Also, the Roman Church seems to take pains to prevent the assimilation of these people. Its parochial schools, its foreign born priests, the obstacles it places in the way of marriage with Protestants unless the children are bound in advance to Romanism, its persistent use of the foreign languages in church and school, its habit of grouping aliens together and thus creating insoluble alien masses—all these things strongly impede Americanization. Of course they also strengthen and solidify the Catholic Church, and make its work easier, and so are very natural, but the fact remains that they are hostile to Americanism.

Finally, there is the undeniable fact that the Roman Church takes an active part in American politics. It has not been content to accept in good faith the separation of Church and State, and constantly tries through political means to win advantages for itself and its people—in other words, to be a political power in America, as well as a spiritual power. Denials of Catholic activity in politics are too absurd to need discussion. The "Catholic vote" is as well recognized a factor as the "dry vote." All politicians take it for granted.

The facts are that almost everywhere, and especially in the great industrial centers where the Catholics are strongest, they vote almost as a unit, under control of leaders of their own faith, always in support of the interests of the Catholic Church and of Catholic candidates without regard to other interests, and always also in support of alienism whenever there is an issue raised. They vote, in short, not as American citizens, but as aliens and Catholics! They form the biggest, strongest, most cohesive of all the alien *blocs*. On many occasions they form alliances with other alien *blocs* against American interests, as with the Jews in New York today, and with others in the case of the recent opposition to immigration restriction. Incidentally they have been responsible for some of the worst abuses in American politics, and today are the chief support of such machines as that of Brennan in Chicago, Curley in Boston and Tammany in New York. . . .

Toward the Catholic as an individual the Klan has no "attitude" whatever. His religion is none of our business. But toward the Catholic Church as a political organization, and toward the individual Catholic who serves it as such, we have a definite intolerance. We are intolerant of the refusal of the Roman Church to accept equality in a democracy, and resent its attempts to use clerical power in our politics. We resent, too, the subservience of members who follow clerical commands in politics. We are intolerant, also, of the efforts of the Roman Church to prevent the assimilation of immigrant members. We demand that in politics and in education the Roman Church abandon its clutching after special and un-American privileges, and that it become content to depend for its strength on the truth of its teachings and the spiritual power of its leaders. Further than this we ask nothing. We admit that this is intolerant; we deny that it is either bigoted or unjust.

● ● ● ● ●

This article, "Gentlemen from Indiana," by Morton Harrison, *The Atlantic Monthly*, May, 1928, p. 676, describes in detail how the Klan almost took over this northern state. Of particular interest is the sales campaign it organized and its use of economic and social pressure to win over the dissident and silence the opposition. Something of the native American's deep unrest with the developing urban culture can be gained from the description of the fervent and almost religious support of the Klan and its leaders in a state which once had known and sheltered Abraham Lincoln. Reprinted by permission of *The Atlantic Monthly*.

A HUNDRED THOUSAND MEN, MOST OF THEM WEARING FLOWING WHITE ROBES and visored cowls, waited patiently about a mound in a field near Kokomo, Indiana. They had been told, "A new Messiah will be born in the ballot box of Indiana." Several doctors of divinity had already climbed the mound—or, as they called it, the mount—and exhorted the multitude to smite the Devil. There were allusions to the Prince, the Sermon on the Mount, the Nativity.

Suddenly a Knight flung a trembling hand toward heaven and shouted, "He's coming!" The sea of white hoods rippled. Every eye was strained toward the southern sky. A flake of the sun itself flashed from behind a cloud.

The Purple Prince was coming to his coronation. Some Knights raised their arms toward him and shouted prayers of thanksgiving. The Prince's chariot of fire was a gilded airplane in which he circled the field and descended in a wide spiral to a stretch of meadow reserved for his advent.

A squat but agile figure clad in a silken robe of purple, embellished with a gold piping and mystic symbols, climbed from the plane and gravely shook hands with several distinctively robed men who stepped forward from the multitude. Armed men cleared a path to the mount. The Prince, bowing stiffly to right and left, was escorted to his dais. He paused until the whole countryside was dead with silence. When every eye was on him he raised his hand so vigorously and imperiously that no sceptre could have improved the effect. With his other hand he flung back his visor, exposing a rosy, chubby face lighted with animal cunning.

"My worthy subjects, citizens of the Invisible Empire, Klansmen all, greetings. It grieves me to be late. The President of the United States kept me unduly long counseling upon vital matters of state. Only my plea that this is the time and place of my coronation obtained for me surcease from his prayers for guidance.

"Here in this uplifted hand, where all can see, I bear an official document addressed to the Grand Dragon, Hydras, Great Titans, Furies, Giants, Kleagles, King Kleagles, Exalted Cyclops, Terrors, and All Citizens of the Invisible Empire of the Realm of Indiana.

"It is done in the executive chambers of His Lordship, the Imperial Wizard, in the Imperial City of Atlanta, Commonwealth of Georgia, on this Tenth Day of the Seventh Month of the Year of Our Lord Nineteen Hundred and Twenty-Three, and on the Dismal Day of the Weeping Week of the Hideous Month of the Year of the Klan LVII.

"It is signed by His Lordship, Hiram Wesley Evans, Imperial Wizard, and duly attested.

"It continues me officially in my exalted capacity as Grand Dragon of the Invisible Empire for the Realm of Indiana. It so proclaims me by Virtue of God's Unchanging Grace. So be it."

Thus did David Curtis Stephenson, Texas printer, confirm his boast that he was the most powerful man in Indiana.

He concluded his oration with a plea for straight Americanism, an admonition to avoid violence, and a word of compliment and farewell. As he turned to leave, a coin was thrown at him. This was a signal for a wild demonstration of fealty and love. Rings, stickpins, pocketbooks, watch charms, coins, were showered upon him. He stood fast until the tribute subsided, motioned his retainers to gather in the treasure, and retired to make merry with his Knights and to discuss the fiscal affairs of his principality.

Ku Klux Klan officials said that this was the greatest assembly of Klansmen in the history of the order. The Klan estimate of the number of people was 200,000. The popular tradition in Indiana is that 100,000 were present.

II

Stephenson's coronation, or sanctification, raised the curtain on a new era in the Indiana Klan. Stephenson was taken into the Klan for the express purpose of applying high-pressure sales methods to increasing its strength. He was soon sent to Indianapolis to build up the membership, and in a few months he seized the power and later the title of Grand Dragon of the realm by going over the heads of his superiors to the Imperial Wizard himself.

The original purpose of the revived Klan, as defined when William Joseph Simmons gave new life to it during the World War, was to stop immigration. The Ku Klux Kreed, as printed in the Kloran, or "THE Book of the Invisible Empire," declared simply for white supremacy and "the sublime principles of pure Americanism." The candidate for membership—or, in the language of the Klan, "for naturalization in the Invisible Empire"—was, however, required to swear, with his left hand over his heart and his right hand raised to heaven, an affirmative answer to these two of eight questions: "Are you a native-born, white, Gentile American citizen?" and "Are you absolutely opposed to and free of any allegiance of any nature to any cause, government, people, sect, or ruler that is foreign to the United States of America?"

In the ritual of the Klan there is no incitement of hatred for the Jew, the Catholic, the negro, or the foreign-born. They were excluded from membership as being the polluting undercurrents and backwash of the sparkling stream of Americanism. "Shut off the poisonous inflow; purify what is here"—that was the battle cry of the Klan as written and preached by its revivalists.

Had the Klan invasion of Indiana been kept on this plane, where it was held until it accumulated a considerable membership of honest men eager to protect the Cross and the Flag, it would have run its course, as it did in neighboring states, thinning out to nothing in the lake-district industrial centers.

The distinctive feature of the Klan of Indiana was the sales plan of
D. C. Stephenson. He sold fright, as he had sold coal, in carload lots. If
the Klan went fairly well on a diet of fear, how would it flourish on
large quantities of it?

He saw in the Klan exclusion feature a combination of the four live-
liest prejudices that inspire men to put upon their fellows. These four
prejudices he made his "sales features."

First came the normal American aversion to alien newcomers speaking
a foreign tongue. The war intensified this aversion to a degree never
known in the history of the country.

Secondly, the original Klan crushed out of the negro all his dreams
of political equality, and left a prejudice which was easily whipped into
fury by his invasion of the Northern labor market during the war and
the elevation of his economic and social position by the immigration
restriction law.

Thirdly, it was easy to make capital of the fact that the Jew money
lender and credit merchant is a red flag in every community where he
prospers.

The fourth sales feature was the well-known rabble-rousing formula
against the Catholic Church. The American Protective Association and
various slanderous anti-Catholic weekly newspapers have kept it in
working order.

But it is a well-known fact that a man cannot be induced to fear the
neighbor near whom he has lived many years in peace and harmony.

The Stephenson sales plan took this fact into consideration. It was the
secret of its success. The campaign was directed, not against the little
band of negroes who lived together down along the river, worked for the
white folks, kept a religious revival in continuous operation, and minded
their own business, but against a mythical wave of black labor sweeping
up from the South to work for a dollar a day, live in squalor, and commit unspeakable offenses against the white people.

No one was urged to lynch Nick, the smiling and busy Greek confec-
tioner whose ice-cream parlor was a high school students' meeting place,
but a terrifying curse was hurled at an unnamed Greek in the next
county who had put an American-born citizen out of business by cut-
throat competition, and especially against remote masses of unassimilated
aliens in large cities awaiting only a Lenin to show them how to abolish
by force the institution of private property.

No voice was lifted against the peace of Solomon Stein, the industri-
ous, amiable clothier, model family man and perhaps faithful attendant,
as a visitor, upon the service of the Presbyterian Church, but the welkin
rang with invective hurled eastward in the general direction of a Jewish
ring of international bankers who started the war and were preparing to

foreclose a mortgage on the world, bankrupting Henry Ford and others. The Catholics were the hard problem. In most Indiana communities there is but one Catholic parish. Catholic children are required by diocesan order to attend Catholic schools. The families live near the church because their religious and educational interest is centered in it. The adults mingle socially but little with the Protestant people, the children less. The Catholic Church ritual is so foreign to anything in the experience of the average American rural Protestant that a skilled agitator can ascribe to it many of the attributes of a pagan incantation and excite religious animosity. But the Catholics are important customers. Acting on the theory that the intensity of a weak man's hatreds is measured directly in terms of his remoteness from his enemy, the Pope was selected as the archenemy of American purity. There are few things a Kokomo Klansman can do with greater safety than stand in the privacy of his own home and shake his fist at Rome, Italy.

For good measure, Stephenson threw in the Devil. To win the Anti-Saloon League, he declared war on bootleggers and "blind tigers." He blacklisted roadside "petting parties" and promised to banish the vice element from every community.

III

Until the day Stephenson wrested the leadership of the realm of Indiana from Joe Huffington, there was no plan for a state-wide membership drive. There were small klaverns in several counties, but much of the state was unrepresented. To cover the state in one sweeping campaign, Stephenson cast about for a group of men skilled in the brand of exhortation required to chill with fear. Ruling out the forbidden classes and the politicians, who in nearly every community were classed as allies of the Devil, he came to the Protestant clergymen. He made every Protestant clergyman in Indiana an honorary member of the Klan. Not all availed themselves of the privilege, but in many communities every Protestant clergyman was a Klan leader.

The war chest was a perplexing problem, but Stephenson knew that few things interest a zealous reformer more than easy money. The Klan initiation fee was fixed at ten dollars. This fee was split on a sliding scale, Stephenson giving as much as six dollars to the solicitor who actually got the cash from a new member. The commission was at times much less. It has been estimated that Stephenson's average share was $4.20, out of which he paid all expenses of the state headquarters.

The sale of Klan regalia and klavern equipment netted large profits. Klan robes cost $3.28 each in large quantities and were sold to initiates at an average price of $6.50.

Stephenson's imperative command was that every community must be split into two factions—a large group of Klansmen, a small group of out-landers. He knew that an active enemy would keep every klavern on its toes and presenting a united front for self-preservation. The membership drive cut a new line of cleavage through lodges, clubs, churches, political parties, labor unions, and farm organizations. The intelligent leadership in nearly every group was anti-Klan, openly at first, silently later. The Klan group fought savagely and incessantly. Often it won, and when it did many of the antis joined in fear of losing their clients, patients, and customers.

Stephenson made no attempt to regulate the propaganda or to censor the speeches used by lecturers and evangelists. He turned them loose and let them talk. Many of the most successful had the advantage of years of training in the pulpit. They were especially good at strafing the Pope. One exaggeration led to another until it was declared that the Pope was coming to Washington, D. C., to lead in person the uprising against the United States of America. For some time photographs of the Protestant Episcopal Cathedral of Sts. Peter and Paul, on Mount Alban, at Wash-ington, were circulated as true pictures of the new Vatican in process of erection. The Cathedral was described as being so placed, four hundred feet above Washington, that field guns could be fired from its vicinity directly upon the Capitol and the White House. Work on the Cathedral being somewhat slow, the orators adopted a detailed description of the Scottish Rite Temple at Washington as the new home of Pope Pius XI. The left-wing leaders even went so far as to move the Pope's new head-quarters to Cincinnati, and some Klansmen exhibited pictures of the Jewish Hospital as his headquarters until he could take over a section of the city suitable to his needs.

The climax came when an overzealous lecturer declared to a crowd at North Manchester, a college town, that for all they knew the Pope might come there any day. "He may even be on the north-bound train tomor-row!" shouted the barker. "He may! He may! Be warned! Prepare! America for Americans! Seach everywhere for hidden enemies, vipers at the heart's blood of our sacred Republic! Watch the trains!"

Some fifteen hundred persons met the north-bound train the next day to the great embarrassment of the lone North Manchester passenger, a quietly dressed and somewhat clerical-appearing traveling man who, believing that he was about to play the part of the victim in a lynching party, started to flee and was forced to identify himself by his possessions as not being the Pope. . . .

The Klan's favorite public demonstration was the parade, or, in the language of the Kloran, "klavalkade." Two of its largest parades were held in Indianapolis—one past the principal negro district, the other past the residence of the Catholic bishop. Although hundreds of persons in the larger cities who had no direct contact with the Klan felt that the whole movement could be laughed out of existence, few ever expressed that view after seeing a robed Klan parade.

Bystanders watching a night parade of robed Klansmen marching four abreast were immediately quieted by the ghostly spectacle. The column extended, in the glare of one street lamp after another, as far as there was any visibility. White-robed figures with heads and faces covered with pointed hoods, bodies completely draped in loose flowing cassocks— the dead whiteness of the uniforms and the dead silence of the marchers; here and there a float picturing stirring episodes of the Revolutionary War, or in the Christian war for the world. A great profusion of fiery crosses and American shields, held on the floats by unmasked men and women, most of them stiff with self-consciousness, but now and then a youth staring defiantly at the crowd, like a small boy making faces at a securely caged circus lion.

In the great mass of marchers there was not an eye or a face or a hand in sight, nothing to read but a broken ripple of old shoes,—square-toed, cracked, run over at the heel,—shuffling in and out of the shadow cast by the robes. Hood tipped forward, each marcher following the old shoes ahead—and at the head of the parade a curious want of pomp and splendor. Grand Dragon Stephenson is not there, nor is Grand Klaliff (Vice Dragon) Walter Bossert, of Liberty (Indiana University, LL.B., 1907), sometime Republican Sixth District chairman, nor the Grand Kludd, or chaplain, the Reverend V. W. Blair, of Plainfield, ordained to minister to the spiritual needs of the Disciples of Christ, but lately without charge, a roving missioner on the Klan's Indiana realm. The Grand Officers are elsewhere, conferring with the Grand Klabee, or treasurer.

The Klan demand for action took the form of demonstrations and Horsethief Detective Association highway patrolling, with now and then a cross-burning near a Catholic church or on some commanding hilltop. A cross was built of lumber, wrapped in burlap, saturated with kerosene, planted upright, and fired. These crosses flashing through dark nights drove many a worthy citizen to the refuge of his home, there to gather his family about him and pray earnestly for deliverance from the wrath of his neighbors.

The Stephenson sales plan got results. Membership cards came in by hundreds. A former Klan organizer testifying in the campaign of Arthur L. Gilliom, Indiana attorney-general, to cancel the charter of the Klan on the ground that it was a political organization disobeying the corrupt-practices law by failing to file an account of its expenditures, testified that the Klan's greatest membership in Indiana was 178,000. It is known from reliable sources, however, that 194,000 names were listed in the roster of the realm at one time. The Klan claimed as many as 250,000 members.

IV

Stephenson chose to strike, not with the lash, the tar brush, and the torch, but with the ballot. As he came into full sway as Indiana's Klan leader, the governor, Warren T. McCray, a farmer, banker, and cattle breeder, suffered serious financial reverses in the post-war collapse of land values and farm-products prices. He engaged in credit methods which the United States district court regarded as a scheme to use the mails to defraud; he was taken from his office and sent to Atlanta prison. This was the first time in the history of the country that a governor was taken from office to serve a prison sentence on a felony charge. The disgrace shocked and humiliated the state. McCray's misfortune was in no way connected with the Klan, but Stephenson made capital of it. He exploited it as proof of his charge that there was corruption in high political offices.

Ed Jackson, secretary of state, became Stephenson's candidate for governor. Arthur R. Robinson, whose law firm served as Stephenson's attorney in several cases and who was Jackson's close personal friend, spent much time with both men. Charles J. Orbison, a Masonic and Democratic leader, came into the deal. These men developed so much power that Senator James E. Watson, former state president of the Epworth League, was forced to recognize their political power, not as a Klansman, but as a politician forming an army to win an election. There was talk about the five sons—Stephenson, Jackson, Robinson, Orbison, Watson.

Although Stephenson once filed for a Congressional nomination in an Indiana Democratic primary, he turned to the Republican Party to gain his political ends. He won the nomination for Jackson in the primary. In the convention a bloc of new faces jumped at the crack of Stephenson's whip and he approved the nomination of every man on the ticket except Arthur L. Gilliom, upstate candidate for attorney-general. In many counties the Klan won a complete primary victory, Democrats by thousands violating the primary law by marking Republican ballots. Stephenson won the state election. He won the Indianapolis city and school elections.

He was so busy winning elections that the old Klan faction outflanked him and persuaded his home klavern at Evansville to banish him from the realm on a charge of immorality. Bossert was elevated to Grand Dragon. The allegiance of the Klan general-assembly bloc was so divided between Stephenson and Bossert that neither could command enough strength to pass the promised laws abolishing private schools, establishing segregated negro districts in cities, requiring New Testament instruction in the public schools, forbidding alien landholding, and other violent class legislation.

Stephenson's goal was the 1928 Republican nomination for President of the United States. He planned to enter the United States Senate as successor to Samuel M. Ralston, Democrat, the incumbent, whose health was rapidly failing. From the Senate he expected to gain enough strength to salt the Republican national convention with a majority Klan bloc, and then, as the Republican nominee, to carry much of the North and nearly all the South, reuniting the country under the rule of the Cross, the Flag, and the Old White Blood.

But when Ralston died Stephenson lay in Noblesville jail, near Indianapolis, awaiting trial on a first-degree murder indictment. The evidence showed that Stephenson kidnapped a girl and so terrified and abused her that she took poison. Her dying statement, admitted as evidence, was that after she took the poison he carried her in his motor car half the length of the state, replying to her appeals for medical attention with a demand on his chauffeur for more speed. She stated that when the chauffeur finally rebelled, saying they would run afoul of the law, Stephenson shouted, "I am the law!" He left her alone in his garage all night and then had her taken to the home of her parents to die. Instead of going to the Senate, he went to the Indiana state prison for life. Robinson went to the Senate, served until the next election, and won the nomination and election.

TO UNKNOWN GODS

Perhaps nowhere else was the struggle between the old and the new America more sharply delineated than in religious controversies between the so-called modernists and the traditional Protestants. As the modernist movement, led by *The Christian Century* and famous preachers like Henry Emerson Fosdick, sought to sharpen the appeal of the church for the sophisticate and the urbanite, the traditionalists fought back with zeal and sometimes fury. Fosdick was himself forced to leave his New York pulpit, and heresy trials dotted the decade. In the deep South and in spots in the Middle West, fundamentalists mounted an attack against all intellectuals and intellectualism, a campaign that expressed itself in organizations like the Ku Klux Klan, in the anti-evolution laws, as well as in a new series of blue laws. But the city would not be denied and consequently many new sects and cults developed which for all their disparities had these things in common: (1) a de-emphasis of traditional dogma and ritual, (2) a promise of a relatively easy way to God or heaven, (3) either an elegance or a sumptuousness lacking in the spare Protestant tradition.

Since the fringe groups and cults on either side of the controversy best illustrate the religious developments of the decade, no attention is paid to the vast body of Protestantism in the following documents. For reasons of space and for contrast, then, the exceptional is depicted at the expense of the normal.

26. THE OLD-TIME RELIGION

The old-time religion, savoring of the frontier and camp meetings, still existed, as attested to by the following colorful description of a Holy Roller meeting on the outskirts of Dayton, Tennessee, where the famous Scopes anti-evolution trial was then being held. Perhaps the most interesting part of the sermon below is its obvious defensive attack upon intellectualism and urbanism. Comparisons should be made between the doctrines expressed on Shin Bone Ridge and those enunciated by the Ku Klux Klan and by the State of Tennessee in its case against John Scopes for teaching evolution in the public schools. The following account, "The Holy Rollers on Shin Bone Ridge," by Allene M. Sumner, appeared in *The Nation*, July 29, 1925, p. 137-8.

THE HOLY ROLLERS OF DAYTON, TENNESSEE, CHOSE THE WEEK OF THE evolution trial for their revival time. "The sin down there in the valley must be wiped out by the glory of the Lamb," said the Rollers.

The Holy Rollers of Dayton have no church. God frowns upon money, they say, and the contractors and carpenters of Dayton refuse to put stone and mortar together without money. The Holy Rollers, therefore, found their "arbor church" on Shin Bone Ridge—two massive elm trees, their huge limbs swollen and cracked with age, their leaves interlacing. Rough wooden benches semi-circled the elms. And crude teapots with fat white wicks crammed into their snouts blew opal flame into the silver of the moonlit night. Night things all about. The screech of the bobcat. The wail of the whippoorwill. A whir of bats' wings, and the staccato of insects. The great mountains like black-robed Druids keeping watch over their own.

The Holy Rollers, a hundred or more, sat on the benches and on the dew-wet grass. Curious folks from the town came to their cars and sat and listened. A deputy sheriff with his pink-dressed girl—sometimes there is trouble.

"Folks, we's only got'n three books an' they ain't all aliken but we can holler somehow," said Preacher Joe Leffew, clad in blue shirt, torn across the back, showing his sun-bronzed flesh, with torn blue overalls reeking of the mule team. The hymn rolled out. A hymn thunderous with rhythm. There was a stamping of bare and hobnailed feet, a swaying of bodies, old men and old women, girls and boys and little children.

> We ain't goin' to sin any more, Lamb,
> We ain't goin' to sin any more, God,
> We's all goin' to glory, God,
> And wash in the blood of the Lamb.

The song became a dirge and the dirge became a fiendish thing, rising in howls and wails and moanings that stilled the wild things of the night.

Preacher Joe Leffew preached. "Some folks thinks as how as we-uns are funny people. They come here, poor sinners that they are, to mock an' revile us. Here's our word of Scripture. 'An' Christ reeled to an' fro, as a drunken man.' Now, children, dear children, some folks think that means the Lamb was a drunkard. T'aint so at all. It says 'as a drunken man.' You cain't tell me God's son ever went home all soused up."

Preacher Joe Leffew assailed education. "I ain't got no learnin' an' never had none," said Preacher Joe Leffew. "Glory be to the Lamb! Some folks work their hands off'n up 'n to the elbows to give their young-uns education, and all they do is send their young-uns to hell."

"Glory to His name," shouted the huddled figures, misty-gray in the night damp.

"I ain't let no newspaper in my cabin for nigh unto a year since the Lord bathed me in His blood," said Preacher Leffew.

"Glory to the Lamb," wailed the chorus of the saved.

"I never sinned enough to look in one of these here almanacs."

"Praise His name," wailed the chorus of the saved.

"I've got eight young-uns in the cabin and three in glory, and I know they're in glory because I never learned 'em nothin'."

"Glory to the Lord," wailed the chorus of the saved.

"I've gotta team of good mules and a wagon an' that's all I have got, but I'd give 'em away tomorrow for more of this good old-time religion."

"Praise God," thundered the chorus of the saved.

Testifying began. An old woman of seventy, her gray hairs straggling over her lean, sun-bronzed face. Hands at her hips, she paced the circle hemmed in by wooden benches. She twisted her sharp-boned old body into gyrations, touched the ground, shrieked and moaned. Ma Ferguson "speaks with tongues" and testifies with strange and stirring words.

"We cain't repine on no flow'ry beds of ease," said Ma Ferguson. "We gotta save the daughters—gotta save their bodies—gotta stop fornycation."

"Glory to God," wailed the chorus of the saved.

A group of calico-gowned mountain women came forward, each about to bring one more potential Holy Roller into this vale of grief and woe, each carrying an infant in her lean, bronzed arms. Like a Greek chorus in the hollow of the night they moaned and swayed and cried together, rocking their babies in rhythm with their "speech of tongues." The hard, dry years that sap the living juice from the bodies of mountain women had leathered their faces. The strange light of a vision was in their eyes. They dropped their little bundles of baby flesh. The moon was high now. Blue and silver and amber it dripped light through the elm leaves. The mountain women dropped to the ground. They clutched hands and kicked and frothed and moaned: "Gotta save the daughters—gotta save their bodies—gotta save their bodies——"

Again the preacher, his eyes popping out like blue marbles, his shock of corn-colored hair on end, preached. He dragged a bench from the outer circle into the central hollow. "Come, sinners," he implored, "come to the moaning bench."

Song after song was wailed in the hollow of the night.

> From the manger to the cross,
> Not a moment's time was lost.

Drama. A spurt of orange. A girl's shrill treble laugh dying into a hoarse sob. A girl of sixteen in a flaming sport dress had thrown herself, a little huddled heap, upon the bench. Her hands dug into the dirt of the ground. Sobs wrenched her. Her voice was piping and shrill. "Jesus, save me; God, help me; Christ, come to me."

The "saved" surrounded her. Ma Ferguson bent her white hairs over the bench, an arm about the sobbing girl. The mountain women huddled about her. Preacher Leffew stroked her white arm: "Save her from fornycation, God; Jesus, put Your mark upon her."

Hour after hour passed, the treble piping was hoarse. Midnight—and the Holy Rollers, damp and limp with exhaustion, lay flung out upon the grass.

27. "EVERY DAY IN EVERY WAY . . ."

During 1922 thousands of Americans were repeating to themselves: "Every day in every way I'm getting better and better." This thumbnail distillation of the thought of Emile Coué, a French pharmacist, took the country by storm. Couéism was scarcely a religion, compounded though it was from some of the doctrines of Christian Science, the Emmanuel Movement, and psychology. But Coué's insistence that the body, mind, and spirit were a unity, and that all could be rehabilitated and perfected through the power of the mind, had religious overtones. And the widespread appeal of this simple self-help doctrine indicated a mass dissatisfaction with the old theology and with the contemporary church. Throughout the decade scarcely a popular religious or quasi-religious movement emphasized either dogma or creed. The following description of Coué and his works by Lyman P. Powell, "Coué: An Estimate and a Comparison," appeared in *The American Review of Reviews,* December 1922, pp. 622-3.

EAST AND WEST THROUGH ALL THE CENTURIES, MEN HAVE BEEN DEMONstrating the quaint verse of Spenser:

"For of the soule, the bodie forme doth take,
For soul is forme, and doth the bodie make."

To this idea Mrs. Eddy gave new impetus. Dr. Worcester, a distinguished Boston preacher, related it both to the historic Christian Church and to scientific medicine. Mr. Hickson, not reckoning with the doctors, came over here five years ago, after a plain man's life in England, and, Bishop Manning said the other day, "gave spiritual help to thousands."

Now Emile Coué is coming, and it looks as though he will be praised and dispraised more than any recent predecessor. Who is this Monsieur Coué? Some aged men still recall the daring Charcot, at Nancy, first to put mental healing on the Continental map, at a time when throughout

Europe mental healers, of one type or another, were doing work of more than local interest.

Coué began modestly. When Liébault and Bernheim were at their best, Coué sat at their feet, an eager student, young, impressionable, winsome, learning how, while he was also independently earning daily bread. His life story would occupy few lines in any Who's Who. He came of humble parentage, and his profession is that of a pharmacist. Like P. P. Quimby—one of whose patients was Mary Baker Eddy, in 1862—nobody ever heard of him till he began his healing work. When Christian Science, New Thought, Emmanuel Movement, and other expressions of drugless healing, were getting under way, Coué made a study of them and at the same time delved deep into psychoanalysis. By 1910 Coué had his New Nancy School going. When the Great War exploded, more than one hundred persons daily were crowding to his clinic, and he was averaging 40,000 consultations every year.

Down to Paris, bruised but still triumphant, Coué took his way in October, 1919, and soon found himself a national celebrity. Last winter in England, for a time at least, he seemed to share public interest with Lloyd George, appeared to help many besides Lady Curzon, and evoked some medical derision summed up in our own *Journal of the American Medical Association* as the purveying of "cloudy stuff."

Back of all his voluble explanations of his methods, is an asset one patient has called "a strong and smiling goodness." Just to see him, just to hear him give assurance with that smile which never seems to leave his face, makes many a sick person better. In fact, the personality of an Osler, a Dubois, a Bastianelli, is often half the battle.

But what after all are the ideas and the methods of this newest champion in the lists of human ailments? Every healer seems constrained to develop his own theory and methods, though as Professor Goddard long since indicated, and the new President of Colgate intimated, all get about the same results. Monsieur Coué is an opportunist. With Bergson's star in the ascendant like William James's star a while ago, Coué takes into account Bergson's distinction between intelligence and intuition, and makes the most of intuition, asserting that "We possess within us a force of incalculable power, which, when we handle it unconsciously, is often prejudicial to us. If, on the contrary, we direct it in a conscious and wise manner, it gives us the mastery of ourselves and allows us not only to escape and to aid others to escape from physical and mental ills, but also to live in relative happiness, whatever the conditions in which we find ourselves."

This unconscious self he considers the general guide of all our bodily functions. Since the will is often misused or misuses us, Coué—like Gerald Stanley Lee in another field—substitutes and cultivates and if necessary re-educates the imagination. "If you can persuade yourself that you can do a certain thing, provided it is possible, you will do it, however difficult it may be." Thus Coué sets the imagination off against the will, and uses imagination through what he calls "self-mastery through conscious autosuggestion."

So many from America and England have visited Nancy that to describe Couéism in operation is not difficult. Mrs. Kirk has just written a whole book of her experiences there last summer. One naturally gets to the clinic early in the morning. Even then the rooms reserved for treatment are likely to be overcrowded. As old Agnew in the days of Garfield always took immediate command of every situation, so Coué opens up his battery without explanation or delay. To the nervous invalid, with compelling cheerfulness, Coué smilingly remarks: "You have been sowing bad seed in your Unconscious; now you will sow good seed." An excitable and overworked woman deluging him with her troubles, Coué interrupts with the sensible comment: "You think too much about your ills." To a former patient who failed to report improvement, Coué remarked: "You must put your trust in the imagination, not in the will." To a blacksmith with a disabled arm, Coué with authority ringing through his voice said, "For ten years you have been thinking you could not lift your arm above your shoulder. . . . Now think 'I can lift it.' Quick! Think I can, I can!" A gentle stroke of the shoulder, a final authoritative word from Coué, and whispering to himself, "I can, I can," the blacksmith went back to his anvil—and work.

But Coué never forgets that body, mind and spirit are a unity, and while treating the specific ill, he deals with ills in general already making trouble for the patient or ever likely to make trouble. He denies that he does more than teach the patient how to help himself by conscious self-suggestion. "We are what we make ourselves and not what circumstances make us," is his favorite expression. Autosuggestion, properly exercised, he is sure will bring "a progressive improvement which little by little transforms itself into a complete cure, when that is possible."

In the same low monotonous voice heard these years past in Dubois' clinic at Bern, in Lloyd Tuckey's hypnotic suggestions in London, in Worcester's induced relaxations in Boston, Coué in his sunny rooms at Nancy, with the birds trilling through the windows and the leaves a-rustling, reinforces the patient's self-suggestions, and also tries to cure the entire personality. Not even structural lesions, before which doctors stand in pause, make him hesitate. He sends his patients home to sing by day and night:

> "Day by day, in every way,
> I am getting better and better."

Monsieur Coué will find a hearty welcome next month in America. Like Mr. Hickson he will do much good. Comparatively few will underestimate his healing powers; for some men have such powers. But he will have to run the gauntlet. Christian Science has besides its cures a serene solidarity, a host of Bible readers, and an organization so effective that in hotels and railway stations everywhere I find the Christian Science literature. In spirit at least, the Emmanuel Movement has certainly returned, and many ministers are following its principle of adding religion to suggestion—auto and hetero—and also deferring to the doctor and strengthening his hands. The action of the Lambeth Conference has been buttressed by the Episcopal Convention, held last September in Portland, Oregon, which appointed a commission to give further careful study to drugless healing, recognized that "special gifts" of healing do exist, authorized such clergy as their Bishop may approve to exercise the same, and very wisely provided for the inclusion of three physicians in the commission.

How does Couéism differ from other movements of a somewhat similar nature? Except in terminology there is no substantial difference. "Each in his separate star," every healer seems to get results. The functional furnishes the most inviting opportunities; but there are organic cases credibly reported to have been improved or cured.

"There's a long, long trail a winding" back to those pre-Christian days when Socrates remarked to Charmides, "there is no cure for the body apart from the soul"; and Monsieur Coué is simply latest in the line. Jesus worked wonders and then promised his Disciples that "greater things than these shall ye do." When Christian Science was under fire some fifteen years ago, and the Emmanuel Movement some thought would divert attention from regular parochial routine, Freud and Breuer opened a new doorway they called psychoanalysis into self-help by suggestion. But "all roads lead to Rome," and though Monsieur Coué points to a new one, which many certainly have already followed and found help, he merely illustrates Victor Daley's words——

> "There is nothing but the human
> Touch can heal the human woe."

Monsieur Coué is doing the same good work many others have been doing. Being human, he has extemporized his own vocabulary, though borrowing from various sources. If on his visit to us he can help more, ill of soul or mind or body, who are we to say he shall not use the terminology he prefers?

28. HEAVEN IN A SILK HAT

The religious and semi-religious inventions of the Twenties were not confined to the masses or to the socially lowly. Buchmanism, later to be known as the Oxford Movement, and still later Moral Rearmament, was aimed at the educated and wealthy, in particular, the undergraduates of the smarter eastern colleges and universities. Frank Buchman, a one-time Lutheran minister, left the uncongenial climate of North Dakota in the mid-Twenties for the Atlantic seaboard where groups of his followers were soon found at Princeton, Harvard, and Yale. The movement rapidly spread to Britain and the continent, especially after it broadened its message to include more mature people. Buchmanism paid scant regard to either religious dogma or ritual. Mainly, it relied upon "God guidance" which the individual secured by "spiritual silence," a time alone to talk with God, and by a process which the initiates called "washing out." The latter was effected through group confession at the famous house-parties by which Buchman's followers spread his doctrines. The group confessionals inspired much prurient gossip about the house-parties, but the meetings seemed to inspire the insiders with an extraordinary zeal. The following account of a Buchmanite house-party, "A Religious House-Party," by Kenneth Irving Brown was published in *The Outlook,* January 7, 1925, p. 27.

THE METHOD EMPLOYED BY MR. BUCHMAN IS THAT OF GATHERING TOGETHER for a week-end house-party men and women (sometimes both, sometimes men or women) who are willing to give a few days to quiet thought and discussion of religion. Religious house-parties! Religious house-parties which college men from Princeton, Yale, Williams, and Harvard, girls from Vassar and Smith, debutantes from Baltimore and Boston, and stranger-guests of all ages and from many States have attended!

I know of few things harder to describe with accuracy and fairness than one of these gatherings. Men who have attended them have told me how impossible it is to give to another a reasonably truthful picture and impression of the party; and the result is that a flock of wild rumors have risen and multiplied until today there are some who profess to believe that the parties are orgies of sex stories or prolonged cases of hysteria, and that the total influence of the movement is pernicious. These rumors have, I believe, been spread by those who, knowing the work only at second hand—for they refuse to investigate it for themselves—have consciously or unconsciously misrepresented facts, or drawn conclusions on isolated examples. The methods employed by Mr. Buchman and his leaders have in some cases brought unwholesome results, but it is manifestly unfair to emphasize these to the exclusion of the hundreds of cases of men and women who through Mr. Buchman's help have renewed those contacts which are the heart of religion. Inasmuch as these house-parties are so difficult to describe, may I take the liberty of setting down in addition to my observations my personal impressions of the one which I visited?

The first house-party for Harvard men was held in March of last year, and so popular did it prove that five others were arranged near Boston, before the end of the academic year, to which Harvard men were among those invited. I was eager to check the curious stories of approbation and disapprobation which had reached me, and accepted with alacrity an invitation to spend the first week-end of April at South Natick, a tiny beauty-spot near Wellesley, easy of access from Boston.

I had been reading Mr. Sedgwick's thoughtful volume, "Pro Vita Monastica," and the promise of a few days away from the hurry of "academic leisure," days free for deeper thoughts than most days seem to allow, pleased me. I journeyed with two Harvard graduate students to the South Natick Inn, and we laughed as we signed the register of "wandering scholars in search of religion." Above the signatures some one had written of the house-party these words:

> An effort to get people to think along right lines, to lead a constructive rather than an aimless and selfish existence, and achieve victory over one's self, to get contact with God, to help America and help the world.

The guests at the house-party gathered at dinner on Friday evening, some thirty-five in number. There were additions and subtractions during the following days, but the number remained substantially the same. After dinner word was passed that there would be a meeting in the parlor of the Inn at seven-thirty, for those guests who might care to come. Everything was most informal, and at no time was any attempt at coercion made. We gathered—Harvard undergraduates and graduate students, Worcester business men, a vestryman from St. Thomas's Church in New York, a professor of theology, and a freshman from Bowdoin—crowding in circles about the fireplace. Until eleven we sat there, while a few of the leaders spoke informally of the purpose of the party, and each member of the group briefly introduced himself. We were asked to give our names and addresses and our reasons for coming. One poor man, less well informed than the rest, had the notion gained from the name of the leader that he was getting into a literary gathering, but he hastened to add: "I like what you're doing, and I'll stay." Curiosity, interest, boredom with college, skepticism of the movement—all of these were reasons offered, but curiously the prevailing reason given was that "my roommate Jack went on a house-party a month ago, and came back with something he didn't have when he went. I want to know what it is"; or, "My friend So-and-so has a power in his life which makes mine seem poor in comparison; and he says it's religion. I doubt it, but I've come to see."

Humor? There was humor aplenty, and the group was entertained hugely by stories of the various members—but they were discussing religion, discussing it with all the ease and humor and naturalness with which they might have discussed the coming election. That was the miracle: no feeling of something uncanny, no conscious emotional exhilaration, no pious solemnity, but perfect naturalness.

That, I suppose, is why we find it hard to describe a religious houseparty, for we Americans except in moments extraordinary do not speak our innermost thoughts; and when we discuss religion we put forth frantic efforts to keep the discussion impersonal. Like the Samaritan woman at the well, we are prone to raise theological questions when religious discussion touches the intimate places of our lives. But these students and business men were discussing religion very personally, for their "I's" were searching.

When the first evening gathering broke up, the men divided themselves into small groups and wandered off into the night. I went with three others, and I can still clearly recall the quiet of that walk as we discussed what had taken place and recognized that something admirable which certain, at least, of the leaders possessed.

The programme of the second day called for a "quiet time" at eight o'clock, for those, again, who cared to come, "a quiet time in which God can say, 'Hello!'" "Spiritual silence" is one of the major points in Frank Buchman's endeavor—time alone with God. He delights to tell of a post-card sent him during the war with the picture of a donkey and this caption: "Man has two ears and one mouth; therefore let him hear twice as much as he says." Mr. Buchman's criticism of our prayers is that they are one-sided; we tell God what we desire, and then leave for the day without offering him a chance to speak his will for us. It is Mr. Buchman's purpose to begin each morning with an hour of silence that he may "get his orders for the day." Whether we explain this experience as the direct intervention of Deity or, resorting to psychology, as the action of our own subconscious selves, such meditation, if regularly and sincerely practiced, brings its spiritual enrichment.

An academic appointment called me back to Cambridge, so that I missed the group and the morning meeting. I returned soon after luncheon only to find the Inn empty; the men were out on the river canoeing, or up in the hills hiking. About four o'clock they drifted back for the afternoon group. That was a story-telling meeting (although stories were absent at none of the meetings), with several of the leaders giving the best bits of their experience as to how God had used men to enrich other men's lives. One of our most puzzling questions today is how can men know the will of God; throughout the gathering the story-tellers were pointing out the way by which they, as well as other men, had found answers to this question.

Mr. Buchman opened the evening meeting with the emphasis on the value of sharing experiences—the so-called "Confessional Meeting." No other part of Mr. Buchman's programme has received quite so much adverse criticism, nor been so misrepresented, if it is fair to judge from the knowledge of a single house-party. "Sin," says Mr. Buchman, "is anything which keeps us from God or from the other fellow." It may be something heinous, or it may be something comparatively trivial, such as intellectual pride or a "play-it-safe conservatism," but in any case until it is recognized and banished the full stature of personality can never be gained. One aid toward banishing it is to bring it out into the open—that is, to "share" it with another.

There was no morbidity in the conversational talks of the evening; I felt no emotional pressure, although I was keenly moved by certain things which were said. It was an exchange of experiences for mutual benefit, and I for one profited by the experiences of those who spoke. And yet I am aware of the dangers courted by such methods. Those who speak need to guard against that feeling of self-righteousness which is so likely to follow public confession, as well as against interpreting the sense of relief which comes with disclosure as satisfactory restitution or forgiveness. But the meeting was valuable for whetting one's consciousness of sin—understanding by sin anything which hurts life. There was for many of us a clearer recognition of the little gray-hued acts which we do so often without question or thought. Often the matters mentioned were seemingly inconsequential. One student from the Cambridge Episcopal Theological School was bothered by a small custom tax evaded by having some vestments intended for personal use sent to the church; another student was troubled for handing in a review of a book which he had only partially examined. In other cases there were graver sins confessed, sins of the flesh; but again there was no pressure brought to bear upon any one to mention that which he felt should not be told.

One young law student said: "I am in no sense conscious of sin. I came through the custom offices a while ago and undervalued my luggage. It seemed to me a good trick, and I still admire it. Is something wrong with me?" No attempt was made in the open group to answer his question, but we all admired his candor.

Here was a spiritual clinic; here were men interested in learning the A B C's of religion. For the Protestant there is no infallible Church; and for an increasing number of Protestants there is no infallible Bible. God speaks to the individual, but how can he be heard unless the individual listens? It is Mr. Buchman's belief that in moments of quiet "luminous thoughts," "dynamic thoughts," "hunches" (he calls them by all these names), come, offering specific guidance for the day. Each thought he would check whenever possible by conference with others or by the daily happenings of life, that he may not act without judgment. "No hunch is a hunch from God unless it is a good hunch." That is the meaning of the phrase "God-guidance."

The afternoon and evening meetings were likewise studies in a spiritual technique. And with the close of the evening group came the end of the house-party. It was as strangers that we gathered, but it was as friends that we parted. Some had come a little contemptuous, others skeptical, and still others with nothing but a conventional religion. But we separated, as a Princetonian has written of a later house-party—

> with the odor of the supernatural lingering in our nostrils, many with a new kind of faith and a new kind of peace, and everybody with the sub- dued feeling which usually accompanies a great cascade of new knowledge about yourself, of realization that there are more things in heaven and earth, Horatio—

I have tried to describe very simply what I observed at the house-party and to offer some personal impressions. I have left unsaid things which might have been said, for criticism comes temptingly easy when one speaks of the matters of the spirit, and Mr. Buchman would, I know, be the first to recognize that his methods are fallible and that his work has been marred by mistakes. To me the house-party was a very vital, constructive force; I shall not soon forget the days of its fellowship; but for myself (and in this I know I am voicing the sentiment of others who were at the South Natick Inn) I crave a larger expression of reason, a more conscious union of intellect and the desirable "mystic experi- ence." . . .

29. SISTER AIMEE AND THE FOUR SQUARE GOSPEL

One of the most amazing religious phenomena of the Twenties was the spectacular rise of Aimee Semple McPherson and her Four Square Gospel. Aimee came from Kansas to California after having been a school teacher, a carnival side show barker, and a missionary. She arrived in Los Angeles, a divorcee with two children, unknown and without money. But within five years she had organized her own religious move- ment supported by thirty thousand members whose contributions built an enormous temple from which numerous evangelists went out to spread the movement along the West Coast and to the Middle West.

From the start to the end of her career Aimee was almost constantly in the newspaper headlines, her most newsworthy incident involving her disappearance while on the beach. She turned up thirty days later in the desert with the implausible story that she had been drugged and kidnapped. But it is doubtful whether such sensationalism was the principal reason for the rapid growth of her following. Her religion was light on theology but heavy on hope and the helping hand. A mixture of showmanship, sensuality, and faith healing, her "religious productions" were calculated to appeal to transplanted Mid-westerners and Southerners, alone and bewildered in the Los Angeles urban complex. The following articles describe a "sermon in the temple" and the essence of her preaching. The first article, "Vaudeville at Angelus Temple," by Shelton Bissell, appeared in *The Outlook*, May 23, 1928, p. 126.

TAKE THE EDENDALE CAR OUT OF LOS ANGELES SOME SUNDAY AFTERNOON toward five o'clock. Ride for a bit less than a half-hour and alight at Echo Park. Here are much shade, cool green water, pleasant grassy glades, and, beyond and above it all, looming stark, ugly, bloated, a huge gray concrete excrescence on this delightful bit of nature. It is Angelus Temple, citadel of Aimee Semple McPherson and the Four-Square Gospel.

At 6:15 the doors swing open. The Temple holds 5,300, and probably one-fourth of that number are in line at this time. Within fifteen minutes the huge auditorium with its two flaring balconies is completely filled. The interior is plain, the stained-glass windows garish, but the lighting is adequate, the opera chairs restful after your long stand in line, and the ventilation through scores of doors and transoms is satisfactory. The platform is arranged for an orchestra of fifty, and the "throne" of "Sister" McPherson on a dais just below the high organ loft, softly bathed in creamy light from overhead electrics. Behind the "throne" is a shell of flowers and greenery. The musicians, mostly young and all volunteers, come in at 6:30.

The service proper will not begin until seven, but with the entrance of the band it is seen that not a seat is vacant, and that hundreds are standing at the doors. When it is remembered that this is only a usual, unadvertised—Aimee carries no church notice in the dailies—Sunday night service, repeated fifty-two times in the year, it will be seen that here we have a phenomenon almost, if not quite, unique in American church life. We are reminded also that this is "Radio KFSG" by two microphones.

For half an hour the band dispenses such familiar secular and quasi-religious selections as Sousa's "Washington Post," Sullivan's "Lost Chord," a waltz-time arrangement of "Mighty Lak a Rose," and a crashing number, announced by the leader as "Radiant Morn March." After each selection there is loud applause. But the performance must at least be tagged as dedicated to the Lord, so at the sound of an electric bell two uniformed young women workers appear on the platform with a banner, "Silent Prayer." Instantly the musicians kneel, a hush falls upon the thousands, and in utter stillness the great throng sits for the space of thirty seconds. Then the bell rings again, the banner is quickly removed, and the band bursts into a lively waltz tune.

Now, at five minutes to seven, the vested choir, half a hundred strong, enters from either side. There is a moment of tension and hushed expectancy. All is in readiness. The dramatic has surely not been neglected by this super-dramatist. Audience, workers, band, choir, even microphones—all are here. But the throne is still empty, bathed in its soft light. Suddenly through a door far up on the wall, opening out on her private grounds, appears Mrs. McPherson. She is clad in white, with a dark cloak thrown loosely around her shoulders; her rich auburn hair, with its flowing permanent wave, is heaped high on her head. In her left arm she carries a bouquet of roses and lilies of the valley, artfully planned to illustrate a point in her sermon (Canticles ii. 1), a description ignorantly applied by her to Jesus; on her face is the characteristic expansive, radiant McPherson smile. She is a beautiful woman, seen from the auditorium, with the soft spotlight shining upon her. Let no man venture to deny it. And, in fact, no man will. The writer has seen screen beauties in his day, and confesses to a slight clutch of the heart as he watched her superb entrance. Assisted to her "throne," she gracefully seats herself, turns to her audience—and her microphone—and is ready to begin.

Of the almost bewildering program which followed there is time and space to say little. The singing was stupendous, cataclysmic, overwhelming. "Jesus, Saviour, Pilot Me," "Stand Up, Stand Up for Jesus," "Rock of Ages," and other favorites followed in swift succession, a stanza or two of each. The more than five thousand voices so filled the temple that the ear-drums were bruised and beaten by the thunderous concussion. "Sister" led with voice and waving arm, though she had choir and organ and trumpeters behind and around her. It is her service, let no man forget that. Not for one moment does she drop the reins. The handshaking, sandwiched in between two hymns, was a clever device to create the illusion that all—sinners, saints, workers, mere spectators—are one huge happy family.

"Every one take the hand of five others all around, in front and in back," shouts the beaming Aimee.

Humming confusion with laughter and motion follow, while the five thousand stand up and stretch. The choir then sings, and sings gloriously, the composition of California's own Charles Wakefield Cadman, "The Builders." Little children file onto the stage, and they sing, too—sing so that all in the temple can hear every word, sing as I have never heard a dozen little tots sing in all my life. And the silent radio catches every note and flings it out to listening thousands. Then Aimee prays, a prayer liberally splashed with "Amens" from the crowd. A small boy, eleven years old, enlivens the occasion by playing on a guitar "made of solid silver," as "Sister" radiantly announces. Only one short encore is allowed the enraptured audience, which applauds until Aimee holds up her hand. Much is coming yet, and the time element bulks large. Mrs. McPherson carries a watch, and she never forgets to look at it.

Next, the audience must judge between the comparative merits of some songs written by workers in the Temple, and sung lustily to different popular tunes, such as "There's a Long, Long Trail" and "Tramp, Tramp, Tramp, the Boys Are Marching." A stereopticon flashes the words on a big bare spot on the left-hand wall, where all can see. Winning words, in the estimation of the crowd, judged by the volume of applause, began thus,

> I was loaded down with sin,
> But my Saviour took me in.

They were sung to "Tramp, Tramp," and it was easy to see that they would be a prime favorite in the Temple thereafter. The prize-winner was called to the platform, and there graciously presented with her reward by Aimee herself. After a rather humorous song by the Male Four-Square Quartet and a piano solo ending with a tremendous crash of all the keys within reach, the platform was cleared for a wedding. The big organ boomed forth the stately chords of the "Lohengrin" march, and the wedding party was discerned crawling at a snail's pace up the long, long aisles. Attention was divided between the procession and the superb figure standing before her "throne" waiting their arrival. Two Temple workers were to be made one and sent forth to preach in a branch of the Four-Square Gospel. Being an ordained minister, "Sister" performed the ceremony, using the full Episcopal service, slipping and faltering once or twice as she read the words.

The microphone is very close here, for the grandmother of the little bride is listening in at Albuquerque, New Mexico, and after the service, which is concluded with a loud "Salute the bride" from Aimee and a shower of rice raining down from the laughing men and women in the choir, "Sister" lifts the microphone and in dulcet tones calls greetings to the listening grandmother.

And now she announces, "The offering will be taken," and is so busy giving orders to her handsome young major-domo at her side that she almost forgets such a minor matter as the prayer over the plates held patiently by the dozen ushers, until the oversight is hurriedly rectified by "Lord, accept the offering we have brought. Amen." The collection is not a copper or even a silver one predominantly. Many bills are heaped in the baskets, for Mrs. McPherson preaches the alabaster box of costly ointment more frequently than the widow's mite, and her followers are all tithers, to the last individual.

"Open all the windows, all the doors," commands "Sister." "We have a rule in the Temple that no one shall leave during the sermon, under any circumstance. I become utterly helpless if there is any motion before me. No one must stir. The ushers will enforce this, please."

Smilingly said, but the tone is that of Napoleon before battle. All settle down as the lights are lowered, and the sermon, the climax of this astonishing religious vaudeville, begins.

Aimee preaches with a beautiful white leather Bible in her right hand. The book is open, and the leaves of her sermon are within it. She is rather closely bound to her notes, yet so deftly does she handle them that it almost seems as though she were preaching extempore. The sermon, from the theme "What Think Ye of Christ?" is crude, rambling, now and then artfully self-laudatory, a handful of proof-texts loosely strung together with commonplace illustrations. Summoning fanciful figures to her side with a vigorous hand-clap, she conducts a court of inquisition. Builder, banker, jeweler, architect, politician, schoolboy—on they come in fancy, with many others, and each is asked the question, "What think ye of Christ?" to be answered with an ecstatically uttered text of Scripture. "He is the door," said the builder. "The pearl of great price," said the banker. "The Prince of Peace," said the statesman. "The rose of Sharon and the lily of the valley," said the florist—it was here that Aimee's bouquet made effective entrance. Even the grocer had to bear his testimony, for Jesus was to him "the fuller's soap." With illustrations, almost all of them more or less improbable, these gentlemen with their testimonies were homiletically strung together. But it was reserved to the schoolboy to make the hit of the evening.

"Schoolboy," shouted Aimee, summoning him with a clap of her hand from the aisles of memory, "what think YE of Christ?"

"Oh, he is the elder brother!"

"Yes," shouts "Sister," "he is. See the poor little schoolboy going home from school. Behind that tree lurks a big, blustering bully. He pounces on the little boy and pummels him. But down the road comes the elder brother on a bicycle. He leaps on the bully, and has him down; he rubs his face in the dirt." The action is graphically illustrated by Aimee, and greeted by the excited laughter of the thousands. "He saves the schoolboy. Amen." "Amen," is echoed by all. "Oh, how often have I been like that schoolboy," she goes on, a note of pathos creeping into her voice. "No husband, no father, no brother—all alone in the world. The big bully, the devil, has me down, He is pummeling poor Sister. But suddenly down the road, on his bicycle of love and grace, comes the Lord Jesus Christ. Praise the Lord! He rescues me." Fervent ejaculations from her auditors.

It was hopeless as a sermon, but it was consummate preaching. She knew her audience. She knew what she was after, and she got it. She is a superb actress. Her rather harsh and unmelodious voice has yet a modulation of pitch which redeems it from utter disagreeableness. To her carefully manicured and polished finger-tips she is dramatic. In her pose, her gesture, her facial expression, her lifted eyebrows, her scintillating smile, her pathetic frown, Aimee is a perfect exponent of the art of how to say a platitude and delude her hearers into thinking that it is a brand-new truth, just minted by her. She sweeps her audience as easily as the harpist close beside her sweeps the wires in soft broken chords while she preaches. And not for one instant of time is Mrs. McPherson unmindful of that great unseen listening multitude "on the air." She moves the microphone from time to time. She rests her hand lovingly upon it. She never shifts her position one step away from it. All her climaxes are enhanced to the listening thousands throughout southern California and near-by States who regularly "tune-in" on Sunday nights. Radio KFSG is as dear to her as the five thousand and more in Angelus Temple.

At 9:25 to the dot the converts fill the platform. Just why they come is a question. But they are there, waiting for " 'Sister' to pray for them."

"Here they come, from all sides; down from the top gallery, up the aisles, here they come," she almost screams through the microphone. (There were perhaps thirty-five out of an audience of 5,500.) But each convert was guided and supported by a personal worker who seemed to spring from the ground by magic the instant a hand was raised. How many remained and sought baptism after being lifted by Aimee to the throne of grace is not known. Doubtless none slipped through the net who could be kept.

At 9:30 to the second she dismisses the multitude with the benediction, inviting all "first-niters" to stay and be shown around the Temple by official guides; to see the commissary department with its store of food and clothing for the destitute to whom the Temple ministers, the carpenter shop where are made the "sets" with which Aimee frequently garnishes her evening performances and the school where more than a thousand students are taught McPhersonism and the Four-Square Gospel, to go out later as evangelists. But it is over three hours since most of those present seated themselves in the opera chairs, and three hours is longer than any church audience in America save Aimee's can be held together night after night.

The vast concourse swarms to the street. Scores of waiting electric cars take all swiftly back to the big city, swallowing up this tiny leaven of 5,500 in a garish, blatant, heedless lump of over a million souls.

What shall be said? Aimee is Aimee, and there is none like her. A religious message utterly devoid of sound thinking, loose and insubstantial in its construction, preposterously inadequate in its social implications, but amazingly successful after five years of running, and still going strong, judging from statistics, the infallible appeal of churchmen. No American evangelist of large enough caliber to be termed National has ever sailed with such insufficient mental ballast. The power of McPhersonism resides in the personality of Mrs. McPherson. The woman is everything; the evangel nothing. There is no way to understand how a jejune and arid pulpit output has become a dynamic of literally National proportions but to hear and see the woman. To visit Angelus Temple, the home of the Four-Square Gospel, is to go on a sensuous debauch served up in the name of religion.

● ● ● ● ●

This analysis of the appeal of Aimee Semple McPherson's Four Square Gospel is from Morrow Mayo, "Aimee Rises from the Sea," *The New Republic,* December 25, 1929, p. 136.

. . . SISTER SUBSTITUTED THE GOSPEL OF LOVE FOR THE GOSPEL OF FEAR. This doctrine was as strange in Southern California as it is elsewhere in Christendom. No ambassador of Christ in that section had ever thought of it until she introduced it; the others had rejected it at once on principle. Sister substituted the cheerfulness of the play-room for the gloom of the morgue. She threw out the dirges and threats of Hell, replacing them with jazz hymns and promises of Glory. The gospel she created was and is an ideal bed-time story. It has a pretty color, a sweet taste, and is easy for the patients to take. She threatens nothing; she promises everything.

Plagiarizing from the Salvation Army, Aimee built Angelus Temple on that great question: "Are You Washed in the Blood of the Lamb?" But Sister went the Army one better. She not only propounded the poser; she answered it. She assured her customers that they were. Next, she invented the Four-Square Gospel. This is a trade-name, based on the supposition that Heaven is surrounded by four walls. Mrs. McPherson describes the Holy City literally—the jewelled walls, pearly gates, golden streets, milk and honey. She says she is not sure—she is not *sure,* mind you—but she has a pretty good idea that Heaven will resemble a cross between Pasadena, California, and Washington, D. C. That will give an idea of what may be expected at Angelus Temple. The atmosphere bubbles over with love, joy, enthusiasm; the Temple is full of flowers, music, golden trumpets, red robes, angels, incense, nonsense and sex appeal. The service may be described as supernatural whoopee. It is balanced by the stronger medicine concocted and dispensed at the Gospel Lighthouse, Sister's third creation. The Lighthouses have been so successful that Sister now has them scattered throughout the United States. Here she introduced a Military Note—the Old Reliable!—with thrills and bold adventure. The Lighthouse was also built to a sure-fire theme-song: "Throw Out the Life Line!" The ladies of the chorus are clad in dapper uniforms so much like those of American Bluejackets that the Navy went to court in a vain effort to prevent Mrs. McPherson from be-littling the dignity of Our Boys. The typical Lighthouse service leads up to a Rescue. The grand finale shows a dozen nightgowned virgins cling-ing to the Rock of Ages, while the wind howls, the thunder roars, the lightning flashes and the waves beat about them. Sister—magnificent in an Admiral-General's uniform—directs the girlish sailors as they throw out the life line, while a corps of male Coast Guard workers for the Lord sweeps a prop sea with searchlights. The virgins are Saved; the curtain descends as the band crashes, the audience stands and cheers, and the American Flag waves triumphantly over all. In New York this spectacle would cost $6.60 in a hellish theatre, run by the Devil and Jake Shubert. Sister merely says: "Put your willing hand in your pocket, praise God, and bring out a five dollar bill!"

Divine healing was not, at first, one of Sister's accomplishments. But it was too tempting to leave to the lesser quacks; it came logically with time, observation and prayer. Sister, I understand, has cured cases of spinal meningitis and club feet. A doctor could never cure a veteran hypochondriac, for none would come within reach of any M. D. But he goes to Angelus Temple, and when Sister fixes him with her large elec-tric eyes, brushes his cheeks with her frankincensed mane, and lays her moist, warm palm upon him, he leaps to his feet, shouts "Glory to God!" and does a Paddock down the aisle: he is cured. He is cured as com-pletely as if he had sat on a red-hot stove, and without the pain.

FREEDOM FOR THE SECOND SEX

Women were one of the dominant forces supporting the reform era from 1900 to 1920, attempting to wipe out prostitution, abolish the saloon, and in general trying to raise the social standards of men to their own. After World War I, however, women sought less to change the other sex and concentrated on changing themselves. Prohibition came about in part because of the insistent demand of women. But with the Volstead Act women appeared in droves in the speakeasies and the new cocktail bars. As the "flapper"—the new woman of the post-war decade—changed her attitude toward the consumption of alcoholic beverages, so she also rapidly changed those pertaining to courtship, marriage, and the rearing of children, the knee length dress, beauty contests, and companionate marriages, all phenomena of the decade.

In essence the flapper of the Twenties demanded the same social freedom for herself that men enjoyed. Consequently she left home and asserted herself in the business world. As she became the major purchaser of consumer goods, whole new industries, such as the cosmetic and beauty industry, appeared. Other manufacturers frankly admitted designing their products to appeal to her feminine taste. Thus she became a major prop for the new mass consumer society.

Many defenders of the social status quo were aghast at the activities of the new woman and protested vigorously that they signaled the downfall of society. Most such people blamed the war for the revolution in the social code. But a more reasonable explanation lay probably in the new urbanism and the mass consumer society. At any rate, after the feminine revolution of the Twenties native culture was never again the same. The following documents attempt to indicate something of the nature of the vast changes made.

30. THE FLAPPER

The "flapper," as the young independently-minded woman of the early Twenties was called, was the subject of much discussion in the press, the pulpit, and periodicals. The following article, "Flapping Not Repented Of," *The New York Times,* July 16, 1922, discusses the nature of this new feminine type. Reprinted by permission of *The New York Times.*

OMAR SANG OF WINE, WOMEN, AND SONG WHEN THE WORLD WAS YOUNG enough to appreciate it, and children still willingly listened to fairy tales of Cinderella and Aladdin, a distant relative perchance of Omar himself. But the time came when the virtuously sophisticated world smiled indulgently at the parody of some witty person who changed the old saying to "Near Beer, Chickens, and Jazz."

. . . Then the war with its sundry excuses for self-sacrifice, bravery and courage—at least we, the future flappers, had the sheer audacity to name our fondest hopes in this way—came upon us and surrounded us all about.

Now with the peace slinking in through every loophole, we turn ourselves around to see just what has been happening. Peace. "Yes," say we who won our freedom in the slippery paths of war. "Peace." And the outcome of it all is the flapper. . . .

As an ex-flapper I'd like to say a word in her behalf. I who have tasted of the fruits of flappery and found them good—even nourishing—can look back and smile. The game was worth it. . . .

A flapper lives on encouragement, and only because these sweet, innocent boys try to go her one better does she resort to more stringent methods. . . .

Of course a flapper is proud of her nerve—she is not even afraid of calling it by its right name. She is shameless, selfish and honest, but at the same time she considers these three attributes virtues. Why not? She takes a man's point of view as her mother never could, and when she loses she is not afraid to admit defeat, whether it be a prime lover or $20 at auction.

. . . She can take a man—the man of the hour—at his face value, with no foolish promises that will need a disturbing and disagreeable breaking.

But here we must distinguish between the different types of flappers. There is the prep-school type—still a little crude. . . . She has not the finish of the college flapper who has learned to be soulful, virtuous on occasions and, under extreme circumstances, even highbrow. . . . But the after-prep and college girl emerges into something you can check up.

She will tell you where you stand in her catalogue, and if she wants you badly enough she will come out in the open and work for you with the same fresh and vigorous air that you would work to win her. She will never make you a hatband or knit you a necktie, but she'll drive you from the station hot Summer nights in her own little sport car. She'll don knickers and go skiing with you; or, if it happens to be Summer time, swimming; she'll dive as well as you, perhaps better; she'll dance as long as you care to, and she'll take everything you say the way you mean it, not getting "sore" as her older sister did when that "pious" older sister rested back seductively in the pretty green canoe with a pink parasol to keep off the healthy tan of the sun. Speaking of canoes, she may even quote poetry to you; not Indian love lyrics, but something about the peace conference or theology. . . .

After all, she checks up pretty squarely, doesn't she? Watch her five years from now and then be thankful that she will be the mother of the next generation, with the hypocrisy, fluff and other "hookum" worn entirely off. Her sharp points wear down remarkably well and leave a smooth polished surface. You'll be surprised at what a comfort that surface will be in the days to come!

31. PETTERS AND NECKERS

"Petting" and "necking" were two of the new terms coined to describe the new departures in courtship. The following article, an account of a summer conference of college women, indicates something of the revolution in the relations of the sexes that had taken place on the University campus. Beyond the comments upon the prevailing social code the author's remarks on the new classes of students coming to the average college campus are of special interest. The new consumer economy of the Twenties not only afforded automobiles to the masses, but also extended to them the possibility of a higher education. The extracts are from Eleanor Rowland Wembridge, "Petting and the Campus," *Survey*, July 1, 1925.

. . . LAST SUMMER I WAS AT A STUDENT CONFERENCE OF YOUNG WOMEN comprised of about eight hundred college girls from the middle western states. The subject of petting was very much on their minds, both as to what attitude they should take toward it with the younger girls, (being upperclassmen themselves) and also how much renunciation of this pleasurable pastime was required of them. If I recall correctly, two entire mornings were devoted to discussing the matter, two evenings, and another overflow meeting.

So far as I could judge from their discussion groups, the girls did not advise younger classmen not to pet—they merely advised them to be moderate about it, not lose their heads, not go too far—in fact the same line of conduct which is advised for moderate drinking. Learn temperance in petting, not abstinence.

Before the conference I made it my business to talk to as many college girls as possible. I consulted as many, both in groups and privately, as I had time for at the conference. And since it is all to be repeated in another state this summer, I have been doing so, when opportunity offered, ever since. Just what does petting consist in? What ages take it most seriously? Is it a factor in every party? Do "nice" girls do it, as well as those who are not so "nice"? Are they "stringing" their elders, by exaggerating the prevalence of petting, or is there more of it than they admit? These are samples of the questions I have asked, and have heard them ask each other in the discussions where I have listened in.

One fact is evident, that whether or not they pet, they hesitate to have anyone believe that they do not. It is distinctly the *mores* of the time to be considered as ardently sought after, and as not too priggish to respond. As one girl said—"I don't particularly care to be kissed by some of the fellows I know, but I'd let them do it any time rather than think I wouldn't dare. As a matter of fact, there are lots of fellows I don't kiss. It's the very young kids that never miss a chance."

That petting should lead to actual illicit relations between the petters was not advised nor countenanced among the girls with whom I discussed it. They drew the line quite sharply. That it often did so lead, they admitted, but they were not ready to allow that there were any more of such affairs than there had always been. School and college scandals, with their sudden departures and hasty marriages, have always existed to some extent, and they still do. But only accurate statistics, hard to arrive at, can prove whether or not the sex carelessness of the present day extends to an increase of sex immorality, or whether since so many more people go to college, there is an actual decrease in the amount of it, in proportion to the number of students. The girls seemed to feel that those who went too far were more fools than knaves, and that in most cases they married. They thought that hasty and secret marriages, of which most of them could report several, were foolish, but after all about as likely to turn out well as any others. Their attitude toward such contingencies was disapproval, but it was expressed with a slightly amused shrug, a shrug which one can imagine might have sat well on the shoulders of Voltaire. In fact the writer was torn, in her efforts to sum up their attitude, between classifying them as eighteenth century realists and as Greek nymphs existing before the dawn of history!

I sat with one pleasant college Amazon, a total stranger, beside a fountain in the park, while she asked if I saw any harm in her kissing a young man whom she liked, but whom she did not want to marry. "It's terribly exciting. We get such a thrill. I think it is natural to want nice men to kiss you, so why not do what is natural?" There was no embarrassment in her manner. Her eyes and her conscience were equally untroubled. I felt as if a girl from the Parthenon frieze had stepped down to ask if she might not sport in the glade with a handsome faun. Why not indeed? Only an equally direct forcing of twentieth century science on primitive simplicity could bring us even to the same level in our conversation, and at that, the stigma of impropriety seemed to fall on me, rather than on her. It was hard to tell whether her infantilism were real, or half-consciously assumed in order to have a child's license and excuse to do as she pleased. I am inclined to think that both with her and with many others, it is assumed. One girl said, "When I have had a few nights without dates I nearly go crazy. I tell my mother she must expect me to go out on a fearful necking party." In different parts of the country, *petting* and *necking* have opposite meanings. One locality calls necking (I quote their definition) "petting only from the neck up." Petting involves anything else you please. Another section reverses the distinction, and the girl in question was from the latter area. In what manner she announces to her mother her plans to neck, and in what manner her mother accepts the announcement, I cannot be sure.

But I imagine that the assumed childish attitude of the daughter is reflected by her mother, who longs to have her daughter popular, and get her full share of masculine attention. And if the daughter takes for granted that what her mother does not know will not hurt her, so does her mother's habit of blind and deaf supervision indicate that she too does not want to know any more than she has to. The college student is no longer preeminently from a selected class. One has only to look at the names and family status in the college registers to see that. If petting is felt to be poor taste in some families, there are many more families of poor taste than there used to be, whose children go to college. Their daughters are pretty and their sons have money to spend, and they seem prodigies of learning and accomplishment, especially to their unlettered mothers, who glow with pride over their popularity. The pleasant side of the picture is that anybody's daughter may go to college and pass on her own merits. The less agreeable side is that more refined, but timid and less numerous stocks feel obliged to model their social behavior on the crude amorousness and doubtful pleasantries which prevail at peasant parties. If anyone charges the daughters with being vulgar, the chances are that the mothers, though more shy, are essentially just as vulgar. The mothers have no accomplishments in which the daughters cannot surpass them, or no alternate social grace or cultivated recreation to suggest, if petting is denied them. Indeed that daughters are really at war with their mothers in point of view, I do not believe. On the contrary, thousands of mothers live all their emotional life in the gaiety of their daughters—having nothing else to live it in, and they suffer quite as deeply as their daughters if maternal strictness threatens to make wallflowers of them. Do not listen to what their mothers *say*, but *watch* them, if you want to know how they feel about their daughters petting! Their protests are about as genuine, as the daughter's, "Aren't you terrible?" when a young man starts to pet.

The sex manners of the large majority of uncultivated and uncritical people have become the manners for all, because they have prospered, they are getting educated, and there are so many of them. They are not squeamish, and they never have been. But their children can set a social standard as the parents could not. The prudent lawyer's child has no idea of letting the gay daughter of the broad-joking workman get the dates away from her. If petting is the weapon Miss Workman uses, then petting it must be, and in nine cases out of ten, not only Mrs. Workman, but also Mrs. Lawyer agree not to see too much. At heart both women are alike. Neither one can bear to see her daughter take a back seat in the struggle for popularity, and neither woman has any other ambition for her daughter but a successful husband. If by any chance, petting led *away* from popularity and possible husbands instead of *to* them, the mothers would be whole-heartedly against it, and if they were—petting, as a recognized recreation, would stop.

32. GALS AND COFFIN NAILS

In the following article, a tobacconist discusses the advent of a new type of customer, the woman smoker. A decade or so before, a President's daughter, Alice Roosevelt, was asked to leave the lobby of a Chicago Hotel after she had lit a cigarette. But by 1920 the woman smoker wasn't unusual even on the streets of major cities. How strong the opposition was can, however, be seen in the following comments, "Women Smokers," *The New York Times,* February 29, 1920. Reprinted by permission of *The New York Times.*

IN SPITE OF PULPIT EXCORIATIONS, IN SPITE OF CAMPAIGNS WAGED BY THE Women's Christian Temperance Union, in spite of warnings from the Peace Societies, the number of women who smoke is on the increase.

"Do you find you are getting any woman customers?" was the question put to the clerk behind the counter of one of the innumerable smoke-shops.

. . . "How many women would you say came in for cigarettes during a day? Would you say there were as many as—twelve? Or maybe—twenty?" The man at the counter began looking interested.

"You're not stringing me, are you? Twelve or twenty? Seventy-five or a hundred is more like it. . . . They come in just the way the men do. And they buy the same kind of cigarettes the men do.

"There's one thing funny about them. You get to know the people that come in to buy stuff. The men change the brand of cigarettes they use. They try out a new smoke occasionally. The women never. They stick to one kind right through. If you happen to be out of stock, they'll leave the store without buying anything. You see, they're still a bit scary about what's what, so they hold on hard to the smoke that their men folks started them on." . . .

(Another clerk at an exclusive Fifth Avenue shop, asked the same question.)

"An increase in women smokers?" he repeated. "Oh, yes; a very great and noticeable increase. I think I might truthfully say that today 50 per cent of our patrons are women. . . .

"Do you know," he said, "it's really very funny. The men who come into the shop to buy cigarettes for their lady friends buy perfumed ones. And when the ladies come in themselves they buy the strong ones. They insist upon getting the same kind as the men. . . . They want a man's smoke every time."

What are the anti-tobacco organizations doing in the face of the spread of this habit? According to the Board of Temperance, Prohibition, and Morals of the Methodist Episcopal Church the increased use of tobacco among women during 1919 was "appalling." In a recent statement the board made an "earnest appeal to women to refrain from the use of tobacco in the name of the country's welfare."

"No nation can maintain the vigor which has been characteristic of the American people after its women begin the use of cigarettes." . . .

This attitude in a large measure is the one taken by the Women's Christian Temperance Union. . . .

"Be it resolved, that the National W.C.T.U. encourages further scientific research into the effects of nicotine and urges all public and private school teachers and Sunday school workers, both by precept and example, to assist in an educational campaign to make these effects known with a view to instructing the youth as to the well-proven facts of science; and

"Be it further resolved, that the National W.C.T.U. brands as untrue the charge made by the Association Opposed to National Prohibition that we are engaged in a secret campaign for an amendment to the Constitution prohibiting tobacco. . . .

[Mrs. Ella A. Boole, President of the New York State organization says:]

"We are working on this question from a scientific standpoint and from an educational standpoint. After all, the duty of motherhood is still relegated to the women of the nation. Just as long as that is true we must protect the coming generation by teaching the present one the effects of the habit of smoking on the unborn. . . .

"The war has in no small measure been responsible for the spread of smoking in this country. Some of our young women as well as some of our young men have developed the habit. The cigarette was found to act as a sedative when no other kind could be found. It may have its uses on the battlefield. But the war is over and the peculiar needs of the war are over. There is no reason why we should carry over into the peace period a habit that was taken up as a war measure. . . .

33. LADIES OF THE TICKER

Before World War I Hetty Green became a national celebrity because she made a fortune on the stock market. But a woman customer in a broker's office was still as rare as one in a barber shop. After the war, however, both of these male sanctuaries were invaded by "a monstrous regiment of women," and although the males complained bitterly, the "customer is always right" dictum of the age prevailed and women soon made their appearance before the stock ticker. The excerpt below from "Ladies of the Ticker," by Eunice Fuller Barnard, *The North American Review*, April 1929, p. 405, is a discussion of the female contribution to the great bull market of the Twenties.

So Wall Street has come to Fifth Avenue. Silently one by one among the smart specialty shops of the Forties and Fifties appear the brokers' signs. With the arts of the drawing room, stock market operators for the first time in history are actually bidding for feminine favor. And woman is at last being made free of those more or less green pastures where men long have dallied.

For a year, indeed, all through the recent bull market, women by the hundreds have sat, and even stood in tense rows in the special stock-brokers' rooms set aside for them in various hotels of Upper Broadway. Day in and day out through a long five hours, aggressive, guttural dowagers, gum-chewing blondes, shrinking spinsters who look as if they belonged in a missionary-society meeting, watch, pencil in hand, from the opening of the market till the belated ticker drones its last in the middle of the afternoon.

Now they are packed into a stuffy, littered back room adjoining the men's, and again ranged in a tapestried parlor, with a miniature beauty salon attached, to raise the spirits in time of loss. Sometimes there are sympathetic young men managers in the latest double-breasted coats of Broadway; sometimes business-like women in charge, looking critically at the references of would-be buyers-on-margin.

Five years ago the average brokerage house still frowned on the woman customer. Some even now do so officially. But they are King Canutes forbidding the rising tide. Around them already is the surge of women investors—stenographers, heiresses, business women, housewives. The financial expert of a metropolitan newspaper recently estimated that in the last decade the woman non-professional speculator in stocks has grown "from less than a two per cent to a thirty-five per cent factor of the huge army that daily gambles in the stock market." Others, more conservative, put it at twenty per cent.

At the same time a brokerage house with offices throughout the eastern half of the country, in advertising for women customers, stated that already one out of five of its many thousands of clients was a woman. "In the past year," announced another firm, "the growth of the woman investor and the woman speculator has been amazing, and it is getting larger almost weekly." In a few instances women now own the majority of stock in large corporations. And there are even brokers who believe that women quite as much as men made the speculative stock market of 1927-29.

However that may be, certainly one of the outstanding social phenomena of that market when its history comes to be written will be the fact that in its course women for the first time in this country on a large scale financially became people. They became a recognized, if minor, factor in the vast new trading capitalist class. For one enterprising Victoria Woodhull in the 'Seventies, and one Hetty Green in the 'Nineties, marked as sports of nature, today there are hundreds of women investing their own funds and often playing the stock market with as bold a front as men.

Nor are they women of any one class or any one part of the country. Some of the most picturesque stories of the recent boom times are told of unexpected types. A woman farmer in the Middle West, for instance, recently telephoned her woman broker in New York to buy her a hundred shares of an automobile stock at a certain price. By quick action the broker secured them for her—the only shares that changed hands that day at so low a figure. By the next day they had gone up twenty points. The telephone call had cost the woman farmer six dollars, but had netted her almost two thousand overnight. To the same woman broker a scrub-woman in a well known club handed over $15,000 in cash which she had made on the stock market, for reinvestment. Indeed, in many instances waitresses and telephone girls, cooks and washerwomen who, so to speak, stood in with the boss, are said to have invested their mites on a wealthy employer's advice and cleaned up modest fortunes.

One thing necessary to woman's participation in the market was of course money of her own to invest. And that, in these last expansive years, she has undoubtedly achieved as never before. Last year some 95,000 women as heads of families made income tax returns on $400,-000,000. Others paid taxes on $1,500,000,000.

One woman broker, for example, who personally handles 300 accounts, has mainly business women as clients—buyers for department stores, small shop owners, advertising writers. Some of them are earning $15,000 a year, living on half, and investing the rest. Often they buy stock in the companies for which they work, or in others whose soundness they know from first-hand experience.

Then there is the growing army of women of inherited wealth—widows, and daughters—who of recent years seem to be given more and more discretion in the handling of their estates. And there are the wives who do not appear separately on the income tax returns, but who are sometimes, so far as investments go, the real disposers of the family savings. Frequently brokers will mention a writer or an artist whose wife attends to all financial matters from paying the bills to investing the surplus or negotiating the loans. More and more commonly, too, it is the wife of a busy professional man who volunteers to watch the stocks in which they are jointly interested.

Quite naturally, it seems, in this world of more and more intense specialization for men, investing, like buying, might slip into the woman's role. Today, it is estimated, 85 per cent of the spending in America is already in her hands. The disposition of income for present goods—for food, clothes, service, and often education, travel, and automobiles—is largely and unquestioningly hers. Why should she not, with her increasing leisure, learn to buy securities for the family's future, quite as well as fur coats and antique furniture?

But before that day could come, of course, women as a class would need far more experience than they have thus far had with stock exchange vagaries. Up to the recent break woman's entry into the market has been almost wholly over a bed of roses. She has yet to show that she can hibernate with the bears when the heyday of quick profits is over, as it already seems to be. She has pragmatically to learn the painful lesson that buying stocks may mean sudden and devastating loss, as well as gain. And if, after the holocaust, she has any money left, she has in many cases to discover for herself the gulf fixed between rational investing and stock gambling as it has been going on the last two years. After the introduction with veil and orange blossoms, in other words, can she compose herself to the dishwashing and the darning?

34. NEW MARRIAGE STYLES

One of the most discussed topics of the decade concerned the proposals of Judge Ben Lindsey of Denver for the legal establishment of "trial" and "companionate" marriages. The advent of the "career woman" and the rising divorce rate made a discussion of the institution almost necessary. But years before Lindsey shocked the conservatives by this reform proposal, a leading woman novelist, Fanny Hurst, publicly announced that she and her husband were establishing separate living accommodations as much to further both their careers as to express their own individual tastes and interests. Miss Hurst's discussion of the arrangement with a reporter from *The New York Times*, December 9, 1923, was reprinted all over the country and called forth an amazing amount of both pro and con comment. Reprinted by permission of *The New York Times*.

"To begin with," she said, "my solution to the marriage problem is not the world's solution of the problem. I didn't set out to do that. I was not inspired with the ardor of the reformer who would bring peace to a badly organized world. There was none of that. I was interested in a highly specialized situation, peculiar to myself. . . . Mr. Danielson and I worked out a formula which seemed to meet our special and individual needs. It happens that we have hit on the right one. For ourselves, it has stood the test of eight years. It works.

"That doesn't mean that our solution must or will be the solution of the world. As long as human beings differ from each other each will have to work out his own salvation. But if we are going to treat the marriage business intelligently then we'll have to begin with acceptance of the idea that human beings are different. . . .

"Take the marriage structure as it now stands. It's old fashioned, it's drafty, it's leaky, the roof sags, the timbers shake, there's no modern plumbing, no hardwood floors, no steam heat. We don't feel comfortable in it. We've outgrown the edifice, but we don't dare get out of it. . . .

"For some strange reason, social custom is the laggard of civilization. . . .

"Those of us who dare shiver at the cold of the old edifice, plan our structure differently. We study the plans of many architects and build our house to suit our own particular and peculiar needs. We put in hardwood floors, sanitary plumbing, steam heat, many windows. We retain much of the charm of the old-fashioned house. We keep the open fireplace, the handsome door, the good pictures, the things that bring ease and comfort and spiritual delight. It's all very wonderful. And very satisfying and sensible.

"Not the least satisfactory arrangement of the new structure, the new marriage structure, is the privacy it gives, the little self-respecting privacies which the old kind of marriage seems to revel in breaking down.

". . . Monogamy, however, is conceded to be a good thing for the social structure. Whether it is or not is not the point of this discussion. But granted that it is, what is the thing which is going to make us happy in a monogamous marriage? Illusion. Monogamy has to be pampered a bit; it has to be made to appear like a many-faceted jewel. A woman must be new to her mate, a man must be a not altogether known quantity to his. Neither can afford to let all the barriers *fall*.

"It is the partitions built up in the new edifice that help maintain the illusion, that help conserve and preserve it. Yet men are afraid to build it and women are afraid to live in it. Fear, fear of living. That is the cause of the slow step of progress in all avenues of life. . . .

"I have talked about this thing to women. I have talked it from the platform. I believe that marriage can be happy, but I am also convinced that the old pattern cannot be made to fit all. But women will not look at the problem from the point of view of the problem as a whole. They argue from the individual. . . .

"You speak about trial marriage. Trial marriage is a logical solution for the problem for some people, but it's a waste of time to discuss it. People take it about as seriously as 'Yes, we have no bananas.' They refuse to consider it. You can't make any headway. It's important, but as long as people are ridiculed and shamed out of it, that won't be a solution to anything. . . .

"Do I think my solution is the solution for the young women who are aware of this wind before the dawn? Yes and no. There is no one solution for all, as I said before. But it's a solution as far as it can be adapted to individual needs. Keeping a double menage is not a prime requisite of the arrangement. Keeping a sense of privacy and freedom is.

". . . Where there's actual freedom it is more likely to be used than abused. There is not so much to fear from a relationship of this sort, because both are kept on the *qui vive* for each other. There is everything to fear from the old-fashioned good-wife-and-mother relationship. It is contrary to the biological instincts of the human race. Its observation is based on the least admirable of human traits—fear of living!

". . . If a woman can sell insurance or run a paying beauty parlor or write a book, the chances are ten to one that she can hire vastly more efficient service to train her children than she could give them. Because I can paint a picture, let us say, does not mean that I can bring up a child. . . .

"No, the place of the woman of intelligence is not inevitably in the kitchen worrying about pot and pan trifles, not at the front door every evening waiting tremulously for the step of her John and fearful lest the roast be not overdone. Her place is where she can give the most service and get the most out of life. . . ."

35. THE END OF THE FLAPPER

By the end of the decade the flapper's rebellion was already over and a new style of woman, the siren, had taken her place. But this did not mean that American women were ready to give up the rights and privileges they had won. On the contrary, the social skirmish died down because the conservatives had vanished and the new freedom for the sex was now the accepted mode. Already foreign commentators were describing the paramount place women had in American society and predicting feminine dominance. The following account from *The New York Times*, July 28, 1929, describes the end of the "jazz age" and essays a prediction as to what will follow for the newly enfranchised sex. Reprinted by permission of *The New York Times.*

PARIS, ENDLESSLY RESOURCEFUL IN FEMININE INVENTIONS, IS BUSILY ENgaged in sending New York a new siren. On the stage and in the subtly lighted salons of the great couturiers, at the races and under the trees of smart midsummer cafes, she takes her graceful way before the attentive eyes of the tourist throng. With her clothes molded to her figure, her draperies that veil line and curve only to accentuate them, her air of knowing much and saying little, her mysterious allure that is at once the oldest and the newest of feminine accomplishments, she spells the death sentence of the flapper.

And the flappers know it. Voices falter in their stridencies and reach for lower notes. Girls from the hinterland clutch at brief skirts in a sudden agony of doubt as to the chic of bumpy knees, and the maidens from Park Avenue register a mental note that smartness has now clothed itself in garments of a fascinating complexity, and that sophistication no longer lies in revealing too much. . . .

But the woman beloved of Paris is more than a thing of clothes and mannerisms, and the eagerness of America to imitate her outward semblances without realizing that it connotes an indefinable inner grace, might well evoke that slow, enigmatic smile which is one of her most charming weapons. She knows very well the ways of the world. She has character and background as well as long skirts and a deep-back decolletage. It is whispered that she has brains under her smooth long hair, and that she is not ashamed of having lived a discreet number of years. . . .

To Europe, the emergence of this new-old feminine type symbolizes the end of the post-war jazz age and the recrudescence of values that for years were crowded out by the nervous intensity of speed and the jeering laughter of saxophones. But that does not mean she has turned back the clock. The siren of 1929 is no more a return to the Trilbys or Sapphos of the 90's than she is like the Theda Bara's of one's childhood movies. She is as modern as the airplane and the backless bathing suit. She is the most versatile thing that ancient tradition and progressive education have yet produced. In her highest development she is a combination of the best of old Europe and young America. . . .

This new siren of the Champs Elysées and Park Avenue is the result of that mutual scrutiny. European in her poise, her knowledge of clothes and of the uses of mystery, American in her clear beauty of slim form, her calm directness, she is an enchanting proof that the Old and New Continents, when they work together, can do better than either of them alone. . . .

And so, being thus equipped, she goes serenely about the main business of being a siren. She handles men with the combined skill of both her parental continents. . . . Ancient wisdom teaches her to be a confidante, but seldom to confide, to understand rather than to seek to be understood, to charm and delight rather than to demand amusement. Newer, franker ways have abolished any "slave complex" she might have inherited along with that knowledge. . . .

She no longer has to bother about smashing tradition or demonstrating her superiority to convention. In this she is the flapper's debtor, for that young person abolishes surplus clothes and surplus manners with the same enthusiasm she devoted to acquiring gin and cigarettes. By sheer force of violence she established the feminine right to equal representation in such hitherto masculine fields of endeavor as smoking and drinking, swearing, petting, and disturbing the community peace. They need no longer to be the subject of crusade. Indeed the incurable flappers who go on fighting for them are as absurd as the good ladies who still carry the hysteric air of martyrs in the cause of woman's rights.

They being won, the new siren may elect to use them or not as she sees fit. She may go on disregarding the old conventions, she may set up new ones as a convenient set of rules which give form and seemliness to the game of life. . . .

The dream of idealists is that the new style means a real chance to follow the sloganeers and "be yourself." . . . It is variety's golden opportunity to step in and banish the monotony of life, to make a change of personality as easy and pleasant as the shift from tweeds to tulle.